ENVIRONMENTAL PLANNING IN THE CARIBBEAN

Environmental Planning in the Caribbean

Edited by
JONATHAN PUGH
University of Newcastle Upon Tyne

and

JANET HENSHALL MOMSEN
University of California, Davis

Routledge
Taylor & Francis Group
LONDON AND NEW YORK

First published 2006 by Ashgate Publishing

Published 2016 by Routledge
2 Park Square, Milton Park, Abingdon, Oxfordshire OX14 4RN
711 Third Avenue, New York, NY 10017, USA

First issued in paperback 2016

Routledge is an imprint of the Taylor & Francis Group, an informa business

British Library Cataloguing in Publication Data
Environmental planning in the Caribbean. – (Urban planning and environment)
1. Environmental management – Caribbean Area 2. Planning – Caribbean Area 3. Environmental policy – Caribbean Area
I. Pugh, Jonathan, 1974– II. Momsen, Janet Henshall
363.7'009729

Library of Congress Control Number: 2006924968

ISBN 13: 978-1-138-27050-3 (pbk)
ISBN 13: 978-0-7546-4391-3 (hbk)

Contents

List of Figures and Tables *vii*
List of Contributors *ix*
Preface *xi*

1 Introduction 1
Janet Henshall Momsen

2 Physical Development Planning in the Anglophone Caribbean: The Re-articulation of Formal State Power 7
Jonathan Pugh

3 'The Bad Old Days Look Better': Enlightened Colonial Land Management Practices and Land Reform in the British Windward Islands 21
Beth Mills

4 Challenges to Promoting Agro-biodiversity in Caribbean Small Farming Systems: A Jamaican Case Study 33
Elizabeth Thomas-Hope and Balfour Spence

5 Disaster Creation in the Caribbean and Planning, Policy and Participation Reconsidered 53
Jonathan Skinner

6 Environmental Planning and Heritage Tourism in Cuba During the Special Period: Challenges and Opportunities 73
Joseph L. Scarpaci

7 'Nuff Respec'? Widening and Deepening Participation in Academic and Policy Research in Jamaica 93
David Dodman and Jane Dodman

8 Corporate Environmental Sustainability: Sandals Resorts International in Jamaica 111
Paul Kingsbury

9 Conservation and Recreation Planning on the Caribbean Coast: Cahuita, Costa Rica 129
Galen Martin

10 Nature, People and Planning on the Coast of Belize 155
Roger Few

11 *Dis Da Fu We*: Conservation, Development and Empowerment in San Pedro Town, Belize 177
Brandon Kitagawa and Janet Momsen

Index *199*

List of Tables and Figures

Figures

4.1	Location of the PLEC Rio Grande Valley demonstration site, Portland, Jamaica	36
5.1	Before and after the eruption of Mount Chance, Montserrat	59
5.2	The integrated planning approach	62
5.3	Logic sequence when creating a scenario according to Senger	66
5.4	MVO scientist monitoring the volcano during a tourist visit (photo by author 2005)	69
6.1	Late sixteenth-century water pipe that drew water from the Almendares River, 9 km west, of Habana Vieja. This section was revealed during renovations near Plaza Vieja, in Habana Vieja in the mid-1990s	76
6.2	A water truck delivery in Cerro, Havana	79
9.1	Cahuita National Park	130
9.2	Regional transportation map	136
9.3	Cahuita Point aerial photo, 1969	137
9.4	Coral National Momument proposal	138
9.5	Lemieux's National Marine Park Proposal	139
9.6	Kutay's (1991) management proposal	146
9.7	Residents' perception of the purpose of CNP by gender	150
10.1	Case study sites in northeast Belize (1997)	159
10.2	The balance of containment	171
11.1	Dimensions of sustainable development	178
11.2	Map of Belize	180

Tables

4.1	Description of land-use stages and field types at the Rio Grande Valley demonstration site	40
4.2	Species richness as a function of land-use stages	42
6.1	Environmental planning administered by Cuba's National System for the Protection of the Environment and the Rational Use of Natural Resources (COMARNA)	78
6.2	Heritage tourism financing mechanisms and environmental planning challenges	86
10.1	Principal planning events in the two case studies	160
10.2	Generalized typology of local actors	162

11.1 Individual empowerment questions 184
11.2 Individual Empowerment Index 185
11.3 Community empowerment questions 188
11.4 Community Empowerment Index 189
11.5 Conservation and tourism questions 193

List of Contributors

David Dodman is a Lecturer in the Department of Geography and Geology, University of the West Indies. He holds a DPhil from the University of Oxford, and his research interests focus on issues of urban management and sustainability in the Caribbean.

Jane Dodman has been a community development practitioner and educator in Jamaica since 1983. She holds a BA from the University of Durham, an MTh from the University of Edinburgh, and a PhD from the University of Sheffield. She is currently the Principal of Mel Nathan College, one of the constituent colleges of the International University of the Caribbean, a recently-formed institution that promotes lifelong learning, educational empowerment, prosperity, peace and wholeness in the region.

Roger Few is Senior Research Fellow in the School of Development Studies, University of East Anglia, UK. His research work on social aspects of environmental change encompasses response to environmental health risks and natural hazards, as well as community participation in natural resource management and conservation.

Paul Kingsbury is an Assistant Professor of Geography at Simon Fraser University. His research draws on psychoanalytic and Marxist theories to examine the geographies of power and enjoyment inherent in the practices of consumption, labour and tourism.

Brandon Kitagawa received his BS in Combined Sciences from Santa Clara University in 1998. He lived in Belize as a Peace Corps Volunteer (1999–2001), returning to complete a MS in Community Development from UC Davis in 2003. He is currently a Community Organizer with an affordable housing organization in Sacramento, California.

Galen Martin received his PhD from the University of California, Davis in 2004. He is currently an instructor in the Environmental Studies Program at the University of Oregon. His research interests are international conservation issues and political ecology, especially in Central America and the Caribbean. He has extensive experience in interdisciplinary courses and curriculum development.

Beth Mills received her PhD in Geography from the University of California, Davis, in 2002. She has travelled, lived and worked in the Caribbean since 1975. Her research interests include trans-national communities, tourism, land use and community development. Currently she is working for local government in Santa Fe, New Mexico where she provides geographic analysis for community and regional planning as well as working on solutions for environmental and conservation problems.

Janet Henshall Momsen is Professor of Geography, Department of Human and Community Development, University of California, Davis. She has previously taught in Canada, Brazil and the UK and worked extensively in the Anglo and Francophone Caribbean. She has edited *Women and Change in the Caribbean* and, with Jean Besson, *Land and Development in the Caribbean.*

Jonathan Pugh is the Fellow in Territorial Governance at the University of Newcastle, UK. He runs the website and network 'Participatory Planning in the Caribbean' (http://www.planningcaribbean.org.uk).

Joseph L. Scarpaci is a Professor of Geography at Virginia Tech. He co-authored (with Mario Coyula and Roberto Segre), *Havana: Two Faces of the Antillean Metropolis.* His latest book is *Plazas and Barrios: Heritage Tourism and Globalization the Latin American Centro Histórico* (2005).

Jonathan Skinner is a Lecturer in Social Anthropology, Queen's University Belfast. He is editor of *Anthropology in Action: Journal for Applied Anthropology in Policy and Practice.* His research has long been focused on Montserrat and in 2004 he published *Before the Volcano: Reverberations of Identity on Montserrat.* He has now moved on to study dance and dance tourism and he is currently editing with Helen Neveu (Oxford) a book on the anthropology of dance, and dance learning and observation techniques (*Dancin' Culture: Knowledge, Transformation and Identity in the Anthropology of Dance*).

Balfour Spence is a lecturer in Geography at the University of the West Indies. He has a BSc and MPhil from the University of the West Indies and a PhD from the University of Manitoba. His research interests involve agriculture and tourism in Jamaica.

Elizabeth Thomas-Hope is the James Seivright Moss-Solomon (Snr) Professor of Environment at the University of the West Indies. She has an MA Hons from the University of Aberdeen, an MSc from Pennsylvania State University and a DPhil from the University of Oxford. Her research interests focus on issues in the Jamaican environment and on migration.

Preface

Environmental planning has become a major thrust of Caribbean governmental and non-governmental organizations across the region. Many courses are offered on how it can be achieved in the Caribbean, billions of US dollars are spent through donor agencies on its implementation. One general trend in environmental planning can be noted as increasingly influential over the last decade. There are still a large number of prescriptive texts and programmes for how environmental planning should be implemented across the region, regardless of different contexts and circumstances. However, many donor agencies, Caribbean lecturers, governments, planners, non-governmental organizations and consultants are becoming increasingly concerned with how environmental planning is produced *through* specific contexts within the region. Concerns are increasingly with how local circumstances shape, appropriate and adopt the wide range of environmental planning discourses associated with the Caribbean.

As illustrated by the general change in emphasis of leading Caribbean environmental organizations, 'the case study approach' is therefore becoming more important as a means to learning about environmental planning in the region and developing best practice. Teaching students in the Caribbean in 2003, the editors discussed this need for more accessible work on how environmental planning is produced through particular cultural, social, geographical, political, economic and historical practices. The various contributors to this volume share this general concern.

With this in mind, the monograph we have produced contains discussions of how the major environmental planning discourses associated with the Caribbean play out in specific contexts. These discourses include: physical development planning, participatory planning, conservation planning, disaster management, sustainable tourism development, community empowerment and heritage tourism. One outcome of this contextual approach is that some of the authors end up challenging stereotypes of how environmental planning plays out across the region: stereotypes associated with tourism, development agencies, participatory planning, heritage tourism and disaster management, for examples.

One contributor shows how tourism does not need to be reduced to its 'dirty failures and dark secrets'; the case in much of the academic literature. Tourist corporations are often essentialized as having unsustainable capitalist motives. But when the contextual nuances are explored, we find that tourists' enjoyment of the Caribbean environment throws up a wide range of conflicting power relations, not all of which have negative effects upon the environment. Another author takes a rather different (and in some ways ironic) approach to the increasing emphasis upon 'the contextual' in discourses of environmental planning in the Caribbean. He looks at how the emphasis upon 'local solutions to local problems' is often re-appropriated and re-articulated across the Anglophone Caribbean, in order to increase the power of a certain limited number of elites in the governments of these countries. Turning to the three case studies of participatory planning that are presented in this volume, all contributors similarly focus upon how participatory planning cannot be seen simply as a 'tyranny' or a 'positive' technique, as is often the case in a wide range of literature at the moment.

Thus, the central theme of this edited collection is that we should not over simplify the effects of specific planning discourses. Rather, there is a need to examine how environmental planning discourses are produced *through* cultural, social, geographical, political, economic and historical factors in given contexts; that is, in an era where grand narratives have become less important, a more grounded approach is required. As shown throughout this monograph, this way of thinking often serves to challenge stereotypes, pointing to the need for a more context-specific approach to how environmental planning can be improved in the future. In providing this collection of individual case studies, we hope to have made some contribution to this approach.

Specific thanks go to Pat FitzGerald for her editorial help in producing the final version. As the publishers of this volume, Ashgate, and specifically our editor Val Rose, are to be thanked for their support for this volume. Jon Pugh also wishes to thank the Economic and Social Research Council for fully funding his three year Fellowship, which involved a range of projects looking at the nature of environmental planning in the Caribbean (2002–2004) (Ref: R000271204). This monograph is one specific output of that Fellowship, to which the Economic and Social Research Council gave full financial support – from conception to publication.

Jonathan Pugh
Janet Henshall Momsen

Chapter 1

Introduction

Janet Henshall Momsen

This collection focuses on postcolonial influences on conservation and planning throughout the Caribbean region. The Caribbean is the oldest colonial area in the world and as such has been influenced by the Dutch, French, British, Spanish and United States systems of planning over many centuries. Postcolonialism, defined as the 'geographically dispersed contestation of colonial power and knowledge' (Blunt and Wills 2000: 170) is linked to the role of imperial and colonial encounters and is used to describe 'an aggregation of critical responses to the historical effects of colonialism and the persistence of colonial forms of power and knowledge into the present' (Kothari 2005).

Postcolonial approaches have been most influential in the fields of cultural studies, history, geography, literary criticism and more recently in development studies. In geography postcolonialism has been used in historical and cultural studies (Blunt and Rose 1994; Nash 2002) and to some extent in urban geography (Yeoh 2001). It is increasingly being employed in development geography (Radcliffe 2005) in research areas of power relations, statehood, social differences and issues of fieldwork (ibid). In this volume we extend this approach to processes of conservation and planning in former British colonies such as Jamaica, Belize, and Carriacou and Spanish former colonies such as Costa Rica and Cuba. We also consider current quasi-colonial societies such as British Overseas Territories (Montserrat) and in this introduction look at the French Départements d'Outre Mer (Martinique and Guadeloupe). The chapters provide grounded empirical studies of the links between colonialism and local planning policies. The empirical chapters are preceded by a theoretical study of planning in the Anglophone Caribbean which provides the context for some of the empirical studies. We consider postcolonial landscapes of the Caribbean in terms of their historical legacies and the environmental footprint of postcolonial planning policies. Or as Willis (2005: 121) puts it 'postcolonialism attempts to understand not only the observable legacies of colonialism, but also the ideas or discourses about 'development' which have been transferred as part of the colonial process'.

Participatory Planning

Participatory planning for development has been widely embraced (Pugh and Potter 2003) but the contributors to this book show how projects hailed as participatory have often become top-down. This may be by choice of the participants as Elizabeth Thomas-Hope and Balfour Spence show. They suggest that small farmers take advice from extension agents and export commodity groups rather than looking to local community leaders. A project to introduce Integrated Pest Management (IPM) to farmers in Jamaica, Trinidad and other parts of the English-speaking Caribbean, though considered participatory by its funding agency, USAID, in fact worked through a local agricultural research organization which in turn trained extension agents who took the knowledge to the field. In an evaluation of the process it was found that the rationale for these new methods was lost as it moved down the hierarchy and so farmers often did not continue using IPM for very long after the training as they found it more time-consuming and less effective than using pesticides (Momsen 2006). Since the underlying rationale of the funding agency was to reduce pesticide residues on vegetable exports to the United States only the few commercial farmers producing for this market found it worthwhile to use IPM. Participation involved linkages between United States-based scientists and a regional NGO and was seen in terms of training West Indian scientists by United States counterparts. Since the focus was on non-traditional export crops such as Jamaican callaloo, Scotch Bonnet peppers and sweet potatoes only these crops were targeted for disease control without the use of pesticides. The aim was to protect American consumers not to overcome local food scarcities or make farming safer for local farmers. The shortage of available extension officers and their lack of time for training and outreach further limited the impact of this project.

Pugh in his review of planning policies identifies a general trend in Anglophone Caribbean planning. He shows how local governing elites from the Cabinets of these countries are particularly adept at re-appropriating the discourses of foreign funding regimes for their own purposes. In many cases, they have done so in order to build up the power of government, at the expense of the power of local planning expertise. He specifically describes the ways in which the formal centralized power of many Anglophone Caribbean states has been maintained through various planning procedures and Acts, and re-articulated in various forms, from the 1930s, to the new era of institutional capacity building which has developed since the 1990s. Marginalization of postcolonial subjects and knowledge is but one consequence of this approach. Such attitudes lead to at best very partial participation, as Skinner shows for Montserrat, in terms of which individuals are asked to participate in planning decisions.

Galen Martin in his study of the Cahuita National Park on the Caribbean coast of Costa Rica shows how ignoring local needs and imposing park planning from the central government led to difficulties and eventually violence. The Caribbean coast of Costa Rica, peopled by Afro-Caribbean people coming originally mainly from Jamaica, is seen as liminal between the Hispanic population of Central America and the Caribbean. The Park was created with little thought for the livelihoods of the local people, and no understanding of local agriculture which was based on agriforestry with cacao and coconuts. Furthermore, compensation for land taken over has still not been paid in many cases. Damage to the reef, the main focus of the Park, was caused by pesticide run-off and plastic bags from nearby banana plantations but local fishermen were blamed. Only after violent confrontations followed by training of local people as guides by a Dutch Bilateral aid agency, was a participatory approach allowed and co-management of the Park introduced.

In Belize Roger Few shows how co-management of a marine conservation area was imposed from above and was often undermined by non-planners. On the other hand, Kitagawa and Momsen, working more recently in the same area, found that local people felt empowered by the marine park. This was especially true of the tourist guides but even those local community members only marginally involved in the protected area supported it and felt that the community as a whole benefited. These two chapters show how attitudes to conservation planning can change over time and be viewed differently by different groups of people. When considered in juxtaposition with Martin's chapter on Cahuita National Park it is clear that protected areas are often seen as spaces of exclusion but when local people become co-managers of these conservation areas then they become empowered and supportive of conservation.

Tourism Planning

As the economy of the region has changed from one dependent on export agriculture to one increasingly involved with tourism, the focus of planning has changed. Whether this is allowing plantations to be turned into golf courses in Barbados or the building of second homes on drier farmland as in Montserrat (Momsen 1977) tourism takes priority over agriculture. Scarpaci describes the importance of heritage tourism in Cuba as a way of conserving old colonial era buildings and cityscapes. External support from UNESCO in the form of declaring old Havana a World Heritage site gave impetus to this activity but grassroots participation has been uneven.

In Jamaica new approaches to planning and the involvement of a variety of stakeholders are considered in relation to both town planning and tourism. David and Jane Dodman look at urban planning for Kingston while Kingsbury considers attempts at sustainable tourism. Both chapters describe interaction between planners, the university and local leaders and show how participation in planning has widened. Some hoteliers have deliberately set out to implement sustainable tourism through such approaches as use of grey water on gardens and purchase of local produce wherever possible. However, the chapter by Thomas-Hope and Spence shows that farmer participation in supplying hotels tends to be limited to the more innovative farmers with the necessary personal contacts.

External Influences

In colonial times planning was undertaken by the colonial masters. Beth Mills shows that this did have a positive environmental impact on Carriacou. The British colonial administration saw social improvement and environmental protection as linked and used an integrated approach to planning. Grove (1995) suggests that exposure to new physical environments simultaneously fuelled scientific inquiry and understanding leading to the development of what he called 'green imperialism'. The Botanical

Garden in St Vincent was established in 1765 and was the first in the Americas. It was seen as a way for Europeans to gain control within a confined space of an unfamiliar environment. The link between trees and precipitation was identified in 'desiccationist' theories as early as 1764 and by 1850 tropical deforestation was recognized as a global problem by the colonial scientific community. In Carriacou at the end of the nineteenth century forest reserves were set up along the ridges and eucalyptus was brought in to dry up the swamp. A few decades later grass barriers were planted in Carriacou and terraces built in St Vincent to prevent soil erosion. Such markers in the landscape were memorials to individual colonial servants and the ideas they brought from other colonies.

On the other hand, Thomas-Hope and Spence suggest that in the Rio Grande Valley of Jamaica it is the small farmers following traditional methods of mixed planting who protect the slopes despite efforts by the Banana Export Company to make them plant bananas in pure stands. Thus they argue small farmers not only maintain the island's biodiversity but also farm in a more sustainable way than the commercial export-oriented farmers.

Contemporary external sources of planning are metropolitan, multinational and international. In the French territories which are politically considered part of France though separated from Europe by thousand of miles, plans are made in Paris or Brussels. Regional development approaches designed for Europe, such as the various LEADER projects, are applied with some difficulty in the tropical islands of the French Caribbean (Dornan 2004). Montserrat, as an Overseas Territory of Britain, also is the recipient of European planning and both Montserrat and the French Caribbean benefit from substantial transfers of funds from Europe. However, when Montserrat's volcano started erupting in 1995 decisions were made in London. As Jonathan Skinner shows in his chapter these decisions were not always the best and were often resented by the locals. The United Kingdom government did arrange evacuation for those living in the affected part of the island and has helped to rebuild the north of the island. However, Britain felt that the people of Montserrat expected too much and there was dissatisfaction on both sides. In this case top-down planning from a distance led to many problems and the alienation of Montserrat as an Overseas Territory (OT).

The benefits of colonial status have persuaded the Montserrat government to reject independence but when natural disasters occur (Hurricane Hugo in 1989 and the volcanic eruption in 1995) the island is restricted to appealing to Britain for support rather than to the United Nations or the world community. However, an independent inquiry showed that there was no contingency planning for dealing with these disasters by the British government and that some of the post-disaster planning problems were 'linked to the complexity of HMG management and the administrative system for Montserrat as a self-governing OT' (Clay et al. 1999: 6).

Cuba is also limited in access to sources of financial assistance for planning improvements as it is alienated from most of its neighbours, except Venezuela, because of American animosity. Planning of all aspects of the economy is centralized in government hands and opposition is not allowed. Improvements in infrastructure are urgently needed and are even becoming a problem for the development of heritage tourism, as shown in Scarpaci's chapter. When additional funds are needed for environmental protection and urban renewal Cuba has to turn to United Nations agencies for assistance.

Conclusion

Other international agencies affecting planning in the region in a less direct way are the World Trade Organization (WTO) and the European Union. As the WTO pushes the integration of the global food economy and the liberalization of trade, the European Union is unable to maintain its trade protection for its former colonies in Africa, the Caribbean and the Pacific, the ACP countries. Soon there will no longer be a protected market for Caribbean bananas in Europe (Myers 2004) and sugar too is losing its traditional colonial markets. For high cost producers such as those of the small Caribbean islands, export agriculture has a very uncertain future (Weis 2004). These global changes demand imaginative solutions from government planners in the region. A better understanding of the planning process may enable these solutions to be found.

References

Blunt, A. and Rose, G. (eds) (2004), *Writing Women and Space: Colonial and Postcolonial Geographies*, London: Guildford.

Blunt, A. and Wills, J. (2000), 'Decolonising Geography: Postcolonial Perspectives', in A. Blunt and J. Wills (eds), *Dissident Geographies: An Introduction to Radical Ideas and Practice*, Harlow: Prentice Hall.

Clay, E., Barrow, C., Benson, C., Dempster, J., Kokelaar, P., Pillai, N. and Seaman, J. (1999), *An Evaluation of HMG's Response to the Montserrat Volcanic Emergency, Volume 1*, Overseas Development Institute report for the Evaluation Department of DFID, London, DFID.

Dornan, D'Arcy (2004), 'Postcolonial Linkages between Agriculture and Tourism in Martinique', unpublished doctoral dissertation, Geography Graduate Group, University of California, Davis, CA.

Grove, R. (1995), *Green Imperialism*, Cambridge: Cambridge University Press.

Kothari, Uma (2005), 'Postcolonialism', in Tim Forsyth (ed.), *Encyclopedia of International Development*, London: Routledge, pp. 541–3.

Momsen, Janet D. (1977), 'Second Homes in the Caribbean', in J.T. Coppock (ed.), *Second Homes: Curse or Blessing?*, Oxford: Pergamon Press, pp. 75–84.

Momsen, Janet H. (2006), 'Gender Perspectives on Sustainable Food for Sustainable Tourism in the Caribbean', in Jennifer Hill, Alan Terry and Wendy Woodland (eds), *Sustainable Development: National Aspirations, Local Implementation*, Aldershot and Burlington VT: Ashgate.

Myers, Gordon (2004), *Banana Wars: the Price of Free Trade. A Caribbean Perspective*, Zed Books: London and New York.

Nash, C. (2002), 'Cultural Geography: Postcolonial Cultural Geographies', *Progress in Human Geography*, 26, pp. 219–30.

Pugh, J. and Potter, R. (eds) (2003), *Participatory and Communicative Planning in the Caribbean*, Aldershot: Ashgate.

Radcliffe, Sarah A. (2005), 'Development and Geography: Towards a Postcolonial Development Geography', *Progress in Human Geography*, 29 (3), pp. 291–8.

Weis, Tony (2004), '(Re)making the Case for Land Reform in Jamaica', *Social and Economic Studies*, 53 (1), pp. 35–72.

Willis, Katie (2005) *Theories and Practices of Development*, Routledge: London.

Yeoh, Brenda (2001), 'Postcolonial Cities', *Progress in Human Geography*, 25, pp. 456–68.

Chapter 2

Physical Development Planning in the Anglophone Caribbean: The Re-articulation of Formal State Power

Jonathan Pugh

Introduction

This chapter is concerned with the ways in which the governments of different Anglophone Caribbean countries have responded to the changing discourses of physical development planning coming from first the colonial office, then 'the West' more generally. It shows how local governing elites from the Cabinets of these countries are adept at re-appropriating these discourses. In many cases, they have done so in order to build up their own power, at the expense of the power of local planning expertise. I specifically describe the ways in which the formal centralized power of many Anglophone Caribbean States has been maintained through various planning procedures and Acts, and re-articulated in various forms, from the 1930s, to the new era of institutional capacity building which has developed since the 1990s. The latter puts emphasis upon creating local solutions to local problems, building up the capacity of Caribbean States to become more proficient in developing their own expertise and solutions for environmental planning, rather than substantive development regimes and policies being dictated from the West.

An important question explored herein is: have these new institutional capacity building discourses emerged because Anglophone Caribbean elites have suddenly become anxious that they need to connect more effectively with their civil servants and planning experts around coherent local visions of development for the nation? Alternatively, is institutional capacity building being adopted in the Caribbean because donor agencies have been so heavily criticized over the last few decades for projecting *their* vision of development, that the emphasis is now placed upon locally based solutions? In agreeing with the second proposition rather than the former, this chapter shows how local elites have seized on the idea of 'local solutions to local problems' in order to increase their power over development further. The chapter therefore shows how local elites in the Anglophone Caribbean have played upon the increasingly prolific development imaginaries of 'context counting', 'local solutions to local problems' and the politically correct anxieties of Western donors, in order to strengthen their positions. Far from Western development agencies dominating the region in a deterministic manner, in practice, it will be shown how local elites from the Cabinets of many Anglophone countries continue to re-appropriate, adapt and mediate Western-planning discourses, as they have since the earliest days of physical development planning in the region. It is not grand narratives of development that are important; but the way in which local governing elites re-articulate these narratives, in order to increase their abilities to govern the people of their country.

Methodology

The work presented in this chapter is part of a wider three-year study into institutional capacity building in the Caribbean, carried out by the present author and funded through the ESRC.[1] This resulted in the collection of an extensive library, covering all of the major planning documents and legislation of Anglophone Caribbean countries. The reader interested in obtaining documents from this library – now housed at the University of Newcastle, United Kingdom – can contact the author. In addition to this library of standard planning documents, emphasis was also placed upon obtaining the major documents and reports concerning institutional capacity building in these different countries spread across the region. To supplement this library further, a series of interviews with leading planners and government officials from all of the Anglophone Caribbean countries covered in this chapter were undertaken between 1999 and 2004. The purpose of these was to ascertain the way in which local governing elites and planners respond to Western planning discourse. Having worked in the region for almost three years in the last seven more generally, it is impossible to put an exact figure on the number of conversations and interviews that have been undertaken in this regard. Rather, this chapter can be seen as reflecting a general trend that I have noticed over this period – that governing elites are particularly adept at engaging with, mediating and re-articulating Western planning discourses, in order to increase their power to rule over the people of their countries, at the expense of the power of local planning expertise. Political discretion appears to come before expertise, as represented in the major planning literature of these countries. And the idea of 'local solutions to local problems' has further supported this development.

The Emergence of Formal Physical Development Planning Systems in the Anglophone Caribbean

One influence on the development of physical development planning in the Anglophone Caribbean was the United Nations. In 1966, the United Nations Development Programme (UNDP) initiated a three-phase programme entitled 'Assistance in Physical Planning' (United Nations Development Programme 1977). This aimed to provide technical assistance for Antigua, the British Virgin Islands, the Cayman Islands, Turks and Caicos, Dominica, Grenada, Montserrat, St Christopher-Nevis-Anguilla, St Lucia and St Vincent. The UNDP phases, which ended in 1992, involved establishing a

Central Planning Unit in each country, formulating physical development plans and strategies, drafting legislation to control land development, and training staff. A total of US$ 2,150,000 was spent on the programme.

Another obvious influence upon the emergence of formal physical development planning systems in the Anglophone Caribbean in the early part of the twentieth century, was the conflict between local elites and the British Colonial Office. Home (1993) argues that in order to appease an increasingly dissatisfied population and maintain their empire during the World War periods, the British Colonial Office passed an Act to improve housing conditions in the Anglophone Caribbean. This centred upon the development of legislation for slum housing, based upon the English 1932 Town and Country Planning Act (Home 1993). The first planning Acts from the Anglophone Caribbean were passed in the 1930s to 1950s in Trinidad (1938), then St Lucia (1946), St Vincent and Grenada, (1946), Dominica, British Guiana, British Honduras (1947), St Kitts and Antigua (1948), Jamaica (1957) and Barbados (1959).

However, as Home suggests, there were more important reasons for the adoption of these Acts, which did not relate to the direct provision of welfare. The central emphasis in the above countries was the appeasement of local governing elites. Thus, whilst Home (1993) notes that a total of £5 million was given by the British Colonial Office for 'welfare provision' through physical development planning, as will be detailed in this chapter, emphasis was instead placed upon the Cabinet re-appropriating and mediating Western planning discourses, at the expense of the power of planning expertise.

The Power of the Premier

The power of the premier in the Anglophone Caribbean over planning expertise is clearly demonstrated through an examination of the operations of the Development Control Authorities of many Caribbean States. With regard to St Lucia for example, the strength of the Development Control Authority, and the Prime Minister who appoints it, draws upon section 7 of the 1971 Town and Country Planning Act. This states that: 'no person shall commence or carry out the development of any land in St Lucia without the prior written permission of the Authority' (Government of St Lucia 1971: section 7). The Development Control Authority is comprised of a Chief Engineer, Chief Technical Officer from the Ministry of Health, a Chairman, an environmentalist, a representative from the Ministry of Agriculture, a legal representative, the Director of Planning, a member of the public (usually a local businessman) and the Head of Planning, who acts as the executive secretary to the Board. Section 3 of the St Lucian 1971 Act states that: 'the Cabinet may at any time revoke the appointment of any member of the Authority if it thinks it expedient to do so' (Government of St Lucia 1971: section 3). Thus, members of the Authority who do not support Government can easily be removed. Furthermore, section 13 of the 1971 St Lucian Act states that 'the Authority shall have the power to regulate its own proceedings' (Government of St Lucia 1971). To summarize, the almost total discretion which is given to the

Authority can be utilized by the government of the day. The Caribbean Conservation Association (1991: 2–3) state that 'this feature of the Act has a long history of being invoked, much to the frustration of the planning process, planners and the general public'.

Similarly, in Grenada, the 2002 Physical Development and Control Planning Act allows for the eight members of the Development Control Authority to be appointed by the Governor General on advice of the Prime Minister (Government of Grenada 2002). In this case, the Authority must include 'the chief technical officers for the time being in charge of physical planning, public works, health services, agriculture and housing' (Government of Grenada 1983: cap. 160, section 3.1). In principle, all of the members could come from the Prime Minister's government.

Moreover, in many cases Caribbean ministers cannot be held liable for decisions made in relation to planning. With regard to Dominica, for example, the Physical Planning Act of 2001 states that: 'The Minister, members of the [Development Control] Authority, the Chief Physical Planner or other public officer shall not be personally liable in any court for or in respect of any act or matter done, or omitted to be done, in good faith, in the exercise or purported exercise of any function under or power conferred by this Act' (Commonwealth of Dominica 2001: Part II.7).

In other countries there is a limited attempt to install some sense of accountability and connection to planning expertise. Section 12 of the 1971 St Lucian Act states that 'a member of the Authority shall not vote upon, or take part in discussion of, any matter before the Authority in which he [*sic*] has directly or indirectly by himself or his [*sic*] partner any pecuniary interest' (Government of St Lucia 1971: section 12). Yet, as the Chief Town Planner of that country told the present author in 2000, there is a long history of members of the Development Control Authority from St Lucia being involved in development decisions in which they have a direct interest. This further illustrates the power of a limited number of elites, particularly those appointed by Cabinet.

In Jamaica, under the Town and Country Planning Act of 1995 (Government of Jamaica 1995), the Development Control Authority is also appointed by, and responsible to, the Minister. There is an accompanying Planning Advisory Committee, also appointed by the Minister, to advise him/her on planning matters. The different functions of these different groups is far from clear, leading to frustration within the planning departments of Jamaica, whilst maintaining the discretionary power of the Minister.

In Jamaica, a consultant reviewing the planning process in 2002 concluded: 'Planners are preoccupied with processing applications and have little or no time available to undertake planning (of course, nor are planners authorized to undertake planning under the provisions of the Town and Country Planning Act)' (KPMG 2002: 18). From the interviews undertaken with planners in Jamaica by the present author in 2003, the following statement of Khan and McDonald's (1995:4 9), made 18 years earlier, therefore still applies: 'many public sector managers are known to gripe about the fact that ministers often disregard their plans and formulate their own to suit their political/partisan needs'.

According to section 4 (3) of the 1981 Town and Country Planning Act of Barbados, the Town and Country Planning Advisory Committee (effectively a Development Control Authority) can advise the Minister on any matter. The Minister can require the Chief Town Planner to consult with the Advisory Committee in respect of any development (Government of Barbados 1981). However, the Minister, who is also the Prime Minister, maintains discretion over proceedings because there is no policy direction for the Advisory Committee. Furthermore, the Prime Minister appoints, and can remove, the seven members that comprise the Committee. Although the Committee does not make decisions that are enforceable by law, it has traditionally been used by the Prime Minister to 'justify' key development issues. In summation, one of the characteristics of planning in the Anglophone Caribbean is therefore that most planning Acts give this premier a strong, if not total, discretion over planning activities.

With regard to Trinidad and Tobago, as a further illustration of the power of the premier, the following two quotes are contained in the Town and Country Planning Act (1990):

> The decision of the Minister on any application made to him under this section shall be final. (Government of Trinidad and Tobago 1990: Part III.11.3. This statement is repeated many times in the Act, in III.12.3, for example)

> If as the result of any objection or representation considered, or public inquiry held, in connection with a development plan or proposals for amendment of such as plan the Minister is of opinion that a local authority or any other authority or person ought to be consulted before he decides to make the plan either with or without modifications, or to amend the plan, as the case may be, the Minister shall consult that authority or person, but he shall not be obliged to consult any other authority or person, or to afford any opportunity for further objections or representations or to cause any further public inquiry to be held. (Government of Trinidad and Tobago 1990: Part III.7.4)

The Cabinet are given further power over development decisions as a consequence of not often formally adopting physical development plans, which could render them accountable to the public. Where plans have been adopted, they are often two decades old, and therefore out of date. Both St Kitts and Nevis' and Dominica's last plan was produced in 1975, St Lucia's in 1977, Barbados in 1983, Trinidad and Tobago in 1984, for examples. Moreover, draft plans produced for St Kitts and Nevis in 1996, for Barbados in 1998, and in 1990 for Antigua, for examples, were not formally adopted.

The Appeals System

In many Anglophone Caribbean countries, the power of the Prime Minister over detailed developmental decisions is further strengthened by the appeals system. In St Lucia, for example, under section 13 of the St Lucian 1971 Act an applicant must appeal to the Prime Minister directly (Government of St Lucia 1971). The

Prime Minister subsequently appoints an appeals tribunal of three people, under the chair of a legally qualified person. However, the Prime Minister can also ask for any application to be referred to Cabinet, even after appeal. The Prime Minister can then agree or overturn the decision of the tribunal. Because the Prime Minister so often intervenes in planning decisions, Suddard (1975: 5) concludes that there is a problem with 'the definition of where town planning begins and ends' in much of the Anglophone Caribbean. The following discussion suggests that this situation remains the same today, 30 years later.

In Barbados, there are no rules or procedures for the approximately 100 appeals hearings that take place per annum. The hearing panel, even more informal than the hearing tribunal in St Lucia, is totally established by the Prime Minister. It is therefore largely a function of personality (Willms et al. 1998).

In Grenada, if an application for development is refused, the applicant can appeal to the Minister within 30 days. The appeal is then referred to an Appeals Tribunal, which includes three persons who have all been appointed by the Minister, the latter always having the final decision (Government of Grenada 2002: Section 11).

In Dominica, the appeals system 'shall consist of not less than three, and not more than five members appointed by the Minister of whom the chairman shall be a legal practitioner of not less than ten years standing' (Commonwealth of Dominica 2001: 74 (2)). Very similar appeals bodies are found across the Anglophone Caribbean, from countries ranging from Guyana to Trinidad and Tobago.

In Jamaica 'the Minister may allow or dismiss the appeal or may reverse or vary any part of the decision of the local planning authority, or the Authority, as the case may be, whether or not the appeal relates directly to that part, and deal with the application as if it had been made to him in the first instance' (Government of Jamaica 1995: III.13.2). As a result of such strong power being given to the premier over planning expertise, a consultant who reviewed the planning process in Jamaica in 2002 stated that 'a concern is the absence of an appropriate appeal process for subdivision and planning decisions, providing an objective and independent review against the provisions of an adopted plan' (KMPG 2002: 12). Moreover, senior planners in Jamaica in 2003 agree with Soler (1988: 32), who 15 years earlier stated that 'the Physical Planning Section [of many eastern Caribbean countries] does not play a major role when other Government agencies invest in projects which have a strong impact on the physical environment …'.

Duplicating Departments, in Order to Strengthen Control

The idea that governing elites can, and should, maintain a strong hold over development reform – at the expense of planning expertise – is illustrated in many Anglophone Caribbean public administration documents. One example of this is the duplication of planning department functions and the associated development of bypass mechanisms. Almost 15 years ago, Williams (1990: 129) noted 'the tendency to continually formulate new plans for change and establish more and more agencies as 'bypass' mechanisms is significant'. Let us briefly take Trinidad and Tobago as another current example of this. At present there is an Environmental Management Committee (set up in 2001), and an Interim National Physical Planning Commission (produced in 1996). These were added to the Town and Country Planning Division, as one leading planner from Trinidad described the situation in 2003. This existence of multiple planning agencies leads to 'complete confusion', as another Trinidadian planner explained in that year to the present author. And the new draft Planning and Development Bill (modifying the Act of the same name of 1996) does not clarify when and how different departmental functions will be established.

Similarly, in Grenada there is a Planning Department within the Ministry of Agriculture, but also a Physical Planning Unit in the Ministry of Finance. Their different functions are also not clear. The reason for maintaining such confusion and duplication is the same as Williams (1990) noted 15 years ago. If a member of Government has friends and contacts in one department, then this department can be used to validate development planning decisions – the more departments concerned with development, the more chances a Cabinet Minister has of increasing their control over development.

Whilst of course by no means comprehensive, the description of formal physical development planning presented in the last few sections illustrates that such systems are often used to strengthen the hand of the Cabinet, at the expense of planning experts and civil servants.

The Re-articulation of Physical Development Planning as a More Inclusive System

Since the 1990s in particular, new political ideologies have been deployed through donor agencies' programmes. These have emphasized the importance of local solutions to local problems, and mark the arrival of the era of 'institutional capacity building' in the Anglophone Caribbean. But they also reflect the strong sense of anxiety that has emerged within the field of development studies more generally over the last few decades. There is a lack of confidence within Western donor agencies that direct substantive prescriptions of development policy are effective, or politically correct (see Crush 1995, Sidaway 2000 and Blaikie 2000 for examples). As Pender (2001: 397) points out, 'Structural Adjustment lending, and the policy conditionality associated with it, is at an end'. Today, there is an emphasis upon *partnership* between the different agencies that are connected to government, as a means of articulating more locally based solutions to problems. It is worth recapping how this situation has historically evolved.

In 1995, writing about the impasse in development studies, Arturo Escobar wrote a paper that started with the following quote:

> If I knew for a certainty that a man was coming to my house with the conscious design of doing me good, I should run for my life … for fear that I should get some of his good done to me. (Thoreau 1977: 328)

The way in which Escobar reads Thoreau illustrates the strong sense of anxiety that has emerged within the field of development studies more generally over the last couple of decades – the lack of confidence that the West can 'do good' in the developing world (see Esteva 1987 and Nandy 1989 as early examples). The general argument surrounding the impasse in development studies is that the people of the developing world become dominated by Western ways of doing development. This, in turn, excludes autonomous 'spaces' for local people to express themselves in, and alternatives therefore need to be found. The idea that 'development stinks' (Esteva 1987: 135) has had a significant impact upon the subject of development studies, which is now dominated by fear: the fear of being accused of producing Western visions and missions for the developing world.

Escobar (1995: 166), a leading critique of development agencies, reflects the wider criticisms which have been made over the last couple of decades, in writing:

> As a pacesetter for the development industry, the World Bank influences decisively the fate of nearly $60-billion-a-year official aid to the South … up to 80 per cent of that aid is spent in donor countries on the contracts and salaries of staff and consultants.

In recent years, such statistics and statements have influenced a status of anxiety within Western donor agencies. Donors no longer have the confidence to project their visions of development onto the developing world (Pender 2001). There has been a shift from the period of certainty which characterized 1980 to 1994 – 'closely associated with the worldview of Western elites' – to a period of 'growing uncertainty within the Western policy prescribing elite' (Pender 2001: 400).

Donor agencies have made unprecedented self-criticisms of their previous approaches to development. This is reflected in the narrow framework of direct budgetary support, pushed forward through the UK's Department for International Development poverty reduction strategies. A draft policy paper *Partnerships for Poverty Reduction: Changing Aid 'Conditionality'* states:

> Our understanding of what makes aid effective is changing. Evidence and experience have challenged traditional approaches to 'conditionality' (where each donor frequently attached conditions to its aid in order to promote particular policies in the partner country). This paper sets out a new approach to building a successful partnership for poverty reduction. We believe that developing countries must have room to determine their own policies. (DFID 2004: 1)

As one example of this, the paper also says that:

> The UK will continue to attach 'process conditions' to improve the quality and effectiveness of aid. For example, we will use conditions that strengthen participation by poor people in decision-making. However, such conditions must be carefully designed so as not to interfere with national political processes. (DFID 2004: 2)

This illustrates Pender's (2001: 408) general point that: 'a more relaxed approach is today regarded as appropriate'. In particular, it shows how the nation state is being prescribed a more autonomous role – one that should not be interfered with too much (Pugh 2005b, 2005c). The strength of certainty and power to control governing elites from these countries is reflected in the new ideologies and discourses that are being supported through regional and international programmes across the Caribbean.

Institutional capacity building is a form of planning which attempts to bring together diverse and fragmented agencies for collective action, in order to increase the power of the nation state to produce coherent visions for development. Examples of the exponentially increasing importance of institutional capacity building are rife in the contemporary Anglophone Caribbean (see United Nations Economic Commission for Latin America and the Caribbean 1998). The Small Island Developing States Programme of Action (SIDsPOA) – the first regional response to the Rio Earth Summit of 1992 – brought together 111 small islands from across the globe. Held in Barbados in 1994, one of its central themes was the development of institutional capacity building. The 1998 review of the SIDsPOA elevated 'institutional capacity building' above 'poverty alleviation' and 'involvement of marginal groups' (United Nations, Economic Commission for Latin America and the Caribbean 1998). Thus, the elites who represented the Anglophone Caribbean at the SIDsPOA formally put institutional capacity building as a very high priority indeed, above the alleviation of poverty. This therefore placed significant emphasis upon bringing together the different governmental departments and civil servants in specific Caribbean countries, in order to prepare more coherent visions for sustainable development.

Building up the Capacity of Local Governing Elites

The following few examples show that Anglophone Caribbean Governments have adopted this new language of institutional capacity building. These Governments have had to formally engage in such Western planning discourses, in order to receive funding. Donor agencies therefore continue to prescribe the planning discourses that are articulated by elites in the region. Yet, as the following shows, the Cabinet of many Anglophone Caribbean countries has also continued to deploy and co-opt these discourses to suit their own purposes – from the earliest days of physical development planning (discussed in the last sections of this chapter) to the present era of 'institutional capacity building' (explored in this section).

Turning firstly to St Kitts and Nevis, the draft 1996 National Physical Development Plan endorsed the concept of institutional capacity building (Physical Development Planning Division 1996). It did so by attempting to bring together the previously fragmented agencies of government, non-governmental sectors, the private sector, churches, special interest groups and the general public. The draft 1996 National Physical Development Plan states that:

> By involving the affected and interested parties in the setting of goals and objectives, defining alternatives, assessing their impacts and selecting the one for implementation, support for the selected action is generated among those responsible for the plan, thus increasing assurance of the plan success. (Physical Development Planning Division 1996: 6)

Such statements of intent demonstrate how institutional capacity building is now seen to be formally necessary for successful planning. In the past, the Cabinet did not take this approach – it was assumed that they spoke on behalf of all. We now see an explicit attempt to connect with what are articulated to be disconnected and fragmented groups, 'thus increasing assurance of the plan success', as the St Kitts and Nevis plan states (Physical Development Planning Division 1996: 6).

It remains the case, as it has since the very early days of formal town planning in the region in the 1930s, that the Cabinet 'must engage in these new fashions' if they are to receive money (as a leading member of the Caribbean Development Bank described the situation to the present author in 2003). And thus, senior Physical Planning Officers from St Kitts and Nevis have vented their frustration at the Cabinet's lack of willingness to actually implement institutional capacity building initiatives. This would have brought together different agencies under the control of the Physical Planning Division, thereby increasing the power of planning experts. Planners have also expressed concern over the lack of collaboration between the Physical Planning Division and the National Housing Commission, with a resulting duplication of their functions. This also has the effect of reducing the power of civil servants more generally and increasing that of the Cabinet. The governing elites must frequently intervene between conflicting departments that have no clear remit, in order to decide which department has the final say. Correspondence between different members of different departments, passed on anonymously to the present author, indicates that the Cabinet has made no attempt to rectify this situation, despite receiving funding for institutional capacity building initiatives.

Guyana is another country that received funding from the Caribbean Development Bank for institutional capacity building. A 10-year plan funded by the Carter Centre 'marks the first time that Guyanese of all races, religions and political persuasions have come together to draft a blueprint for our future' (Government of Guyana 1996: 2). Yet, there is a sense that the 'new era of co-operation' (Government of Guyana 1996: 2) does not involve ministers cooperating with planning departments, as the latter could challenge their power. According to the Chief Town Planner of Guyana, there is a 'lack of political will' to support the development of his department; and, more generally, to 'continually bypass Government departments'. There are many more examples which illustrate how the re-articulation of planning, with the purpose of widening the formal sphere of influence over development decision-making, is more a reflection of the anxiety of donor agencies, than of the wishes of local governing elites to increase the power of local planners.

In 1998 and 2000, using funds from the European Union, the Government of Dominica commissioned the Organization of Eastern Caribbean States – Natural Resources Management Unit to prepare a study entitled 'Institutional Arrangements for Integrated Development Planning for Dominica' and 'The Establishment of an Integrated Development Planning Process'. Yet, in that country, the Chief Physical Planner (one of only two planners in the Physical Planning and Development Authority) assumes the roles of public officer responsible for administration and operations, the secretary and chief executive. As the Chief Planner described the situation to the present author in 2002, 'two planners cannot challenge' the power of Cabinet 'on any issue'. Government does not want to share power with its planning experts in some sort of collaborative process of decision-making. It wants to maintain firm discretionary control.

The point is not that Anglophone Caribbean governments suddenly feel the need to reconnect to different departments and their civil servants through capacity building. As stated, the discourses of institutional capacity building have largely arisen in response to the concerns of anxious donor agencies, which have been criticized over the last few decades. The result is that 'local' solutions are now considered the only politically correct solution, and funding is given accordingly. In practice, due to the maintenance of particular power structures, these local solutions are more often than not offered by the Cabinet, rather than planning expertise.

The following example from Barbados – which is seen by many public servants from across the Caribbean as most effective in rearticulating Western planning discourses to suit the needs of the Cabinet – perhaps best illustrates the point that the era of institutional capacity building is used to increase the power of government, in the face of an anxious and criticized donor agency community.

In 1997 the Government of Barbados, with assistance from the IDB and a Canadian environmental consultancy, undertook the Environmental Management and Land Use Project (EMLUP), at a cost of US$ 1.795 million. EMLUP ran from April 1997 until December 1998. The project involved not only the production of the third (draft) PDP, but also an Environment and Natural Resources Management Plan, the development of a Geographical Information System (GIS), a National Park Plan for the Scotland District in the northeastern part of Barbados, an Area Plan covering agricultural issues, and a series of Institutional Strengthening Reports. The institutional strengthening component concentrated upon the enhancement of the Department of Environment and the strengthening of the Town and Country Planning Office. The outputs are therefore widespread, and a more comprehensive review is presented in Pugh (2002). Various documents associated with the EMLUP attempt to challenge the power of ministers. These include reducing their abilities to modify development plans, make development orders and regulations, control appeals and planning compensation, make decisions on development applications and intervene in the actions of the Chief Town Planner (Willms 1998). Yet, all of these suggestions have been rejected by Cabinet. The discretionary power of government is thus maintained through new institutional capacity building projects that are being funded by Western donor agencies. It is unlikely therefore that planning experts will have a greater say over the substantial issues associated with the planning process, as such donor agencies leave countries to find their own 'local solutions to local problems'. Expertise thus remains secondary to ministerial power. Ministers will be able to continue to dominate planning decisions, including, as another example, the new Environmental Impact Assessment panel that will be established to oversee Environmental Impact Assessments undertaken in Barbados. The political influence of local elites from the Cabinet will be placed above local technical expertise and the wishes of foreign consultants funded by donor agencies.

Five 'Community Plans' were produced for Barbados as part of the EMLUP. However, these simply reiterate, rather than detail, the policies for the national level. There has been no devolvement of power into the communities, and no processes have been put in place for continuous community consultation. Illustrating the point that formal development continues to be dominated by the Cabinet, there has also been no massive backlash from the public or civil servants. In effect, community plans are produced for the community by central government in order to support the discretionary power of the Cabinet.

Conclusion

In this chapter I have not sought to demonstrate whether local elites mediating, adapting and re-articulating Western planning discourses for their own purposes has 'good' or 'bad' outcomes for the people who they govern. Rather, my purpose has been more modest. I have simply sought to show that, in the era of 'local solutions to local problems', local elites have found another way of working *with* Western planning discourses – something that they have done since the earliest days of the physical development planning system in the Anglophone Caribbean. They are not dominated by Western donor agencies in a deterministic manner; but, instead, reflect upon and mediate such discourses, in order to increase their power to rule their countries. One consequence of this is that planning expertise is reduced to a relatively minor role.

Moreover, whilst Western funding agencies now articulate the more 'democratic' discourse of institutional capacity building (which, in contrast to the era of structural adjustment, does not demand substantive development policies be implemented), this is more reflective of the politicized anxieties of the 'West'. Put bluntly, it is not the elites from Anglophone Caribbean countries that are suffering the anxiety of disconnection from their different government departments and planning experts – but donor agencies who have been criticized for taking too much of a top-down approach in the past. By co-opting the new discourse of institutional capacity building, the Cabinets of Anglophone Caribbean countries fulfil the specifications of international funding agencies, and receive funding that increases their power in return.

Note

1 I am grateful to the Economic and Social Research Council for supporting my PhD (Ref: R00429834850) and my three-year Research Fellowship (Ref: R000271204). Thanks also go to Pamela Richardson, for helping to catalogue the planning library that I have collected over the past eight years. This library is now housed at the University of Newcastle Upon Tyne, UK. Contact JnPugh@aol.com for details.

References

Blaikie, P. (2000), 'Development, Post-, Anti-, and Populist: A Critical Review', *Environment and Planning A*, 32, pp. 1033–50.

Caribbean Conservation Association (1991), *Environmental Guidelines for Caribbean Planners*, Barbados: Organization of Eastern Caribbean States, United Nations Development Programme, United Nations Centre for Humans Settlements (Habitat).

Commonwealth of Dominica (2001), Physical Planning Act, Dominca: Commonwealth of Dominica.

Crush, J. (ed.) (1995), *Power of Development*, London and New York: Routledge.

Department for International Development (2004), *Partnerships for Poverty Reduction: Changing Aid 'Conditionality'. A Draft Policy Paper For Comment*, London: DFID, Foreign and Commonwealth Office.

Escobar, A. (1995), *Encountering Development: The Making and Unmaking of the Third World*, Princeton, NJ: Princeton University Press.

Esteva, G. (1987), 'Regenerating People's Space', *Alternatives*, 12 (1), pp. 125–52.

Government of Barbados (1981), Town and Country Planning Act, Barbados: Government of Barbados.

Government of Grenada (1983), Land Development Control Act, Grenada: Government of Grenada.

Government of Grenada (2002), Physical Planning and Development Control Act, Grenada: Government of Grenada.

Government of Guyana (2001), 'National Development Strategy: 2001–2010, A Policy Framework, Eradicating Poverty and Unifying Guyana', a civil society document, Guyana: Government of Guyana.

Government of Jamaica (1995), The Town and Country Planning Act, Jamaica: Government of Jamaica.

Government of St Lucia (1971), Land Development (interim control) No.8 Act, 1971, St Lucia: Government of St Lucia.

Government of Trinidad and Tobago (1990), Laws of Trinidad and Tobago: Town and Country Planning Act, Chapter 35:01, Trinidad and Tobago: Government of Trinidad and Tobago.

Government of Trinidad and Tobago, Development and Planning Bill (draft), Trinidad and Tobago.

Griffin, C.E. (1997), *Democracy and Neoliberalism in the Developing World: Lessons from the Anglophone Caribbean*, Aldershot: Ashgate.

Home, R., (1993), 'Transferring British Planning Law to the Colonies: The Case of the 1938 Trinidad Town and Regional Planning Ordinance', *Third World Planning Review*, 15, pp. 397–411.

Khan, J. and McDonald, W.A. (1995), 'Political Dominance and Public Sector Management', *Bulletin of Eastern Caribbean Affairs*, 20 (2), pp. 47–55.

KPMG Consulting LP (2002), *Discussion Paper; Modernizing the Planning Framework for Jamaica*, Jamaica.

Nandy, A. (1989), *Traditions, Tyranny, and Utopias*, Delhi: Oxford University Press.

Pender, J. (2001), 'From "Structural Adjustment" to "Comprehensive Development Framework": Conditionality Transformed?', *Third World Quarterly*, 22 (3), pp. 397–411.

Physical Development Planning Division (1996) National Physical Development Plan (draft), Government of St Kitts and Nevis.

Pugh, J. (2002), 'Deconstructing Participatory Environmental Planning: Dispositions of Power in Barbados and St Lucia', unpublished PhD thesis, Royal Holloway, University of London.

Pugh, J. (2005a), 'The Disciplinary Effects of Communicative Planning in Soufriere, St Lucia: The Relative Roles of Governmentality, Hegemony and Space-Time-Politics', *Transactions: Institute of British Geographers/Royal Geographical Society*, 30 (3), pp. 307–22.

Pugh, J. (2005b), 'Environmental Planning in Barbados: A Confident State, Isolated Environmental Movements, and Anxious Development Consultants', *Southeastern Geographer*, Special Edition on the Caribbean, 45 (2), pp. 28–41.

Pugh, J. (2005c), 'Social Transformation and Participatory Planning in St Lucia', *Area*, 37 (4), pp. 384–92.

Sidaway, J.D. (2000), 'Post-Development', in V. Desai and R.B. Potter (eds), *The Arnold Companion to Development Studies*, Arnold: London, pp. 16–20.

Soler, F. (1988), *Development Control and Physical Planning, the Case of Saint Lucia*, St Lucia: Organization of American States Executive Secretariat for Economic and Social Affairs Department of Regional Development, Natural Resource Management Project.

Suddard, R.W. (1975), *Planning Law and Administration in the Eastern Caribbean: A Continuation Report*, St Lucia: United Nations Development Programme.

United Nations Development Programme (1977), *Assistance in Physical Planning (Phase II); Caribbean: Multi-Island Country Project, Prepared for the Governments of the Caribbean Region*, New York: United Nations.

United Nations Economic Commission for Latin America and the Caribbean (1998), *National Implementation of the Small Islands Developing States Programme of Action: A Caribbean Perspective*, Trinidad: United Nations Economic Commission for Latin America and the Caribbean.

Williams, G. (1990), 'The Effectiveness of Newly Established Agencies and Institutions: Caribbean Public Sector', *Social and Economic Studies*, 39 (2), pp. 105–33.

Willms and Shier, Carnegie, A.R., Berridge Lewinberg Greenberg Dark Gabor Limited, Bird and Hale Limited, Halcrox Fox (1998b), *Ministry of Health and the Environment, Government of Barbados, Environmental and Natural Resources Management Plan, Environmental Management and Land Use Planning for Sustainable Development*, Canada: Willms and Shier, Berridge Lewinberg Greenberg Dark Gabor Limited, Bird and Hale Limited, Halcrox Fox.

Chapter 3

'The Bad Old Days Look Better': Enlightened Colonial Land Management Practices and Land Reform in the British Windward Islands

Beth Mills

Introduction

For many people the image of daily life and social structure in the Caribbean during colonial times is dominated by the suffering of African and Afro-Caribbean people under slavery. These negative reminders of the past often provide the framework for thinking about the experiences of individuals during that time. Unfairly or not, it is easy to dismiss the acts of the colonial officers by equating them with a system fraught with oppression and abuse. Furthermore, when colonial governments exited the region after independence in the twentieth century, a vacuum of leadership and skills was created that slowed the economic and social progress of the region in the modern global economy. These harsh realities are one facet of the legacy that European governments left in the islands.

Another, more positive facet of the colonial legacy, is the subject of this chapter. That is, the positive results of sound environmental and land reform policies, both proposed and implemented, by the progressive thinkers of the British colonial administration in the Windward Islands. These men saw the opportunity to preserve island forests and control soil erosion. Their ideas and actions offer a bright spot in colonial history and are instructive for contemporary conservationists in the region. In the case of the British colonial administration in the Windwards, conservation measures were often paired with land reform; social improvement and environmental protection were perceived to be mutually dependent. The historical records shows, and current land use patterns testify to, the sound environmental policies generated during this time. The scope of their integrated and holistic approach is surprising.

Scientists and Administrators

The revolution in scientific thinking that occurred in Europe in the last decades of the nineteenth century is the context within which environmental management projects were realized in the colonies. Grove (1995) provides a solid background for understanding the intellectual milieu of the times in his discussion of 'green imperialism'. The age of discovery and the imperial expansion of European nations into the Western Hemisphere, Africa, the Near and Far East, marks the beginning of the process of globalization. People and ideas, as well as flora and fauna, were moving across oceans in unprecedented numbers. As European colonial powers began to establish plantation economies in the tropics they came directly into contact with complex and unimagined ecosystems. What they experienced lead to a new European evaluation of nature and '... the growing awareness of the destructive impact of European economic activity on peoples and environments of... colonial lands' (Grove 1995: 3). The colonial administrators' reaction to the environments they encountered reflected the dominant religious and philosophical thinking of the time, while the exposure to the new physical environments simultaneously fueled scientific inquiry and understanding.

The founding of the Botanic Garden at Kingston, St Vincent in 1765, with support from the London Society of the Arts, is illustrative of contemporary thinking about nature in the tropics. It was the first such garden in the Western Hemisphere and provided the blueprint for later gardens in Calcutta, India, and South Africa. Plant materials from the Indian Ocean island of Mauritius and various other tropical locations were collected and brought to St Vincent for propagation. The garden not only provided an opportunity for botanical study and experimentation, but in a metaphorical sense, a way for Europeans to gain control within a confined space of an unfamiliar physical environment. The garden organized the unfamiliar. (Grove 1995).

As colonization progressed there was a shift in attitudes towards nature and the environment. With the spread of the plantation economy there was also an 'awareness of the ecological demands of emergent capitalism and colonial control' (Grove 1995: 6). The choice of Alexander Anderson, a 'radical Scottish physician and botanist' (Grove 1995: 265), to head the St Vincent botanic garden is also illustrative of the general intellectual atmosphere of the times. He was in many ways representative of the group of colonial officials in the tropics during the eighteenth century.

Many colonial officials of the time were professional scientists and environmental commentators; frequently they were also medical surgeons. They were the products of the 'Scottish Enlightenment' and graduates of the major universities at Edinburgh and Aberdeen. This group is credited with the introduction of experimental land management techniques to the islands. Many of these experimental techniques would have been difficult to introduce at the same time in Europe (Grove 1995), and their tropical assignments provided them with perfect experiment stations. Among this group of land managers was W.E. Broadway, the curator of the Grenada botanical garden, who visited Carriacou in 1897 and made many insightful suggestions about forest and water conservation. His experiences and observations are detailed below.

This community of thinkers analyzed the physical processes they observed around them and, as a result, by 1850 tropical deforestation was recognized to be a global problem by this scientific community. The connection between vegetation and climate had been suggested in desiccationist (the concept that trees attract precipitation) theories as early as 1764. It was becoming accepted scientific thinking that forests ensured rainfall. Furthermore, the pioneering work of Pierre Poivre in Mauritius in the 1790s tied conservation to radical social reform. He linked the ideas of political reconstruction to tree planting, forest protection, climate preservation, and agricultural improvement. (Grove 1995: 10). Alexander Von Humboldt's writings in the 1820s also make the connection between deforestation, water supply, famine, climate, and disease. These visionaries were laying the groundwork for the modern concept of sustainability in the context of the tropics.

Forest Conservation and Management in the Windward Islands

In the Caribbean, forest conservation policies emerged in the wake of the large scale clearing of native vegetation in the sugar colonies of Barbados, Antigua, and to a lesser extent Jamaica. The Windward Islands, which were ceded to England by the Treaty of Paris in 1763 (including Dominica, St Vincent, the Grenadines, and Grenada), were among the more mountainous and less developed of the islands, and consequently had more forest cover than the other flat and easily accessible islands.

Carriacou, the southernmost and largest of the Grenadine islands, was an exception to this pattern. Although consisting primarily of steep terrain, the original forests had been almost completely cleared during the eighteenth century (Richardson 1975). The larger islands in the Windwards (Dominica, St Vincent and Grenada) contrasted with the Carriacou conditions in that significant acreages of forest, especially in the higher elevations and on the windward coasts, remained undisturbed.

It was clear to scientists during the nineteenth century that the ongoing success of economic activities in the tropics was dependent upon forest conservation. Further, it became clear to some that deforestation in the tropics had global consequences. Apparently, colonial states were peculiarly open, at least until the mid-nineteenth century, to the social leverages and often radical agendas of the contemporary scientific lobby (Grove 1995: 7).

Colonial administrations were also to find the conservation of forests to be a useful tool for controlling peripheral and troublesome indigenous groups. Forest conservation programs, and the survey and allocation of remote areas on the islands as designated forest preserves, provided the colonial government with the legal mechanism to justify bringing indigenous groups under control. These policies are evidenced in the relocation of the Garifuna (a mix of indigenous and African people) from the forested windward coast of St Vincent to the coastal areas of Central America. In the case of St Vincent, government surveys of forest reserves on the windward coast met with fierce resistance from the indigenous people. Another good example of such policy is the changing relationship between people and land in Carriacou, Grenada during colonial times.

Colonial Land Use Policy in Carriacou

The changes brought about to the environment of Carriacou in the eighteenth century with the introduction of plantation agriculture were all encompassing. As the existing forest cover was cleared for plantation crops, the ecosystem was disrupted and severe ecological damage was set in motion. By 1776, 6,041 out of a total 6,927 acres had been cleared, leaving only 886 acres in forest (Rhodes House Library, Oxford 1949). Most slopes were cultivated by this time and soils were exposed to the erosive agents of wind and water as a result of seasonal cultivation. With the failure of the plantation economy after the double blow of emancipation (1834) and the Sugar Duties Act of 1846, subsistence cropping and overgrazing sustained the pattern of environmental degradation. It has been suggested that the island ecology was irreversibly altered by the 'overdevelopment' inflicted on the resource base by first, the plantation economy and it's demands and second, by overstocking cattle, sheep and goats by subsistence farmers (Richardson 1975).

By the late 1800s the colonial government began a series of land reforms that subdivided former plantations and made them available to local people to purchase. It is at this critical juncture that the British colonial government organized to control environmental impacts by implementing forest conservation measures and sustainable land use and water management policies. The higher elevations of the estates were set aside as forest reserves 'to encourage the rain' and common pasturage with fencing was provided in each new village.

Linkages between Resource Conservation, Land Tenure and Social Reform

The period of time between emancipation in the British Caribbean in 1834 and 1900 was one of social upheaval and disruption as planters and former slaves adjusted to the changes shaking the region. While British planters struggled to exert control over the labor supply on which their livelihoods depended, the freed slaves sought ways to acquire land and determine their own future. By the end of the nineteenth century the Eastern Caribbean was in economic depression, in large part tied to the Sugar Duties Act of 1846, which eliminated protections. The region was also reeling from a series of environmental disasters including volcanic eruptions, earthquakes, and hurricanes (Richardson 1997).

Scholars describe a mixed set of conflicts, constraints, resistances, and resolutions between the White plantocracy and freed Africans during this time period (Olwig 1995). Suddenly freed slaves were expected to fend for themselves. The customary support of food and medical care for the former slave was no longer provided. Rights to the cultivation of small plots known as provision grounds, so important to most former slaves (both in terms of meeting basic dietary requirements and as a source of cash from the sale of surplus) were either eliminated or had to be renegotiated. The planters were forced to give in to changing policy regarding slavery at the national level, but they still controlled the all-important access to land.

Planters were typically at the core of and certainly dominated most local government after emancipation. In many cases they were able to enact local legislation regarding taxes and licenses meant to circumvent the intention of the metropole (and colonial adminstrators) to create a new society based on the 'peasant' farmer (Momsen 1987). On many islands there was a tension between the colonial administrators and the local plantocracy over the need for social reform in contrast to what the planters' perceived as unavoidable economic realities.

Legislated controls on African labour and a determination to deny Africans' access to land were strongest and most successful in Antigua, Barbados, and St Kitts, where essentially all land was planted in sugar. On the larger islands of Jamaica and Trinidad there was, physically, more room for the newly emancipated to find land to cultivate, and to some extent purchase, in the more remote, highland areas. In Jamaica there was a pre-emancipation tradition of African villages in the highlands, established by runaway slaves. On some islands, including the British Virgin Islands (Mauer 1997) and Jamaica (Besson 1984) the church was the institution that facilitated the sale of freehold property to the emancipated slaves. Even before emancipation, small farms had been the rule rather than the exception in Grenada, primarily as a result of the success of tree crops over sugar due to the island's mountainous terrain. This fact shaped the evolution of agriculture and land tenure after emancipation on Grenada in a unique way within the region.

To the members of the West Indies Royal Commission of 1897, the poverty and suffering of the post-emancipation laborers was most striking on St Vincent and the Grenadine islands of Union Island and Carriacou (Momsen 1987, Richardson 1997).

On Montserrat, the struggle for land and the brutality and poverty suffered by the emancipated slaves was striking, instigating mass emigration from that island immediately after emancipation. The extent and character of emigration from Montserrat (Berleant-Schiller 1995) is similar to the circumstances found on Carriacou. Local people on these islands (St Vincent, Montserrat, Union and Carriacou) were reduced to squatting and sharecropping (also referred to as *metayage*) arrangements throughout the nineteenth century. Most landowners were absentee by the end of the century. So dismal was life on these islands that land reform was imposed by the colonial government on St Vincent and Carriacou at the end of the nineteenth century, in part, as a result of the deplorable conditions the commissioners of the 1897 survey reported.

When land reform was instituted in St Vincent and Carriacou at the end of the nineteenth century it was done at the recommendation of the West India Commissioners and various other colonial administrators who were familiar with the plight of the local population. Many of these same colonial officials also demonstrated a concern for conservation of the environment, especially as it related to forest resources. Their vision for land use in the new settlements demonstrates their increasing belief in the interconnection between vegetation and climate and was supported by the work done by colonial officials in other parts of the tropics, especially in Mauritius and the other islands frequented by the East India Trading Company.

Land Reform and Conservation on Carriacou (1885–1905)

The historical context for land resettlement on Carriacou was a result of the economic depression in the region resulting from collapse of the sugar market. The political climate for land reform was set in motion by the recommendations of the aforementioned West Indies Royal Commission of 1897 (Richardson 1997: 222–5).

The stage was set for land reform on Carriacou in 1897 with a visit to the island by the curator of the Grenada Botanical Garden, W.E. Broadway. In his report to the colonial government, Broadway outlines the state of agriculture on the island and recommends the purchase of some of the estates by the government in order to redistribute the land to the 'peasantry' (Colonial Office Paper No. 11, Grenada 1898).

Broadway was primarily interested in promoting a plan to improve agricultural production on Carriacou by introducing cacao, coffee and tobacco. He visited some farms along the main ridge of the island, and also the estate at Dumfries, where individual farmers were having some success with cacao. Tobacco was being cultivated on a small scale on the estates at Hillsborough and at Mt Pleasant.

Broadway's report provides a description of the Carriacou landscape in 1897. He complains that trees were cleared to the point of there being no shade available along the roadsides. Mahogany was still growing in some upland locations, but much of the island had been completely cleared of forest cover. He notes that most of the land was being used as pasture for sheep, cattle and horses. Following the tour, he made several important observations and suggestions. Chief among these is his recommendation that the government purchase and divide some of the existing estates. He notes:

> Carriacou is owned almost exclusively by absentee proprietors, and the estates rented out to lessees. All whom I consulted on the subject avowed that the great hindrance of the agriculturalist was the way in which the land is owned by absentee proprietors. They--the lessees--have at present no encouragement to plant permanent products such as cacao and coffee, because it is open to doubt whether the proprietor will take the land from them at the end of their term of lease, which I understood averaged about 5 years.
>
> What they suggest is some radical change be effected whereby the land can be so allotted that these doubts no longer have room for existence. The lessee is not in a position to lease land for a long number of years, when some years owing to drought they make little returns, but still have to continue to pay their rents as they fall due. So far as I could gather, absentee proprietorship is the principal cause for the want of progress made in the agriculture of the island. There is no alternative then, but a rearrangement of the ownership of the land, and, in fact, this is imperative before the advancement can be made in agriculture in Carriacou. Possibly if the absentee proprietor was approached on the subject by the Government, arrangements to the advantage of himself and the lessee might be made. It seems only fair, and reasonable, that if a lessee, took up seriously the cultivation of cocoa and coffee, and if after its establishment it was desired on the part of the absentee proprietor to take over when the lease expired, full compensation should be made to the lessee.
>
> This is the burning question, which, if it meets with immediate attention from the government and is settled favorably for the residents of Carriacou, will remove the

greatest impediment for the progress of the island. Minor reasons there are also which delay progress but which can be removed by perseverance in object lessons, to bear on the primitive methods now in vogue among the majority of the peasantry. Besides this question, there is that relating to the strange and ruinous system of allowing stock to roam at will during the dry season, due I was informed, to the scarcity of fodder when the dry season comes around. These animals have free access to all unenclosed property according to the custom of the island. (Grenada, C.O. Paper No. 11 1898: 7–8)

At this early date there is evidence of the problems that have plagued agricultural development on Carriacou throughout the years. Although Broadway's recommended changes in land tenure were soon implemented, cacao, coffee, and tobacco were never established on the island. The basic components of the mixed cropping system of corn, pigeon peas, and root crops (ground provisions) such as manioc and sweet potatoes, already established by the small farmers at this time, persist in a much diminished fashion, to the present. Cotton became significant after the failure of sugar. It was inter-planted with the corn and peas. Stock trespass during the dry season has remained a problem and expanded in the second half of the twentieth century to become a year-round nuisance, despite government efforts at control of grazing.

In the 1898 report the need for 'reafforestation' efforts are emphasized. Broadway reports that during his 1898 visit he observed:

... on the southern side of Chapeau Carre very near the top I noticed, whilst riding through Grand Ance, a newly cleared piece of land, intended, no doubt, as a provision garden, presently to be extended on, and thus do the hilltops become denuded of their trees slowly, but all the more surely; it is a fact that deforestation is recklessly carried on in Carriacou. (p. 8)

Today we see that the efforts to establish forest reserves over the years, with government supervision, have basically proven successful. Much of the land comprising the ridges and uplands of the island is now forested in secondary growth as a result of setting those areas aside as government reserves during the land reform. There were then subsequent reafforestation efforts by the government agricultural office.

In his report Broadway expresses the colonial view. He is clearly well-intentioned in his efforts to find a way to increase agricultural production and help alleviate the poverty of the islanders. He states:

Once a flourishing sugar producing colony, Carriacou is now in a distressful state. If the people will but accept the assistance of the government which is being extended to them, there is little reason why it should not soon, at any rate, be in much better and prosperous condition. (p. 9)

The attitude expressed in the quote is indicative of the approach to economic development taken toward the residents of the colonies by colonial administrators of the time. The subtext throughout is that if only the 'peasants' would listen and do what they were told they would meet with success. Consistent with this tone, Broadway notes:

> Messrs. John Grant Wells, John McNeilly, and Steill are doing an immense amount of genuine good in the island by the kind and reasonable advice they give the peasantry, and residents in general, from time to time in agriculture. (p. 10)

Broadway's other recommendations included introducing Eucalyptus (an Australian import) to dry up the swamp near the hospital where mosquitoes were breeding, and the planting of white cedar, mahogany, saman and almond. He also speculates that pineapple should be introduced as a crop. It seems that none of these recommendations were ever acted upon.

However, the colonial government did move forward on the recommendation of the settlement of local people on the estates under absentee ownership and implemented the push for reforestation of the uplands. At the end of the nineteenth century the British colonial government and its administrators in Grenada (who also administered Carriacou) began a process whereby failing or unproductive plantations were purchased by the government in order to be subdivided and the allotments sold to local residents. This land reform was initiated in 1898 on three estates on Carriacou. During the first half of the twentieth century several more estates on Carriacou and Grenada were bought by the government in an attempt to settle landless tenants and workers on their own property.

Despite Broadway's great enthusiasm for cacao and coffee cultivation on Carricaou, the market prevailed and cotton was the primary cash crop by 1901. It continued to be so throughout the first half of the twentieth century. A detailed report on the progress of the land settlement scheme at Beausejour prepared by Edward Drayton in 1903 gives a clear picture of the circumstances under which small farmers or the 'peasantry' came to land ownership (Colonial Reports, No. 24, Grenada 1903).

On 1 May 1901 the colonial office in Grenada specified the regulations for allotting the land at Beausejour, one of the larger plantations on Carriacou. From the outset the officials experienced complications at Beausejour because they were unaware of what was happening on the ground. They discovered that 147 acres of the estate had already been sold in small parcels some time before without the knowledge of the government. It was then necessary to ask all those landowners to prove their claim to the government's satisfaction. Time was then taken up with surveying these allotments where they impinged on the estate. Because of these complications the survey was not completed until April 1903.

The total valuation of the settlement was £3,860. Local people responded immediately to the sale of land and during May at least 275 requests were processed. The government decided to reduce the size of the allotments from five acres to two or three acres in order to try to accommodate as many people as possible. Drayton also notes that under the *metayer* system of cultivation most people were accustomed to working about 1 acre of land. In the end, more than one-third of the lots were more than three acres in size, the rest being less. Basically, all purchases were settled by the end of August 1903.

At this time Drayton also reports on initiating the survey for Harvey Vale, another of the large plantations (approximately 300 acres). He states:

> So great is the desire among the peasants to purchase land, that I fear this property will be altogether inadequate to meet the wants of those now occupying holdings thereon. As soon as it became known that the Government intended to purchase Harvey Vale, there was an inrush of tenants, the owners offering no opposition, and I found 120 actually cultivating plots. Every effort will be made to settle as many of them on their holdings as is possible, but there must inevitably be much disappointment. (Colonial Reports, No. 24, Grenada 1903: 7)

In his recommendations Drayton calls for the establishment of an 'Experimental Plot' in order to test cultivation of cotton and corn. Five acres was set aside at Beausejour for this purpose, including a large pond and a well with pump. This site was later to become the Carriacou Botanical Garden. A resident agricultural officer was to be assigned to work under the guidance of the Grenada Agricultural Staff.

Other recommendations made by Drayton at this time demonstrate his concerns for the settlement scheme and reflect the contemporary view in regard to agricultural development in the Windward Islands. These included: improving the quality of livestock, setting aside acreage for pasturage and providing fencing, assisting small farmers to acquire lumber for house construction, protection of forest reserves, reforestation, a plan for improving the water supply, and other suggestions for economic development conserving the available resources.

Conclusions: The Impact of Colonial Policies on the Environment of Carriacou

British colonial policies have shaped the current landscape of the Windward Islands. On Carriacou, the positive results of the policies can be seen today in the successful reforestation of the steep upper slopes of the island. These forest reserves were designated at the end of the nineteenth century when the first land reform initiatives were implemented and the plantations began to break up. The colonial government seized the opportunity to designate the portions of the plantations on the steep upper slopes as forest reserve. They are now good examples of mature tropical forest all along the main ridge that composes the 'spine' of the island at an elevation of just under 1000 feet. The forest is deciduous, trees are adapted to the annual dry season, from January to June. The continuous management of these forest, first by the colonial government and later by the government of Grenada, has been a critical factor in stabilizing soils, preventing erosion, reducing runoff, and providing wildlife habitat.

The colonial administrators had common lands of up to approximately 20 acres set aside for government agricultural projects and experiments at the time land reform was being implemented on three of the large plantations at the end of the nineteenth century (Mills 1987). In addition, the colonial government bought several more estates from absentee land owners in the 1930s to serve as agricultural experiment stations. These projects were important for the introduction and propagation of new crops and the distribution of plant materials to island farmers.

It was also during the 1930s that grass barriers were planted under the supervision of the colonial agricultural officer (Mr Edward Kent, personal communication).

They were planted along the contour line on many hillsides and helped to control erosion on slopes cleared for planting cotton. After the failure of the cotton market in the 1970s, animals were turned loose to graze on the hillsides (Hill 1977). Where the grass barriers are left intact, they continue to protect against soil loss. The large upland water catchments for storage of runoff during the rainy season were also constructed during the 1930s. These structures have fallen into disrepair and are no longer functional for agricultural use.

Colonial officials recognized the need for improved pasture and fencing on Carriacou. Common grazing areas were planted with grasses and access was controlled during the first half of the twentieth century, while the cotton market was sustaining the local economy. With the failure of cotton, small farmers turned to increasing their livestock production for export to Grenada and Trinidad (Hill 1977, Mills 1987). Because of severe dry season conditions, the lack of irrigation for pastures, and the overstocking of the island, tremendous damage was done to the soil resources of Carriacou in the latter part of the twentieth century.

Unfortunately many of the land use practices aimed at conservation introduced by the visionary colonial officials around the turn of the nineteenth century were abandoned or ignored during the last half of the twentieth century. The greatest loss has been in soil conservation. On the windward coast of Carriacou, where wind and severe precipitation events at the start of the rainy season can move a lot of soil very quickly, the effects have been most noticeable, particularly where grass barriers have been eliminated. Overgrazing of pastures, followed by the cultivation of peanuts (groundnuts) in the 1970s and early 1980s, stripped the topsoil from some areas. Lowland portions of the windward coast still exhibit severe gullying.

As the local economy on Carriacou moves away from agriculture and toward tourism and the construction of retirement homes, an opportunity is created for the land to rest and to be restored (Mills 2002). Today's environmentalists working in the Windward Islands stand to learn much from reviewing the assessments of the colonial administrators, the earliest European conservationists in the region.

References

Berleant-Schiller, Riva (1995), 'From Labour to Peasantry in Montserrat after the End of Slavery', in K.F. Olwig (ed.), *Small Islands, Large Questions: Society, Culture, and Resistance in the Post-Emancipation Caribbean*, London: Frank Cass.

Besson, Jean (1984), 'Land Tenure in the Free Villages of Trelawny, Jamaica: A Case Study in the Caribbean Peasant Response to Emancipation', *Slavery and Abolition*, 5 (1), pp. 3–23.

Colonial Office Papers:

C.O. (1898), Miscellaneous Paper No. 11, Grenada.

C.O. (1903), Miscellaneous Paper No. 24, Grenada.

Grove, Richard H. (1995), *Green Imperialism*, Cambridge: Cambridge University Press.

Hill, Donald (1977), *The Impact of Migration on the Metropolitan and Folk Society of Carriacou, Grenada*, New York: Anthropological Papers of the American Museum of Natural History, 54, Part 2.

Mauer, Bill (1997), *Recharting the Caribbean: Land, Law, and Citizenshiip in the British Virgin Islands*, Ann Arbor: The University of Michigan.

Mills, Beth (1987), 'Agriculture and Idle Land in Carriacou, Grenada with a case study of the Village of Harvey Vale', unpublished MA thesis, University of New Mexico.

Mills, Beth. (2002), 'Family Land in Carriacou, Grenada and its Meaning with the Transnational Community: Heritage, Identity, and Rooted Mobility', unpublished dissertation, University of California, Davis, CA.

Momsen, Janet (1987), 'Land Settlement as an Imposed Solution', in Jean Besson and Janet Momsen (eds), *Land and Development in theCaribbean*, London: Macmillan.

Olwig, Karen F. (1995), *Small Islands, Large Questions: Society, Culture, and Resistance in the Post-Emancipation Caribbean*, London: Frank Cass and Co.

Rhodes House Library (1949), State of Carriacou and the other Grenadine islands. 1776, Francis Edward's Catalogue No. 695, 1776.

Richardson, Bonham (1975), 'The Overdevelopment of Carriacou', *Geographical Review*, 65 (3), pp. 390–99.

Richardson, Bonham (1997), *Economy and Environment in the Caribbean: Barbados and the Windwards in the Late 1800s*, Gainesville: University of Florida Press.

Chapter 4

Challenges to Promoting Agro-biodiversity in Caribbean Small Farming Systems: A Jamaican Case Study

Elizabeth Thomas-Hope and Balfour Spence

Introduction

For the past 50 years, the global trend has been towards the practice of depending upon a few high-yielding crops to increase agricultural production and thus decreasing the variety of crops and plants that contribute to food supplies and other needs. The concentration on high-yielding varieties (HYVs) or hybrids has resulted in a significant reduction in the variety and abundance of crops and uncultivated plants. Further, single management systems and procedures have been employed over vast tracts of land to deal with production (Brookfield et al. 2002). The corollary of this has been the need to increase greatly the applications of agrochemicals, both pesticides and fertilizers, in order to manage the status of the crops. Even reforestation projects have been characterized by stands of single species of trees to facilitate harvesting and meet commercial demands.

As a consequence of increased dependence upon selected species, it has been estimated that about 70 per cent of the genetic diversity of agricultural crops has been lost in the past 100 years (Brookfield et al. 2003). It has been pointed out that only about 150 plant species are now commonly cultivated for food, and that only three of these provide some 60 per cent of the calories derived from plants (Fowler and Mooney 1990). Loss in species' variety has further resulted in reduced varieties of farm management practices and techniques. Crop breeding as well as the loss of markets for many varieties of crops has led to reduced diversification in all aspects of farming and land management.

While the increase in productivity that has occurred up to the present time on account of crop breeding cannot be denied, the commensurate loss in genetic biodiversity that has resulted worldwide and the intense dependence on chemical inputs on which the hybrid crops have been engineered to be dependent, has become cause for concern. Whether or not countries were part of a green revolution, or whether the new crops were successful in solving the food security of vast and increasing populations, the resultant monoculture and the attendant dependence on agrochemicals for pest control and fertilizers have become the hallmark of modern agriculture worldwide. Those who engaged in these practices have been lauded as progressive farmers. The effect of this has been to decrease biodiversity and reduce agrodiversity to isolated pockets of the world where modernization has either been resisted or not yet arrived. (Brookfield et al. 2003).

The tragedy of the association made between the practice of agrodiversity and backwardness was that it obscured the fact that agrodiversity was adaptable and for this reason had the resilience that enabled it to survive, in spite of pressures to the contrary. At the same time, these same global trends failed to recognize that agrodiversity was generally accompanied by the promotion of greater varieties of plant and animal species in farm systems, thus securing livelihoods locally while also promoting the broader international goals of biodiversity conservation.

Examples of existing small-farmer practices relating to agro-biodiversity have been provided from evidence gathered by a group of scientists engaged in a United Nations University (UNU) international project, the People, Land Management and Environmental Change (PLEC) project (Brookfield et al. 2003). In the study sites of small farming systems in Africa, Asia, Latin America and the Caribbean, the overwhelming observation was that skilful and diverse methods were employed by farmers not only to sustain biodiversity and improve soil quality, but also to increase production and provide greater security of both food supply and incomes (Pinedo-Vasques et al. 2001). It was also commonly observed that the local environments of many small farming systems, both in terms of topography and the security of the market, were not suited to monoculture and single agricultural systems. Under such conditions, monoculture created greater vulnerability of farm landscapes to natural hazards, land degradation, and agriculture to the uncertainties of both the domestic and international markets.

A critical issue to emerge, therefore, was how agro-biodiversity practices might be incorporated into environmental management planning in general and land management planning in particular. The challenges to achieving such an objective varied with the particular context, but in all cases the overwhelming impact of global patterns of crop concentration and practices associated with monoculture on which international markets for agricultural goods were largely based, provided a momentum that was difficult to counter. This was the case despite the existence of countervailing local circumstances of the physical environment, infrastructure and pattern of social and economic development. What follows is an examination of the situation as it pertains to small farming in Jamaica, with special reference to a study of the Rio Grande Valley, Portland.

The Jamaican Context

Jamaica's history of biodiversity loss, like that of the rest of the Caribbean, began early in its modern development. The emphasis on monoculture started in the seventeenth century with the introduction of sugar by the British colonizers of the island (Watts 1987). Sugar was produced on vast plantations that in the peak years of production extended over all areas of the coastal plain and over much of the plateau of the interior. Mixed farming to supply domestic needs was left to small farmers who largely fended for themselves, most of the time without official support. As a consequence, however, there was greater retention of diversity in farming systems.

Diversification of agriculture in the early twentieth century was characterized by the development of new crops produced on former sugar plantations. Thus bananas, coconuts and citrus fruits replaced sugar on the coastal lowlands and coffee was expanded in monoculture stands into the high altitudes of the Blue Mountain range. On the plantations, wherever possible management became increasingly dependent upon mechanization that required an increase in field size. Because much of the land was owned or used by small farmers, the production of export crops was extended to this group of farmers, who had to produce under the conditions prescribed by the export agencies to which the crops were sold for the export market.

The notion that the promotion of these agricultural systems had resulted in the serious loss of species biodiversity, agricultural management or organizational diversity (and thus flexibility to market and other needs), has never been a matter of concern among those responsible for national development policies. This has been the case despite the significance of such losses for severe deforestation and extensive land degradation, and their implications in terms of the sustainability of farming.

Agro-biodiversity in the Rio Grande Valley, Jamaica

A study of agro-biodiversity practices among small farmers of Jamaica was conducted in the lower Rio Grande Watershed in the Parish of Portland, Jamaica, as part of the international PLEC project (Thomas-Hope and Spence 2003) (Figure 4.1).

Agro-physical Profile of the Rio Grande Valley

The Rio Grande Valley covers an area of approximately 286,000 ha., or about one-third of the parish of Portland. The watershed is characterized by high elevations, steep slopes and is the wettest area in Jamaica. Over 75 per cent of the valley lies above 1500 metres and more than 50 per cent of the area has slopes exceeding 20 degrees. Although highly seasonal, rainfall in the watershed averages 2,250 mm annually. The combination of rainfall, humidity and temperature regimes results in a diversity of flora which is unmatched elsewhere in Jamaica. The Rio Grande, which drains the area, is bordered for 50 per cent of its length by alluvial deposits consisting of carbonaceous and silica-rich sands. The geological characteristics, prevalence of steep cultivated slopes with minimal conservation strategies, and high intensity rainfall contribute to high levels of vulnerability to landslide and flood hazards as well as high levels of soil loss and land degradation (Mines and Geology Division 2000).

Agriculture is the primary economic activity in the Rio Grande Valley and although an estimated 80.4 per cent of the watershed was forested in 1998, pressure for increasing agriculture, especially for banana monoculture, has until recently, been

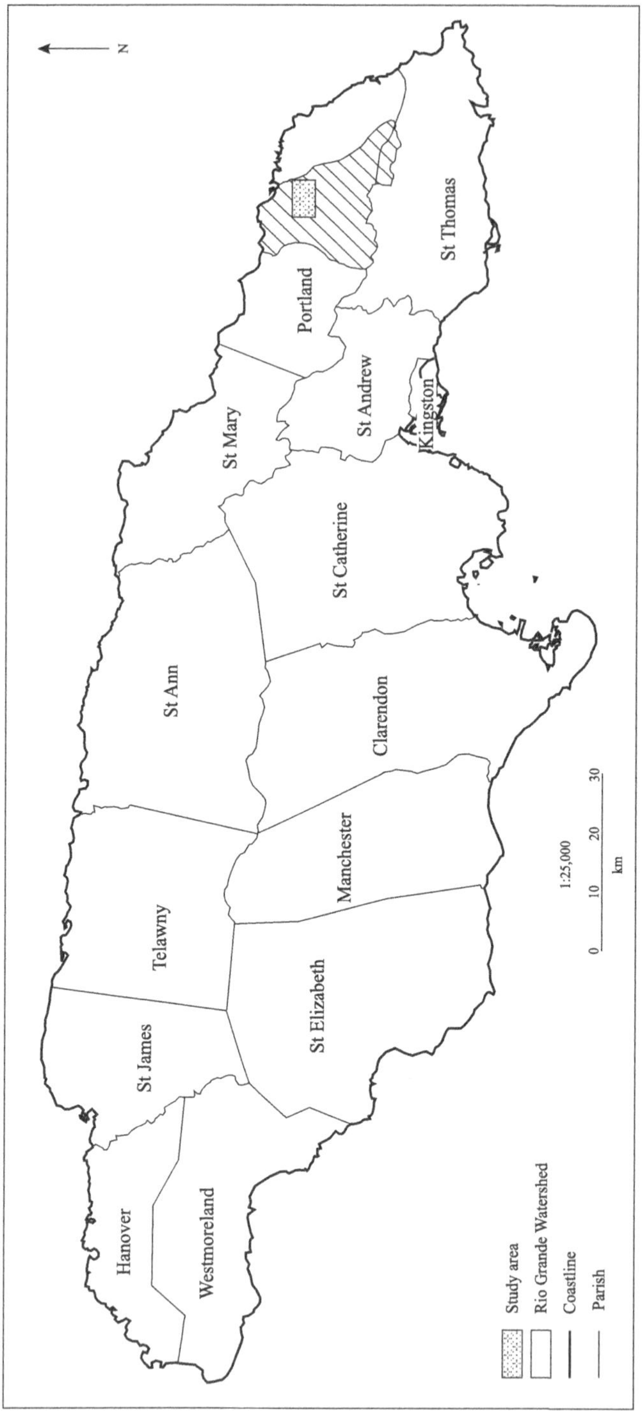

Figure 4.1 Location of the PLEC Rio Grande Valley demonstration site, Portland, Jamaica

rising at an alarming rate. The area utilized for all land-use activities, except forest, expanded between 1986 and 1998, with an overall increase amounting to about 8 per cent (1,866.9 ha.). This expansion in land area utilized for human livelihood has come at the expense of the forested area which declined by about 847 hectares over the 12-year period. This pattern of land-use change has implications for flood and landslide susceptibility in the Rio Grande Valley because the removal of forest from steep slopes and disturbance of these slopes for cultivation increases rainfall run-off and reduces slope stability.

Small farming as a livelihood activity in the Rio Grande Valley of Portland, as elsewhere throughout Jamaica, is associated with poor economic returns. This is largely explained by the vagaries of the market and the difficulties related to transport and access to new market opportunities. In addition, recurrent flooding and landslides cause repeated damage to crops and other property. Agricultural practices, especially those related to monoculture banana production , further aggravate hazard impacts because the practice of removing undergrowth from banana fields allows more rapid water run-off.

The Rio Grande Demonstration Site

Although the Rio Grande Valley continues to be an area of high agro-biodiversity, increased emphasis on specialized crops such as banana (*Musa sapientum*), and the tendency towards reduced inter-planting are major contributors to biodiversity loss in the area. It was important therefore, that efforts made towards the promotion of biological conservation at the demonstration site be firmly integrated into these developmental issues, as well as the social dynamics of target communities.

Promotion of agro-biodiversity at the demonstration site was also based on recognition of the economic uncertainties associated with the monocultural production of bananas by small farmers and their implications for sustainable livelihoods. These uncertainties are related to four factors:

i) the virtual absence of crop insurance among farmers;
ii) recurrent problems of crop diseases;
iii) frequent damage to crops by natural hazards, especially hurricanes, floods and landslides;
iv) erosion and the impending loss of the preferential market in Britain.

Crop insurance among small farmers in the Rio Grande Valley is virtually absent and as a result recovery from the effects of diseases and natural hazards is severely hampered. Farmers can ill afford the cost of such recovery and assistance from official sources is unreliable, severely affecting the sustainability of livelihoods. In addition, the end of the Cold War and the formation of the World Trade Organization (WTO) in 1994, heralded the erosion of the former preferential market for West Indian bananas in Britain as the alignment in global political economy shifted from the traditional North–South towards North–East. This realignment is occurring in a global economic environment of increasing trade liberalization that seriously undermines the competitiveness of West Indian bananas (Joseph 1997). In the absence of agricultural diversity, the cumulative effect of these changes in the global geo-political economy is to erode the livelihood activities of those farmers who rely heavily on banana monoculture (see Introduction).

The work commenced with a general landscape and socio-economic characterization of the study area, which was then established as the project demonstration site within which a sample of plots were selected as demonstration plots. At the site, the scientists and farmers of the PLEC team focused on the evaluation of existing practices and the development of new methods that would promote agro-biodiversity and that could be used strategically in land management as well as improving household economic levels.

The demonstration site encompassed five communities in the lower Rio Grande Valley. These communities included – Fellowship, Toms Hope, Stanton Harcourt, Berridale, and Golden Vale – collectively comprising some 1,000 farm-households and a total population of approximately 5,000 people. A sample of 20 per cent of the households from these communities provided the frame of reference of the study, and the information on agro-diversity relating to both crops and farm-management practices. The household sample also provided the basis for selection of sample plots used for measuring biodiversity with respect to the occurrence and richness of plant species (Thomas-Hope and Spence 2003).

As is typical of the social landscape of Jamaica's small-scale agriculture, the farm population was predominantly older, although there were a number of younger persons who actively farmed. The modal age of the population represented by the household sample was 43 years with the majority of the farmers being male. It is important to note that even where the principal farmer was male, there were important female contributions to the farming process, particularly in the areas of field maintenance, planting and marketing. A significant number (> 60 per cent) of the demonstration-site farmers had been involved in farming for at least 25 years, having been initiated int this activity in childhood (Thomas-Hope et al. 2000).

For most farmers, traditional export crops were the main sources of income although over 40 per cent indicated that farming was supplemented by other income generating activities such as shopkeeping, eco-tourism activities like rafting, and employment outside of the Valley. Remittances from relatives abroad or those who worked outside the Rio Grande Valley were also an important source of income for some older farmers. Farm income was difficult to assess as farmers rarely kept records of costs and expenditures. In addition, expenditure and income generation varied from month to month depending on the stage of crop development. Although the farmers and members of their households provided much of the farm labour input, over 64 per cent of farmers at the study site hired additional help. Generally, farm households cultivated one to two plots, amounting to a total of less than five acres, though the more successful export farmers tended to operate two to three plots, ranging in area from 5.5 to 12 acres.

Characterization of the farm units associated with the households sampled demonstrated the existence of five dominant land-use stages. Within each land-use stage, the identified field types varied as a function of farm management and reflected a complex mix of different types of cultivated and non-cultivated crops as well as trees and shrubs promoted by each farmer. Field types within land-use stages ranged from 1 to 18, with agro-forest and edge land-use stages showing the highest variations in field types (Table 4.1). A total of 235 different species of plants were identified on the farms in the study area. These plants included roots and tubers, vegetables, legumes, cereals, fruits, condiments, ornamental and medicinal plants and timber trees. Local residents used approximately 70 per cent of the plants for food, building material, erosion and flood-water control, mulch, medicine, spices, stimulants and fencing material.

Assessments also showed that field types on some farms changed frequently, primarily as a function of the farmer's crop and land management decisions. For example, one farm was initially characterized as having three dominant land use stages with six field types. This farmer occupied flat lands on the floodplains of the river where he inter-cropped plots of banana, coffee and coconuts, along with a variety of vegetables (including pumpkin, cucumber, cabbage, pack-choi (bok-choy) and peppers). The farmer indicated that his decision to farm this mix of crops was based primarily on the availability of markets, access to technical assistance, the availability of land and proximity to water sources. Subsequent visits with the farmer showed that changes in market availability and other socioeconomic pressures led to a change in his cropping system. He had converted his vegetable stands to banana monoculture (banana orchard land-use stage). This case also highlighted the dynamic nature of the farming activities at the demonstration site, and hence the need for long-term monitoring as a means of accurately capturing the occurrence of diversity and the impact of change.

The Plant Diversity of Land Use Stages and Field Types

The results of agro-biodiversity assessments of farming systems in the Rio Grande Valley indicated that species occurrence and abundance varied according to land-use stages and field types (Zarin et al. 1999). The agro-forest, house garden and edge land-use stages were the most commonly observed within the demonstration area, constituting over 80 per cent of the total sample units. These cultivated land-use stages also displayed the highest diversity of crops, fruit trees, shrubs and other valuable plants as the Margalef species richness index reflected (Table 4.2).[1] The Margalef abundance index showed that the agro-forest, edge and house garden land-use stages respectively, showed a higher abundance index than that of the orchard. Individual farm Margalef index values for the dominant land-use stages ranged from 20 to 58, while that of the banana orchards were as low as 6. From this index it may be concluded that type of land-use stage has implications for the abundance of species found on the farm plots. In those cases where banana fields were intercropped (generating the agro-forest or house garden land-use stage), the Margalef index increased dramatically, sometimes threefold. Another land-use stage showing high species diversity was the fallow, including areas not actively managed due to their susceptibility to flooding.

Table 4.1 Description of land-use stages and field types at the Rio Grande Valley demonstration site

Land-use stage	Field types	Field type(s)	Frequency of incidence
House garden	**FT 1**	Spontaneous growth of grasses (*Commelina diffusa*, *Panicum maximum*), shrubs (*Gliricidia sp.*) and ornamental plants (*Croton sp.*)	1
	FT 2	Multi-storied mixture of staple crops (*Musa sapientum* (banana), *Colocasia* (dasheen), *Xanthosoma sagittifolium* (cocoyam), *Artocarpus altilis* (breadfruit)) with herbs/medicinal plants (*Aloe vera*) and fruit trees (*Mangifera indica*) Ornamental Plant (Croton sp.)	5
Shrub-dominated fallow	**FT 3**	Multi-storied mixture of abandoned staple crops (banana, dasheen, cocoyam, breadfruit) with herbs/medicinal plants and fruit trees	1
Orchard (banana plantation)	**FT 4**	*Musa Sapientum* (banana) fields with little or no intercropping of other crops and undergrowth of shrubs	3
Agroforest	**FT 5**	Mixed crop of *Musa sapientum* (banana) between which *Colocasia* (dasheen), and *Xanthosoma sagittifolium* (cocoyam) are intercropped and other food crops (yams, corn, pumpkin) and fruit trees (*Ananas comosus* – pineapples) are planted randomly	1
	FT 6	*Musa sapientum* (banana) dominant farm intercropped with (*Colocasia*) dasheen	1
	FT 7	Dormant *Musa Sapientum* (banana) Plantation and actively farmed vegetable ground	1
	FT 8	*Musa Sapientum* (banana) / (Musa paradisiaca) Plantain dominant field	1
	FT 9	Mixture of *Musa Sapientum* (banana) plantation and vegetable farming	1

Table 4.1 cont'd

Land-use stage	Field types	Field type(s)	Frequency of incidence
Agroforest (cont'd)	**FT 10**	Mixed Array of *Musa Sapientum* (bananas), dasheen (*Colocassia*)/ (*Xanthosoma sagittifolium*) cocoyam and a number of fruit trees	1
	FT 11	Mixture of food crops e.g *Colocassia*, *Musa Sapientum* (banana) and *Musa paradisiaca* (plantain)	1
	FT 12	Timber intercropped with *coffee sp.* (coffee) and *Musa sapientum* (bananas)	1
Edge	**FT 13**	Grassy verge around edge of agroforest with a mixture of grasses, ornamental plants and fruit trees	3
	FT 14	Grassy verge and mixture of shrubs (e.g. *Sida acuta* – broomweed) and medicinal plants (e.g. *aloe vera*)	5
	FT 15	Grassy verge around edge of agroforest with a mixture of grasses, ornamental plants and fruit trees and food crops (*Musa sapientum*, *Xanthosoma sagittifolium*)	4
	FT 16	Grassy verge mixed with a number of wild growing herbs and shrubs (*Gliricidia sp.*, *weldelia trilobata*), food crops (*Xanthosoma sagittifolium*) and fruit tree (e.g. *Syzgium malaccense*, and *Cocus nucifera*)	1
	FT 17	Spontaneous growth of grasses (*Commelina diffusa*, *Panicum maximum*), shrubs (*Gliricidia sp.*) and ornamental plants (*Croton sp.*)	2
	FT 18	Verge around farmhouse dominated by shrubs e.g. *Gliricidia sp.*, *weldelia trilobata* and *Boerhavia cocinea*	2

Table 4.2 Species richness as a function of land-use stages

Land-use stage	Average species richness	Incidence of the land-use stage
Agroforest	26	9
House garden	27	6
Edge	16	20
Fallow	26	1
Orchard	12	3

The higher diversity in the occurrence of crops and trees common to the agro-forest, house garden and edge land-use stages could be attributed to the intensive management practices employed by farmers as physical and economic coping mechanisms. In many ways these strategies permitted the diversification of agricultural production, allowing for better market access, which in-turn assisted in fulfilling the needs of the farmers and their household for food and cash. The management practices associated with the coping mechanisms allowed for the variations in cropping types and patterns from farm to farm, further increasing agro-biodiversity at the site.

These approaches to crop production, land management and livelihood security formed the basis of the 'good practice' identified in the PLEC project and models developed by the farmers and scientists.

The field types of the sampled areas again supported the observation that variations in diversity were a function of farmers' management practices. The sample area showed species richness that ranged from 7 to 59, with the observed variations following the trends in the land-use stages discussed above. The agro-forest land-use stage showed the highest variation in field types, with over 9 field types identified (Table 4.2). Field type species richness within this land use stage ranged from 13 to 59. However, on farms where there was an emphasis on a mixture of banana, root crops, vegetable, fruit and timber trees, there was greater organizational diversity and the species richness index was above 25. The field type showing the highest species richness (59) was found on a farm divided into a number of subplots upon which crops were planted for sale to the local market. This farm also showed the highest level of species abundance within the agro-forest and edge field type.

This farm and the farmer's management practices also reflected the relationship between market orientation and the occurrence of diversity as this farmer sold all his produce locally. On the contrary, farmers targeting export markets received technical support from the Banana Export Company (BECO), which promoted a reduction in diversity to facilitate greater banana-producing efficiency and to reduce production costs. For example, the banana farmer producing for the export market had to keep his banana plot clear of under-storey to reduce 'wastage' of nutrient inputs through uptake by other plants, and reduce the incidence of diseases on the farm. This approach promoted a reduction in diversity and was reflected in the uniformity in field type observed in the banana plantation or orchard land-use stage. The single field type within this banana plantation (or orchard land-use stage) showed the lowest species richness values, which ranged from 7 to 19, with an average of 12. Most of the other farms had species richness of 20 and above.

The field types of the house garden land-use stage showed less variation within field types. Other assessments of the observed field types showed that the edges also had a significant contribution to make to diversity, as in many instances the edge contained crops, fruit trees, ornamental plants and medicinal plants not commonly grown in the main farming area.

Crops and Cropping Systems at the Study Area

Diversity within the demonstration site was also examined at the level of the crops and crop management systems employed. The banana crop dominated land-use stages and field types of the demonstration site. With respect to the farming systems sampled, over 75 per cent of the farmers indicated that a second major crop was cultivated alongside the main income-generating crop. In addition, 61 per cent of the farmers indicated that they also farmed a third income-generating crop alongside the first and second main farm crops. Commonly observed secondary and tertiary crops included plantain, yam, breadfruit and dasheen. Some farmers also included vegetables such as tomato and legumes. Thirteen different types of vegetables were observed on the sampled farms. These included cabbage, cucumber, pumpkin, tomato, cauliflower, okra and spinach. Legumes were both widely cultivated and consumed in the Valley, but farmers grew limited varieties, mainly kidney beans, string beans, gungo peas, cow peas and broad beans.

Non-cultivated species commonly grew within each land-use stage (with the exception of the banana orchards). Where non-cultivated species were allowed to thrive, namely within the edges and the house garden, there was an associated increase in diversity. Again, it must be emphasized that this diversity was directly a function of the farmer's farm management practices for weed and wild plant control as well as crop and plant choice. Most of the agricultural surplus was sold in local markets Overseas marketing of bananas and coffee was normally organized by commodity associations and tended to be preferred by farmers because it was easier than selling locally.

The Uses and Benefits of Agro-biodiversity in Land Management

Agricultural diversity undoubtedly increases the extent to which biodiversity is conserved on farmed landscapes. Biodiversity within the context of farming is a means used by most farm households to enhance food security and, through the medicinal properties of many plants, to contribute to health care. Additionally, some farmers strategically use diverse plants to reduce flood and landslide occurrence and mitigate impact. Biodiversity is also associated with reduced levels of agrochemical usage on farms. The conservation of biodiversity in farming systems thus contributes to the enhancement of human health as well as ecosystem health and is therefore the basis on which efforts have to be made to incorporate such approaches into the land management practices of farming systems.

Utilization of Agro-biodiversity in Flood and Landslide Control and Impact Mitigation

Farmers at the demonstration site used a variety of cultivated and non-cultivated species to mitigate the impact of floods and landslides (Morrison 2001). Not all plants thus utilized were actively cultivated. Non-cultivated plants commonly included bamboo, coconuts, fruit trees, grass, 'growstick', hibiscus, timber trees, pineapple, sugar cane and wild cane. These plants were utilized in a number of ways. By reducing water velocity, non-cultivated plants not only enhanced slope stability and thereby reduced landslide susceptibility, but the reduced rate of runoff also mitigated the impact of inundation in the 'bottom lands'. Without non-cultivated plants and in the absence of mechanically engineered mitigation structures, farm drains and riverbanks were susceptible to soil erosion and slumping, both of which normally resulted in crop loss which aggravated the impact of these hazards. The farmers utilized larger trees, particularly those with high moisture absorption capacity in the regulation of soil moisture. Trees used in this manner included various types of timber trees and in a few cases, eucalyptus. Timber trees were the preferred variety because of their commercial value. The planting of these species in waterlogged sections of farms served to reduce soil-moisture levels and thereby to reduce the probability of flooding during periods of sustained rainfall. Farmers who did not utilize species with high moisture absorption capacity explained that these species could result in excessive moisture depletion during periods of low rainfall. Other species such as 'growstick', which is a leguminous plant known for its nitrogen fixation capacity which helps to improve soils, were cultivated.

The use of plant species to mitigate the impact of floods and landslide can be either active or passive. Passive use implies that non-cultivated species are allowed to remain on the plot because they provide some measure of protection from the hazard and their value to the farmer in this regard is indicated by the fact that the farmer does not remove them from the plot. Active responses involve the planting of species in a deliberate attempt to stabilize slopes and reduce the effect of flooding. The arrangement of plant species on selected plots demonstrates the active and passive use of biodiversity in hazard mitigation.

Biodiversity and Agrochemical Usage

As is common in farming communities across Jamaica, use of agrochemicals by farmers at the PLEC project demonstration site was prevalent, with over 82 per cent acknowledging the application of chemical fertilizers and pesticides to their crops. Seven different types of fertilizers and 20 types of pesticides were used by farmers throughout the demonstration site (Spence and Thomas-Hope 2005). The chief chemical fertilizer used on all the farm plots was sulphate. Second in terms of usage was potash. The popular fertilizer commonly known as 'Miracle Grow' was made up of nitrogen, phosphorous and potassium in a ratio of 15:5:35. In all cases, at least two and in some cases four different types of chemical fertilizers were regularly used (Smith 2003).

The farmers all indicated that things had changed from what had pertained in the past and while some farmers practiced methods of pest control that included chemical pesticides as well as mixed cropping combinations and the removal of pests by hand, most of them had adopted 'modern' techniques in their farming practices and felt that agrochemical use was essential for successful food production. This was despite the fact that the cost of these chemicals was high in relation to the profits derived from farming. This was particularly true of bananas for export. The banana-marketing agency insisted on clean-weeding and the use of chemicals, which they sold to the farmers.

Despite the general acceptance of the necessity for agrochemical use among the farmers, comparison of the different plots showed that there was a distinct relationship between levels of agro-biodiversity and amounts of agrochemicals applied. While greater biodiversity on plots facilitated reduced agrochemical usage, the converse was also true, with low levels of biodiversity increasing the need for higher levels of pesticide and fertilizer usage. This had the effect of reducing both species variability and abundance on those plots. Thus, within the agro-forest and house garden land-use stages fewer agrochemical inputs were used as compared to the banana plantation/orchard land-use stage. Since agro-forests and house-gardens represented higher levels of agro-diversity than the orchard land-use stage, there was clear indication that increased agro-diversity coincided with lower demands for agrochemicals. For example, on plots that fell within the orchard land-use stage farmers routinely utilized more than one and sometimes as many as five types of fertilizers. The regular use of pesticides as well as the number of pesticides employed was also higher for this land-use stage.

Problems associated with agrochemical use and their environmental impacts are well documented and the desirability of farming systems to become less reliant on agrochemicals is constantly promoted. One of the foci of the PLEC team was therefore to encourage agro-biodiversity within small-scale farming systems at the demonstration site as a strategy for reduction in agrochemical use through the greater use of biological diversity. Farmers knowledge of the nitrogen-fixing ability of leguminous plants was also promoted as a 'best practice' and scientists at the demonstration site encouraged farmers to include peas in the cropping system.

Challenges to Promoting Agro-biodiversity in Land Management

Relationship with External Agencies

The Jamaica Agricultural Society is an association of farmers that meet to discuss common problems in relation to agriculture and to promote the highest standards of managment practices through an annual national agricultural competition. The topics of discussion in the case of the farmers at the demonstration site were usually those relating to problems faced by government and government agencies in relation to externally controlled factors such as the price of seeds and agrochemicals, the problems of the fluctuating market for their major crops, and those of poor road access to farm plots. There was virtually no communication on matters such as farm management and crop selection. In particular, there was obvious tension existing between the farmers who maintained the the diverse cropping system tradition of small farmers, and the Rural Agricultural Development Agency (RADA), which, according to the farmers, usually advocated the establishment of monoculture in their agro-forestry plots (Thomas-Hope and Spence 2003).

The Banana Export Company (BECO), which was the sole channel for exporting the bananas, required farmers to produce the crop as a monoculture, with farms clean weeded and with the intensive use of agrochemicals for both pest control and fertilizers. The company itself sold and distributed the agrochemicals. The farmers complained that the price of agrochemicals was high and that despite their best efforts, the level of rejection of their bananas grown for the export market left them perpetually impoverished. Nevertheless, though working against the odds, many farmers felt that they had no option but to keep producing for BECO since there were apparently no other market opportunities available to them. Besides, farmers who had rejected the traditional system of diversified farm plots and complied with the requirements of BECO were deemed to be 'good' banana growers and held up by the extension officers of RADA as models of good practice. This case of disjunction between the traditional practices of small farmers and the views and policies of the national authorities is not unusual, and a similar situation was observed among fisherfolk in the eastern Caribbean (Pugh 2003).

It is significant that one of the collaborating farmers in the Jamaica-PLEC project who produced bananas for export at the beginning of the project, had persisted in his practice of inter-cropping bananas with a wide variety of other plants, ranging from timber and fruit trees to a ground cover of condiments and medicinal plants. His rationale, which he explained to the other farmers at the demonstration site, was based on the economic advantages of having alternative cash crops to supplement his variable income from bananas as well as increasing the range of crops available for household consumption. He was also aware of the ecological benefits of mixed cropping in providing shade, ground cover and some measure of pest control.

Despite the ongoing problems associated with the production of bananas for the export market, this was not an issue of discussion between the extension services and farmers, nor was the rationale for practicing diverse agricultural systems defended by those farmers engaged in such practice. Not surprisingly, these farmers had been reluctant to defend their practices because they felt that there had been no support or acknowledgement of agro-diversity as a model of good practice by the agents with whom they had contact. Furthermore, the poor state of the main access roads within the area reflected the general neglect on the part of government authorities of small farming. Poor roads, some dangerous to vehicular traffic, made market access for agricultural produce from localities such as the Rio Grande so difficult and costly in damage to produce that the low economic benefits of agricultural diversity were simply made worse.

The Social Dynamics of the Communities

Support and conflict

There were strong networks based on family and kinship groups within the respective communities. Church affiliation also formed the basis of networks of friends and supporters in times of difficulty. In addition, associations, such as the Burial Scheme Society and other informal 'fraternities' and 'partner' groupings, provided various levels of assistance especially in times of grief or other personal distress (Thomas-Hope and Spence 2002).

Sources of conflict in the communities were chiefly related to political differences. Disharmony and suspicion were based on the dominant affiliation of the communities to one or other of the two major political parties. Though most of the time the negative feelings were not openly expressed, nevertheless they were sufficiently strong that some farmers would not interact with those from other communities. This meant that it was not possible to establish a unified team of farmers across all communities at the demonstration site.

Despite the social networks that existed in the communities they had generated little social capital in the context of providing support for agriculture. Even the old practice of labour exchange among farmers had largely disappeared. There was a tendency for farmers to work independently of each other, and this largely prevented the sharing of ideas and hindered the development of any openness about new market opportunities or strategies for dealing with problems such as the mitigation of hazard impacts faced by farmers in the area. The PLEC demonstration activities, in particular the field-based work experience days, gradually broke down these barriers for the farmers who participated in the project. The sharing of information among the farmers contributed greatly to the building of confidence with regard to the benefits that could be derived from the agricultural diversity of the farming systems in which they engaged. For such cooperation to continue and the ideas to be disseminated more widely would undoubtedly require evidence of economic benefit and not solely of the environmental benefits that could be derived. Furthermore, a combination of support from the national agencies and the consolidation of local commitment would also be necessary. However, the external agencies have not been supportive of agrodiversity, and are not principally concerned with the conservation of biodiversity within farming systems. While local commitment could be increased, it requires local leadership from those who are aware of its benefits.

Leadership

Tensions existed within communities concerning the acceptability of the persons who could play a lead role in the organization of activities of any kind. Added to the rejection of persons from a community supporting the rival political party, there was a general lack of confidence in anyone from the area. This reflected an entrenched belief that leadership and new ideas of any value had to come from outside.

Mistrust of leadership from within the community, despite the potential that existed, was evident at the demonstration site in the attitude towards one of the farmers who was a return migrant. As a young man he had migrated to the UK and returned after living abroad for some 30 years to his home district in the Rio Grande Valley where many of his relatives still lived. Though he had returned to farming, he had a more sophisticated approach than the other farmers. He engaged in organic farming and introduced a number of non-traditional plants and livestock that had greatly increased the agricultural diversity on his land. He specialized in growing exotic fruit for the hotel industry, and sought out the marketing outlets and organized the process himself. He demonstrated potential leadership qualities and seemed willing to share his skills and ideas with other farmers. Although he had been born and raised in the area and had retained his family connections there, he was so resented by other farmers that he could not effectively demonstrate anything to them (Thomas-Hope and Spence 2002). There was no way of removing these barriers in the short run. This was not an exceptional case, for as Rubenstein (1987) observed elsewhere in the Caribbean, so also as commonly found in Jamaica, the obvious success of one who had migrated and returned provided the basis of exclusion and a significant barrier to the community's acceptance of them in a leadership role.

While there was general suspicion of leaders that emerged within the community, including those of the community itself who had become successful farmers, people were ready to accept leadership from outside – and the further away, the better. The feeling was that a person from the same locality and background as everyone else had no authority to assert leadership over the rest. Those from outside were assumed to be genuinely more knowledgeable and seen to provide a means of generating social capital that could have other benefits. Networks established with persons 'outside' were therefore valued while those established 'inside' were seen to be of little use except for social support. The negative side of this relates to the lack of confidence that the communities had in themselves. Outsiders and national agricultural policies play a critical role in perpetuating this situation and in preventing genuine empowerment.

Conclusion

The conservation of species found or cultivated in agricultural landscapes is necessary for the maintenance of the plant genetic reservoir. Additionally, plant and animal diversity can be strategically used in hazard management and the mitigation of hazard impacts. Other benefits of the use of biodiversity within farming systems have been shown to include the reduced need for agrochemicals. Issues relating to agrochemical use and their environmental impacts are well documented and the desirability of farming systems to become less reliant on agrochemicals constantly promoted. Still other benefits include the use of biodiversity on farms in enhancing food security. It is important that if the promotion of agro-bioversity were to become part of the process of planning for sustainable rural development, it has to be part of a participatory process based on collaboration between national agencies and farmer communities.

The promotion of agro-biodiversity in the small farming systems of the Rio Grande Valley, Jamaica, brings to the fore the nature of the wider challenge of participatory planning for sustainability. To achieve this, both external factors and those within the farmer communities themselves play a critical part. The matter of community involvement in planning presents a difficult challenge but so too is the relationship with external agencies is also a critical aspect of the success or failure of planning

The absence of support from the external agencies is conditioned by the prevailing agricultural policies that have traditionally favoured monoculture for export combined with the negligible value placed on agricultural diversity and its role in biodiversity conservation. Biodiversity conservation has been widely seen solely as a matter of endangered species protection in uncultivated landscapes. The critical importance of biodiversity conservation within farmed landscapes has been missed by those agencies that fund biodiversity initiatives and by government policies alike. The marginal value placed upon small farming systems especially as it relates to mixed farming is seen in various ways. A principal element of neglect is reflected in the poor condition of access roads to the small farming communities. Overall, national agencies show a lack of awareness of the importance of agro-biodiversity in environmental management in general and land management in particular.

Internal factors that are a challenge to participatory planning are associated with inter-community suspicion, lack of leadership and the rejection of leadership potential within the community itself. Although farmers in the Rio Grande Valley are in many cases applying various forms of agrodiversity, recognition of the value of this needs to be consolidated and disseminated to others. The benefits have to be demonstrated to policy makers as well as to farmers, with opportunities given for farmer communities to recognize and increase good practice and cease farming methods that endanger both community and environmental health.

The dominance of monoculture in rural development discourses at the global level has led, within Jamaica, to the articulation of that perspective in agricultural policies and models of rural development. The evidence that farming systems based on monoculture is neither suited to the environmental or socio-economic conditions under which small farmer communities have to function, has not been used to counter the received view. Furthermore, that mixed systems of farming also contribute to the conservation of biodiversity, is a powerful reason for national authorities to review the externally received rural development imaginary of monoculture. This has not occurred largely because the global discourse has led to the creation of a space that excludes alternative ways of thinking at the national level. The contradiction this presents to traditional small farming practices contributes significantly to the dis-empowerment of the communities which are then, through the lack of confidence and organizational framework, never able to challenge the external view. It is therefore essential that small farmers be assisted in developing successful models of agrodiversity so that an alternative development discourse can emerge. Such a discourse must be appropriate to the environmental and socio-economic conditions within which Jamaica's rural development has to take place and be sustained. Biodiversity within agricultural systems needs to be supported locally to the extent that it provides the basis of an alternative vision and a model of good practice that can challenge the dominance of the external view.

Note

1 A count of the number of species in a particular sample.

References

Brookfield, H., Paddoch, C., Parsons, H. and Stocking, M. (2002), *Cultivating Biodiversity: Understanding, Analysing and Using Agricultural Diversity*, London: ITDG Publishing.

Brookfield, H., Parsons, H. and Brookfield, M. (eds) (2003), *Agrodiversity: Learning from Farmers Across the World,* Tokyo: United Nations University Press.

Fowler, C. and Mooney, P. (1990), *The Threatened Gene: Food, Policies and Loss of Genetic Diversity*, Cambridge: Lutterworth Press.

Joseph, M. (1997), 'Post Lome IV arrangements Must Mirror Principles and Instruments of LOME: A Perspective from the Banana Sector of the Windward Islands', *ECDMP Working Paper* No. 18, April 1997, <http://www.oneworld.org/ecdmp/pubs/wp18_gb.html> (20 June 2003).

Mines and Geology Division (2002), 'Landslide Susceptibility Map of the Rio Grande Valley, Portland. Government of Jamaica', unpublished report.

Morrison, E. (2001) 'Agrobiodiversity Response to Flood and Landslide Hazards in the Rio Grande Watershed, Jamaica', unpublished MSc dissertation, UWI Mona, Kingston, Jamaica.

Pinedo-Vasques, M., Gyasi, E. and Coffey, K. (2001), 'Demonstration Activities: A Review of Procedures and Experiences', *PLEC News and Views*, No. 17, February, pp. 12–30.

Pugh, J. (2003), 'Participatory Planning in the Caribbean: Developing Institutional Capital in the Fisherfolk Communities of the Caribbean' Project Report, <http://www.planningcaribbean.or.uk>.

Rubenstein, H. (1987), *Coping with Poverty: Adaptive Strategies in a Caribbean Village*, Boulder, CO: Westview Press.

Smith, H. (2003), 'Agrochemical Use by Small Farmers in the Rio Grande Valley, Jamaica', unpublished MSc thesis, Environmental Management Unit, Department of Geography and Geology, University of the West Indies.

Spence, B. and Thomas-Hope, E. (2005), 'Agrobiodiversity and the Economic Cost of Agrochemical Use among Smallholder Farmers in the Rio Grande Valley, Jamaica', *PLEC News and Views* New Series, No. 6, March, pp. 3–7.

Thomas-Hope, E., Semple, H. and Spence, B. (2000), 'Household Structure, Agrodiversity and Agro-biodiversity on Small Farms in the Rio Grande Valley Jamaica', *PLEC News and Views*, No. 15, June, pp. 38–44.

Thomas-Hope E. and Spence, B. (2002), 'Promoting Agro-biodiversity under Difficulties: The PLEC Experience', *PLEC News and Views*, No. 19, March.

Thomas-Hope, E.and Spence, B. (2003). 'Jamaica', in H. Brookfield, H. Parsons and M. Brookfield (eds), *Agrodiversity: Learning from Farmers Across the World*, Tokyo: United Nations University Press.

Watts, D. (1987), *The West Indies: Patterns of Development, Culture and Environmental Changes since 1492,* Cambridge: Cambridge University Press.

Zarin, D.J., Huijun, G. and Enu-Kwesi, L. (1999), 'Method for the Assessment of Plant Species Diversity in Complex Agricultural Landscapes: Guidelines for Data Collection and Analysis from the PLEC Biodiversity Advisory Group (PLEC-BAG)', *PLEC News and Views*, No. 13, April (Special Issue).

Chapter 5

Disaster Creation in the Caribbean and Planning, Policy and Participation Reconsidered

Jonathan Skinner

> As I understand it, the report was financed by the United Nations during the 1980s when there was a decade for the reduction of disaster in small territories. According to the paper itself, the report was handed to the Government of Montserrat at the end of it which would have been 1986–87. Hurricane Hugo struck Montserrat in 1989. If the Governor of the day had a copy of the report the Governor's office was blown totally into the sea in Hurricane Hugo, all the library was lost. A lot of the records of the Government of Montserrat were lost also. I can only assume the corporate memory on island had forgotten about this document. (IDC 1998a: 90)

> [D]isasters do not simply happen; they are caused. (Oliver-Smith 1999a: 74)

Introduction

The first quotation above is from Frank Savage, former Governor of the British colony of Montserrat in the Eastern Caribbean, Foreign and Commonwealth Office (FCO) appointee, facing detailed cross-examination before the International Development Committee of the House of Commons concerning the handling of the eruption of Mount Chance which has been ongoing since 1995. At this stage in the proceedings, Savage was trying to explain why it was that post-Hurricane Hugo development work had completely ignored a report by Wadge and Isaacs (1988) which warned of potential eruption and warned against extending development work in areas which they considered to be 'at risk' such as the capital Plymouth, wasting millions of pounds following the eruption of the volcano and subsequent destruction of Plymouth with its new jetty, hospital, library and Government Headquarters in 1997 (see Skinner 2003). The second quotation is from Anthony Oliver-Smith (1999a: 28; see also 1986), an anthropologist who has used his study of the 1970 Peruvian earthquake to assert that '[d]isasters occur in societies. They do not occur in nature'. For Oliver-Smith, a disaster should be read for its longevity and causation in that it is the result of human maladaptation to an environment; it is a 'convergent catastrophe' in the words of Moseley (1999). A volcano, for example, such as that on Montserrat, is a 'trigger' to a disaster (see Zaman 1999: 192); a flood in Bangladesh is precipitated by a colonial legacy of land ownership which had forced the population to the coast (Zaman

1999: 194); an earthquake is a 'cultural artifact' (Doughty 1999: 235), a 'classquake' (Oliver-Smith 1999b: 75) often several hundred years in the making. The 1970 7.7 Richter scale earthquake in Peru – often referred to as one of the largest natural disasters in the Western hemisphere – directly killed 70,000 people, injured another 140,000, destroyed 160,000 buildings, made homeless a further 500,000, entombed entire cities such as Yungay, and radically altered the environment of the north central Andes. Taking a *political ecology* approach to this disaster, Oliver-Smith analyses it as long time in the making, a disaster stemming from patterns altered and re-set ever since colonial conquest fostered urbanization in the valleys, and encouraged the change of building materials from thatch to stone. These non-indigenous adaptations – centralized settlement patterns and inappropriate environmental building materials and techniques – inadvertently caused, produced and induced disaster.

This chapter makes a contribution to the environmental planning theme of this volume by pressing Oliver-Smith's anthropological approach above to the environment, and by considering a contemporary colonial case study of governance, science and disaster on the island of Montserrat in the Eastern Caribbean. There is the potential here for ambiguity surrounding the use of the term 'disaster', as to whether it refers to the natural and environmental disaster caused by the ongoing eruption of Mount Chance from 1995, or to the management of the volcanic eruption. However, in my examination of the eruption of the volcano and the subsequent responses and policy developments to that eruption, it should become increasingly clear that – after Oliver-Smith (1999; 2002) – the Montserrat disaster is an evolving cultural process, a 'Foucauldian' event woven over time, precipitated by poor British colonial policies and practices.

First, this chapter looks at the creation of environments ripe for climactic disaster – hurricane in particular – 'natural' disasters which have characterized much of the twentieth century on Montserrat, but also other Caribbean islands. Second, this chapter goes on to explore in more detail the case of the eruption of Mount Chance on Montserrat, a tectonic disaster riding six years later upon the back of Hurricane Hugo, one which was complicated and exacerbated by Montserrat's colonial status, and one which could have been ameliorated by effective environmental planning. Finally, the chapter closes with a discussion and critique of environmental planning, processes and participation.

Creating Climactic Disaster Environments

Whether considering ecotourism or water pollution in Mexico, or pest control, sustainable tourism development or coastal erosion in Jamaica, the case studies in this volume attest to the need to examine the context behind environmental problems and the planning to offset, reduce or even overcome these environmental problems. These case studies give us ethnographic detail and local insight which is what anthropologists and many geographers seek. But just what does 'the environment' mean for an anthropologist? Common academic and lay use of the term 'environment' suggests that the term refers to 'non-human influences on humanity' (Thin 1996: 185), that it is shorthand for the natural world, our 'biophysical context'. Through the 1960s, Julian Steward's (1955) cultural ecology approach gained academic and popular support, an approach which sought levels of causation between culture and the environment. To some degree, this approach relies upon static notions of both nature and culture, a position rejected by constructionists who fall along a continuum of ever-increasing levels pertaining to the construction of either one, the other, or both. Social constructionism can be criticized generally for its relativism (Skinner 2004), and more specifically, in this context, for imposing 'a barrier between the environment and our understanding of it' (Milton on Ingold 2002: 41). More recently, Tim Ingold's (2000: 20) Gregory Bateson-inspired thesis that the self and the other, mind and body, nature and culture are inseparable from each other, that 'I am a part of my environment', to paraphrase, has gained in acceptance. This means that the environment is more than simply 'that which surrounds'.

With this expansion of the notion of the environment, it is possible to describe the Caribbean as a dedicated 'pleasure periphery' (Turner and Ash 1976) environment. It is a tourist destination where '[o]ur tourism product is our environment', according to Caribbean Tourism Organization spokeswoman Jean Holder (1988): a constructed natural environment of beaches, coral reefs, wetlands and climate, where the tourist can 'gaze' (cf. Urry 1990) and be grazed by the sun's rays. Unfortunately, according to Polly Pattullo (1996), author of *Last Resorts*, the Caribbean has become Milton's poetic 'Paradise Lost', a region of environmental destruction which 'includes the erosion of beaches, the breakdown of coral reefs, marine and coastal pollution from watersports, the dumping of waste and the non-treatment of sewage, sand-mining and the destruction of wetlands and salt ponds', not to mention the social friction, alienation and indigency of the local populations. Further to these manmade environmental impoverishments are natural disasters arising from a convergence of hurricane weather patterns and human settlement and land management patterns.

Records show that there have been more hurricanes in the Caribbean than there have been years of colonial or postcolonial government in the region (Cordeiro 1900: 249). Though unable to significantly control or alter the pathway or intensity of a hurricane (a seasonal tropical storm [June 1 to 30 November] exceeding 33m/s [74 mph], so named after the Carib Huracan God of Evil), the hurricane disaster is one which can be prepared for. This is a necessity of life in the Caribbean Basin and East Coast North America, considering that half of all the 80–100 annual tropical storms turn into hurricanes. Hurricanes are fuelled by the warm waters of the tropics, and hurricane disasters are fuelled by a range of factors from agricultural practices to waste water systems, construction practices and political policies. And in turn, hurricanes can work as catalysts for change: *Winds of Change*, according to historian of Cuba Louis Pérez (2001) who has shown how hurricanes hitting Cuba in 1842, 1844 and 1846 caused a coffee production crisis and impacted upon Cuban politics and relations with colonial Spain. A hurricane wrings devastation upon an environment and brings instability to the cognitive psyche of its human and animal inhabitants.

To give an historical example, in between the US intervention in the Caribbean in the 1898 Spanish-American War and the eventual overthrow of Spanish rule which led to Cuban independence in 1902, Puerto Rico faced one of the worst hurricanes in recorded history. On 8 August 1899, 3,000 people were killed by hurricane San Ciriaco blowing across the island at 115 mph. Though the winds were unpreventable, Schwartz (1992: 314) notes that 'the nature of the island's political and economic structures determined the impact of the hurricane'. Under Spanish colonial domination, the islanders were accustomed to 'poor rations', 'precarious housing' and moral, financial and intellectually bankrupt *ayuntamientos* (municipal administrations) (Schwartz 1992: 313, 309). The plantation system which had barely survived the abolishment of slavery in 1873 had created a landless seasonal workforce with low levels of public health and life expectancy. The hurricane simply added pressure to the island's weak infrastructure, its misguided crop/livestock agrarian structure which relied upon food imports, and the unconvincing government and colonial controls over the labouring classes.

> Puerto Rico was a food importer and already food-deficient. San Ciriaco intensified that situation and underlined the dangers inherent in the island's colonial status. The export agrarian structure, the general poverty of the rural population, its lack of adequate housing, and a fragile infrastructure of transportation, health services, and communication turned San Ciriaco from a natural hazard into a major human disaster. For Puerto Rican patriots, it was not difficult to lay the responsibility for these underlying conditions at the feet of the old colonial power, Spain. (Schwartz 1992: 318)

Furthermore, the hurricane's effects were also felt more by the poor. San Ciriaco had a 'differential impact' (Schwartz 1992: 318):

> Well-constructed houses in San Juan and other urban centers that did not also suffer flooding received damage but withstood the brunt of the storm. The mud and palm-thatch shacks of the rural population were simply blown to the ground; and to make matters worse, the uprooting of trees left the poor with no materials for new roof. The destruction of the bananas, plantains, potatoes, and other 'minor crops' on which the rural poor depended created potential famine conditions, although the government acted quickly to provide immediate relief and to order the planting of food crops. (Schwartz 1992: 318).

Monoculture on many of the Caribbean islands is still a problem. Deforestation in favour of open-land agriculture of sugar cane or coffee, bananas or pasture land for grazing lead to nutrient depletion, soil erosion and landslides. These changes in the land and tree canopy environment also raise levels of water runoff, resulting in flooding and the loss of a clean water system. Land use was found to be a significant factor influencing the location and level of hurricane damage on Puerto Rico during the 1936 and 1989 hurricanes. Recent silvicultural policy in the US Forest Service on Puerto Rico has shifted in the wake of these findings to encourage hardy primary forest growth (Foster et al. 1999: 569).

For Puerto Rican poet Luis Pales Matos, the power of the hurricane is akin to the power held by a musician drawing open a 'fierce accordion of winds'. For Montserratian poet and historian Howard Fergus, the hurricane is '[a] wraith wrapped in grey clouds'. In a more recent example of a climactic disaster, Hurricane Hugo besieged the Caribbean Basin and East Coast North America with winds in excess of 136 mph September–October 1989, a storm surge 16–20 feet above the mean tide, and a pressure of 934Mb – a category 5 hurricane, shattering all previous hurricane records held for landfall. Hugo hit Guadeloupe and Montserrat on 17 September 1989, killing 21 people and leaving 12,000 homeless before laying waste to the US Virgin Islands, Puerto Rico and then South Carolina where evacuation was mandatory and 56,000 inhabitants returned to empty plots where their houses once stood. In all, Hugo precipitated the death of 76 people and damages in excess of (US)$10 billion. In the Carolinas, a Federal Disaster Area was declared and, on Montserrat, the British Governor invoked emergency colonial orders which passed day-to-day control of the island away from the locally-elected Chief Minister.

Whilst the US has an effective federal support structure and, since 1970, has had an 18,000 strong Environmental Protection Agency 'to protect human health and the natural environment' (EPA 2004), Montserrat, with a 1989 population of but 12,000 has to make do with a Government Ministry of Agriculture, Lands, Housing and The Environment. Whilst the powerful US EPA remit includes air and global climate change, water, land, communities and ecosystems, and compliance and environmental stewardship and, since 1985, a Chemical Emergency Preparedness and Prevention Office (CEPPO) to assist with homeland security, Montserrat's Ministry covers areas such as animal welfare, forestry, fisheries, plants and backyard farming. Its aims are as follows:

> To redevelop agriculture and the other natural resource sectors in the north, using traditional and emerging techniques and technologies, to satisfy local demand and to target specific markets for export of fresh commodities and value added products. (GoM 2004)

Because of Montserrat's status as a British Dependent Territory, relying upon British development aid filtered through a Country Policy Plan, and the island's relative poverty (–1 per cent GDP real growth rate and only $3,400 GDP per capita in 2002), Montserrat relies to a large extent upon an island-based NGO, the Montserrat National Trust. The Trust was created in 1969 as a non-profit statutory body and was 'charged with the responsibility of conservation, preservation and presentation of the island's historical and cultural resources and the promotion of public awareness' (MNT 2004). Whilst carrying out anthropological fieldwork on Montserrat between 1994 and 1995, I worked for the Trust which ran the local museum, sponsored and encouraged environmentally friendly initiatives such as the Best Kept Village competition, managed sites of interest and beauty such as the Galways Soufrière and slave plantation, and cared for the rare Montserrat Oriole and its habitat. Local critics of the Trust, however, complained that it was an expatriate organization modelled after the English National Trust, with tourist and Eurocentric concerns over and above the struggling welfare and survival of the Montserratian population.

Post-Hugo recovery Trust activities involved the development of archaeological, forestry (bamboo) and coastal sites and the encouragement of marine protection areas. Though most of the trees were swept clean from Montserrat by the hurricane, Fergus

(1994), in his history of the island, celebrates the fact that within two years, apart from the trees, the island was well-healed with lush green vegetation and many plots of well-constructed housing by a resilient and hardy population. He adds that post-Hugo disaster planning influenced the establishment of a new British Secretariat in Barbados to assist with development activities and to reduce aid 'bottlenecks' (1994: 238). In a chapter devoted to 'Disasters and Recovery', Fergus (pp. 220–38) chronicles the various floods, earthquakes and hurricanes which have perennially ravaged the island. The hurricanes of 1766, 1816, 1866, 1899, 1924, 1928 and 1989 all gain prominence in his account of the struggle to survive and colonize Montserrat (the term colony is derived from the latin for farmer, *colonus*, which refers to an inhabiting and working of the land [Young 1992: 31]). An important point which Fergus makes is that many Montserratians did not learn, or had forgotten the lessons, from the 1928 hurricane by the time that Hugo hit the island. Many constructions were the work of '[a]mateur architects' (p. 234). In Fergus's (p. 234) words:

> Noticeably, some small houses with galvanised covering and hip roofs survived Hugo, while loftier modern structures crumbled. It is evident that the post-1928 generation built with hurricanes in mind. By 1989 the country had become careless and architectural attractiveness was not combined with hurricane worthiness.

It was only post-Hugo that UNDP architects came in to work on the island and to introduce construction policies recommending roofs with pitches 20–35 degrees and with the superstructure bolted down to a substructure. If Montserratians and the Montserrat government had been more careful in their construction rather than relying upon hurricane shelters – which proved to be very effective – then the damage from Hugo would have been minimized. Clearly then, climactic disasters past and present are just as political as they are ecological.

Creating Tectonic Disaster Environments

Interestingly, volcanoes (3.14) share a similar position on the event type variability/number killed score with storms (2.91) (Davis and Seitz 1982: 558). Montserrat is one of the volcanic islands in the Caribbean. Thirty-nine square miles in size and shaped like a teardrop, Montserrat rises 3,000 ft above the black sand beaches at sea level with hot springs and Soufrière Hills, finally peaking with the aptly named Mount Chance. Despite its volcanic aspect, Montserrat has been considered a dormant volcanic island, only occasionally studied after bouts of earthquake activity (1810 to explore the soufrières; 1902 when Pelé erupted on Martinique causing over 100 tremors/day on Montserrat, and 1934 [Fergus 1994: 5]). In 1995, whilst I was on Montserrat working with the Montserrat National Trust and the British development workers who were just finishing the touches of a multi-million pound bilateral development post-Hugo aid project of a new port jetty, hospital and government headquarters, Mount Chance suddenly erupted as a creeping pyroclastic volcano (Skinner 2000; 2004). The volcanic activity went on to destroy the capital city, Plymouth and hillside villages (including

19 villagers in June 1997), the island airport and 25.5 square miles (64 per cent of the island's surface), forcing some 6,500 islanders (62 per cent of the pre-volcano population) to rebuild their lives elsewhere (SDP 1998: 1; see Figure 5.1) and another 1,500 to live in temporary shelters in the north.

Because Montserrat is a British colony, and has been since the 1630s, the island naturally looks to the motherland on matters of jurisdiction and assistance. On occasion, this is beneficial to the island and the islanders eking out a '*rentier*' remittance status (Baldacchino 1993: 40), a strategic positioning such as Chief

Figure 5.1 Before and after the eruption of Mount Chance, Montserrat

Minister W.H. Bramble's rejection of Statehood in Association in favour of colonial status and continued 'budgetary dole' (Fergus 1994: 212). At other times, this can be a disadvantage such as when a disaster is created (Hugo in 1989 and the volcano from 1995), and the island is restricted to appealing to Britain for support rather than to the UN or world community as an independent country – though Montserrat does often receive some gift aid from members of the international community such as Venezuela, Jamaica, the US and Canada.

Following the deaths of Montserratians from pyroclastic mud flows, tensions between the British government (HMG) and the Montserratian people and Montserrat government (GoM), and a series of related development disasters – '"anti-social" social development' policies as I refer to them elsewhere (Skinner 2003) – the House of Commons International Development Committee reviewed and questioned the government's activities and handling of the Montserrat crisis, finally recommending that the Department for International Development (DFID) commission an independent inquiry into the affair. The Overseas Development Institute (ODI) in London conducted that evaluation (Clay et al. 1999), involving myself as a token external party in this whitewashing Whitehall exercise (see Skinner 2003). They wrote a cautious exoneration of 'HMG' in terms of contentious factors such as the appropriateness (limited emergency aid, non-hurricane proof shelters), cost-effectiveness (double-billing and 40 per cent of aid spent on consultancy fees) and coherence (GoM vs DFID vs FCO and other HMG departments) of their disaster responses. Though the report starts with a positive statement ('[t]hroughout the emergency, involving four major evacuations at little notice, everyone has had a roof over their head, no one has gone hungry and there have been no reported cases of child malnutrition, and social order has been maintained' [Clay et al. 1999: 1]), the Summary contained the following selection of buried comments:

> MAIN FINDINGS … There was apparently no contingency planning on how FCO and the then ODA [now DFID] would manage the emergency in an Overseas Territory (OT) in circumstances that raised difficult issues of governance and risk management as well as the detailed practicalities of emergency management. (p. 2)
>
> There was initial indecision and public disagreement between HMG and GoM. (p. 3)
>
> BUILDING SCIENCE INTO POLICY … inappropriate. (p. 40)
>
> APPROPRIATENESS … messy detail. (p. 5)
>
> TIMELINESS … too slow. (p. 5)
>
> CONNECTEDNESS … Addressing urgent emergency requirements, through measures which had a joint objective of promoting development, proved a flawed concept. (p. 6)
>
> COHERENCE (CO-ORDINATION) … Many of the delays, omissions and shortcomings in HMG's response are linked to the complexity of HMG management and the administrative system for Montserrat as a self-governing OT. (p. 6)

> In the early stages of the emergency the overall co-ordination of HMG's response was weak. (p. 6)
>
> KEY LESSONS ... Both FCO and DFID experienced difficulties in posting staff for urgent assignments in Montserrat through normal procedures. (p. 7)
>
> PROMOTING PARTNERSHIP IN THE OVERSEAS TERRITORIES ... There are no agreed standards for infrastructure, social assistance or social service provision, health and education in OTs. There is an urgent need to clarify appropriate standards to which the "reasonable claims" of the OTs on British aid are to relate, especially in an emergency. (p. 8)
>
> DISASTER PREPAREDNESS IN THE OVERSEAS TERRITORIES ... The risk assessment for Montserrat prepared in 1987, which considered the possibility of an eruption, was overlooked. (p. 9)

There is little in the two volume evaluation of HMG's response to the Montserrat volcanic emergency about the conservation of the environment. It is all reaction to the volcano situation, reaction which monitors and also compounds the disaster situation.

It is the Sustainable Development Plan (SDP 1998), produced by the Montserrat Development Unit in conjunction with HMG and non-governmental organizations, which caters expressly for the physical as well as the sociocultural environment on Montserrat. These documents are medium term policy and strategy documents constructed every five years or so by using an integrated planning approach (IPA), a methodology which links the national development goals to individual government goals, to achieve consistency and coherence. The 1998–2002 SDP, subtitled *Montserrat Social and Economic Recovery Programme – a Path to Sustainable Development: 1998 to 2002. The Key Policies and Strategies to Move the Island of Montserrat from Crisis to Development* (SDP 1998), is currently under review and evaluation.

Once an SDP has been agreed on Montserrat, it is then taken forward for use as the basis of a Country Policy Plan which is adopted and funded by HMG. The planning approach thus moves from the people and the GoM through to DFID and HMG and then back to GoM as work programmes which are specified in the local budget (see Figure 5.2). This document is the development strategy, policy and planning backbone on Montserrat for social, economic and environmental concerns.

> The SDP shows a clear commitment to the re-development of Montserrat by GoM and HMG in conjunction with the people of Montserrat ... Following agreement of the SDP, it is possible for the GoM to formulate a Country Policy Plan (CPP) with HMG. ... Whereas the SDP sets out the policy framework for social and economic recovery, the purpose of the CPP will be to outline in detail the specific projects and other activities to be funded by HMG and which will lead to the achievement of the objectives of the SDP. (SDP 1998: 4)

Significantly, the SDP document contains a section on environmental planning for Montserrat. It thus conforms, in its way, to an anthropological notion of the

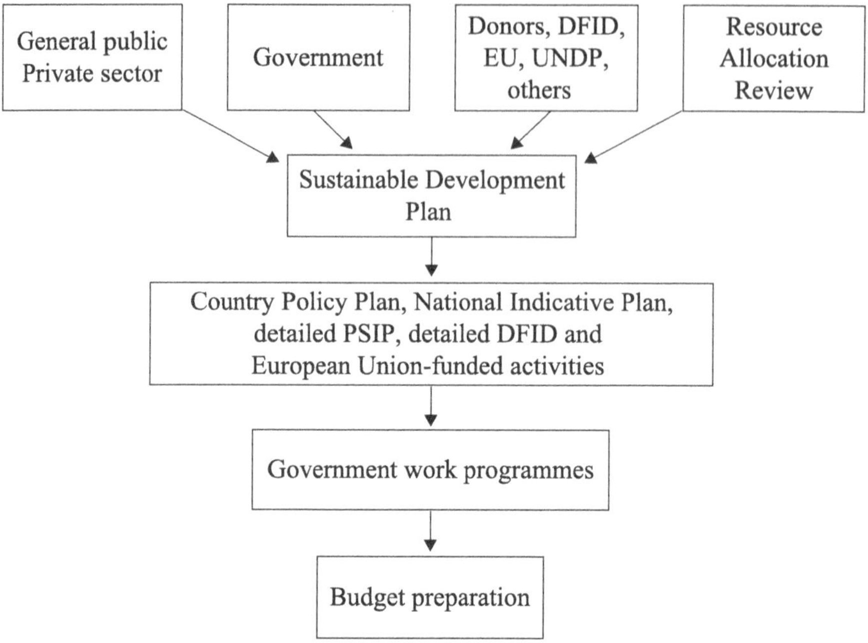

Figure 5.2 The integrated planning approach

Source: SDP 1998: 3.

environment with its holistic approach. Alongside objectives such as the provision of primary health care facilities and direct references to the environment are the following:

> [s]trengthening the systems for the management of the physical environment; … [t]he sustainable management and further development of marine resources; … [t]he consolidation of the economic contribution of the tourism sector with minimal environmental degradation. (p. 6)

In these references, we see, again, the typical Caribbean development initiative, one which is tied to tourism, tourism as the old 'passport to development' philosophy which were first coined in the late 1970s (de Kadt 1979). This line, one recently re-charged under the ecotourism niche, has now been rejected as the 'lipservice' (Pattullo 1996) that it is, short-term gain over long-term pain (Butler 1993).

Further on in the document are the strongest expressions of environmental consideration and planning – a desire for 'responsible approach to environmental and disaster management' (SDP 1998: 7). After addressing the physical planning of the north of the island, the safe zone, environmental health and tourism, fisheries and agriculture, for example, the SDP goes on to tackle environmental protection in detail.

It should be noted how this environmental section is introduced, and what the local notion of the environment is and how it should be considered. The section begins:

> [t]he watershed protection function of forest remains as important as before the volcanic crisis, especially since the Centre Hills spring sources are now the island's only reliable water supply. In terms of biodiversity, most species and ecosystems survive in the Centre Hills and should be protected in situ. (p. 24)

Risk of soil erosion and the loss of soil fertility feature amongst the key issues identified in this part of the SDP, as well as the risk of damage to the forest and to wildlife from ash fall, acid rain and related volcanic activity. As the report goes on to show, '[t]he Forestry strategy centres on ensuring that key forest catchments can collect and store water and that critical forest resources are preserved as new development in the north progresses' (p. 24). In other words, one of the few environmental planning documents on Montserrat reveals that the environment is a resource to be used, largely because of the needs of the island population for fresh water. This example of environmental planning on Montserrat places the people first and looks upon 'the environment' as a physical resource base to be used, managed, developed and sustained as far as is possible. In these examples, neither Hugo, nor the eruption of Mount Chance have altered substantially the overall environmental plans for the island in terms of the conceptualization and deployment of the environment notion. Sustainable development, as surmised by the approach to development in this plan, is for the sustainable development of the colonial citizens of Montserrat. The environmental planning is an anthropogenic projection of needs and desires. The environment is a political and planned environment.

Participation and Environmental Planning

The above case studies are of disaster environments constructed: the climactic hurricane disaster such as San Ciriaco across Puerto Rico and Hugo across Montserrat and the east coast US; and the tectonic disaster on Montserrat. Both types of disaster have been created by a 'convergence of catastrophes' (Moseley 1999) and have been compounded by a lack of 'environmental' planning. Like diseases, such convergences exert stress upon the biotic communities they change – the living environment. What the examples show are the difficulties associated with effective planning, predication, preparation, execution and communication. There are effective hurricane shelters and radio warnings from meteorological offices to warn of the impending arrival of the hurricanes, and to provide some shelter from the hurricane. But the other building constructions are less resilient, relying instead upon the resilience of the citizens to rebuild. As mentioned above, more effective environmental planning would include more stringent building regulations so that the collective memory of the particularly severe hurricane-turned-disaster does not wear off. Land management planning is also important because it features highly in the construction of the disaster. Crop rotation, tree planting and careful animal husbandry would maintain the soil and drainage systems and reduce hurricane follow-up problems such as erosion, flooding and stripping.

In both types of disaster creation, but the tectonic in particular, there is a tendency to personalize the disaster. Many disasters are understood, given meaning, in terms of the 'victims'' cosmology. Andean villagers call their volcano 'a savage', hurricanes are often anthapromorphized or turned into roaring dragons and devils (Hoffman 2002: 127), and many Montserratians refer to the volcano in the south of their island as, simply, 'the Beast'. This type of response to a disaster is frequently discouraged as a primitive logic, a simple response to a complex happening to be suppressed in favour of rational scientific explanations. However, as Hoffman points out, such a response is very telling. It is a response indicative of recovery. The imagery of calamity 'gives an orbit of persuasion on how to cope with and survive it' (p. 114). The shift is cognitive and is one which we can understand from Clifford Geertz's (1973) work on religious systems, from our working with models 'of' the world and models 'for' the world: the former being the existing environment – one of change, disorder and difference; and the latter, an ideational, notional reality, one postulated, desired and worked and prayed for. This distinction is important not just for working with people who are coming to terms with a disaster, but also with the planning stages before and after a disaster. Anticipating and knowing how people are going to react to a hurricane or a volcano, and taking appropriate preventative and palliative care, and working with the models people have for their future and their future environment is what environmental planning is ultimately about.

Wild and uncontrollable, the Oakland California firestorm of 1991 studied by Hoffman (2002) is seen by many of the sufferers to be a phenomenon of nature, set apart from the cultural. And yet a disaster is a convergence of the natural and the cultural according to the thesis central to her approach to disasters. And the environment is constituted of both the natural and the cultural, to return to Ingold and Bateson. Though I have been arguing that the disaster is a created phenomenon, Hoffman goes on to make a valid point when she adds that if a disaster is seen to come from the cultural as opposed to the natural, then it is far harder for the sufferers to recover. This is because the disaster is seen to be 'closer' to them if it is perceived to be more in the cultural realm. This is why it might be harder to 'recover' from an explosion than a hurricane, from a plane crash than a volcano. When applied to the Caribbean and to environmental planning, it is thus useful to identify markers for recovery, and to encourage and foster the natural interpretation of events, particularly when there is a cyclical narrative to the event, the perennial hurricane for example. Environmental and disaster planning should thus 'gear up' rather than 'gear down' the symbolic interpretations and meaning making cosmologies which can sit alongside the scientific.

Though the Sustainable Development Plan and aid negotiations on Montserrat claim to be 'participatory' and integrated, they are an example of belated environmental planning, activities which Moseley (1998: 68) refers to as 'political instruments used ... on the basis of hypothetical pollyannaism'. Certainly, many of the development programmes and plans on Montserrat were examples of bilateral development work and were seen to be strategic and political, such as the marking of evacuation zones to give house preferences to DFID workers (Skinner 2003). And, as Gardner and Lewis (1996) note, the proliferation in the number of social development workers (SDAs) at DFID and on Montserrat has not resulted in integrated – accountable, equitable and appropriate – development. Instead, another level of bureaucracy has been added to an increasingly colonial situation. This layer is often an audit culture layer which needs objective, quantifiable outputs (Gardner and Lewis 1996: 131). After the disaster, Hoffman (2002: 138) suggests that a board of inquiry can be used as an event which acts as a 'ritual of reassurance'. In her example, the Oakland community was reassured by the probing and analyzing of the firestorm disaster. The future was made safe by ritually raking over the ashes, a ritual way of understanding the disaster to correct and prevent it from recurring: 'Culture taking care of a cultural problem'. In my example of the DFID dealings with the tectonic disaster, the reassurances are for the British public, to ensure accountability in overseas development practice; in other words, in the chains of command, in the structures of control, and not in the work itself or for the Montserratians themselves.

In *Living with the Unexpected: Linking Disaster Recovery to Sustainable Development in Montserrat*, Anja Possekel (1999) explores how scientific ideas about complexity and uncertainty can be applied to the understanding of natural hazards and disasters. For Possekel (see p.66), scenario planning is an evolutionary and participatory approach which assists with the reconstruction process. Figure 5.3 is an example of scenario planning. The process is loosely divided into three iterative phases which move from a *phase of analysis* in which the question and/or problem is formulated, through to a *phase of prognosis* when assumptions are made, and finally a *phase of implementation* when the scenario is tested. These phases shift from a definition of the research object which is largely descriptive, to the second phase which deals with assumptions and visions about future developments. The process then ends with implementation and analysis of the effects. As a planning process, scenario testing has internal logic to it, and can be broadly participatory, incorporating the views of a large number of people. It is a consensus-building activity.

Because scenario building and testing works in this inclusive fashion, it delivers results which appeal to the lowest common denominator. This can mean that innovative thinking and planning is stifled. In other words, there is an inherent – and sometimes slow – conservatism to the process. With caution but also with common sense, the drafting of scenarios and their alternatives in order to develop appropriate measures can turn out to be both practical and visionary, but can also turn into a rhetorical exercise of persuasion. As I have argued in my critique of social development work on Montserrat (Skinner 1996; 2003: 113), frequently, participatory work is a subtle form of local or indigenous co-option, a technique for imposing colonial or neo-colonial will and governmentality. Possekel (1999: 112), for example, used this participatory approach when considering environmental planning on Montserrat, their perceptions of the natural environment in particular.

Possekel set a questionnaire for a select group of Montserratians to answer and for those answers to inform a focus group on the perception of the natural environment

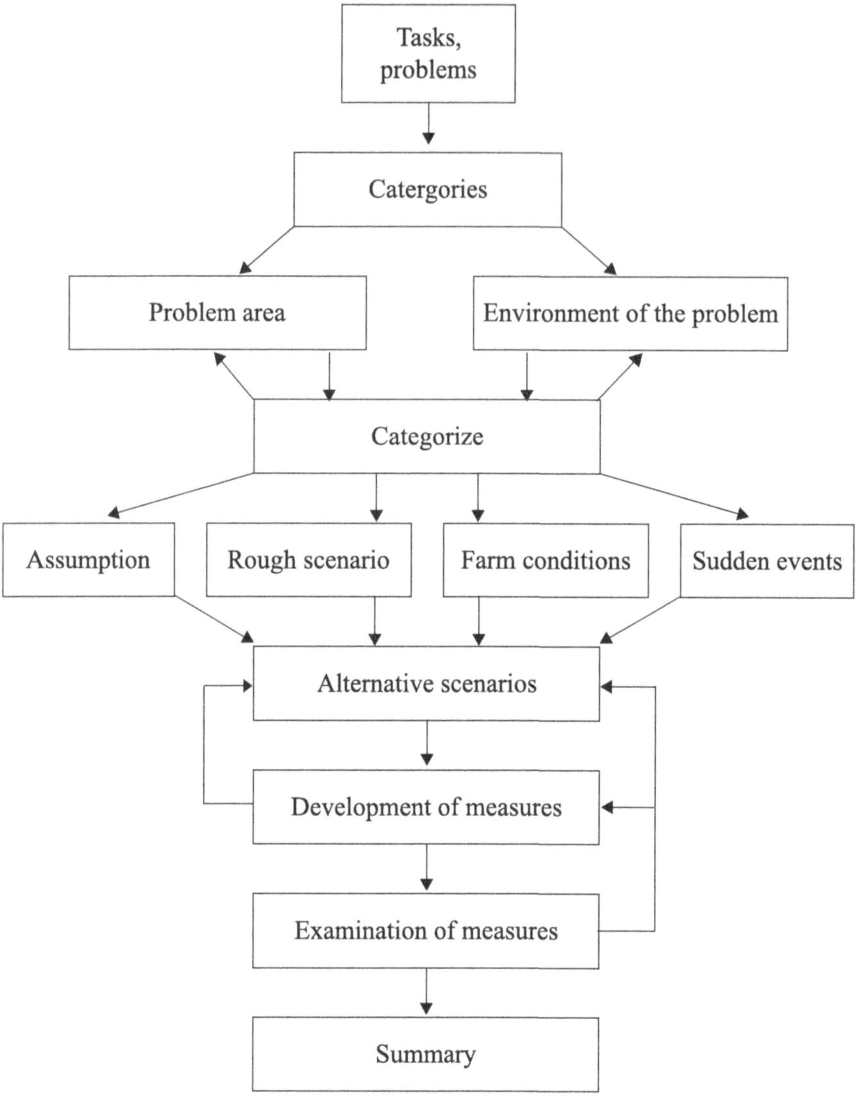

Figure 5.3 Logic sequence when creating a scenario according to Senger

Source: Possekel 1999: 67.

and resources. These answers reveal that the volcano was considered to be an island resource before the volcano erupted and that it subsequently turned into a threat and a curse (p. 113). Again, like the Sustainable Development Plan, the perceptions and notions of the environment are as a resource to be used, used carefully and judiciously so that it might continue to be used in the future.

> About half the people interviewed answered the question 'What is your personal view about the environmental situation on your island?' as follows: 'The environment in Montserrat is still pretty unspoilt'. The environment was on the whole evaluated positively. The people's impression was that there had so far been hardly any overexploitation of the natural resources. Comparisons were made, pointing out that the environment on neighbouring islands was often in a critical state. (p. 112)

To some degree, Possekel's questioning is participatory: it draws in the participants and facilitates a discussion. However, the questions and interpretations are set and determined by Possekel. She controls the initial and final stages of the planning process. Further to this, Possekel selects the participants in the process. This pseudo-bottom-up approach to development is a mid-way position between Rapid Rural Appraisal (RRA) and Participatory Rural Analysis (PRA), the former consisting of data collection by outsiders eliciting information, and the latter consisting of local data collection, correlation and interpretation with the assistance of outsiders.

The PRA methodology – devised in opposition to traditional Rapid Rural Appraisal (RRA) questionnaires – is used elsewhere to better effect by the anthropologist Hermann Tillmann in Panama where the Ngobe people use village level planning initiatives to tackle the infringement of agro-forestry technology upon their cultural and physical environment. There, PRA is considered to be locally satisfying as indigenous voices predominate: the indigenous exercise control of the development process and funds. However, PRA is an expensive and time-consuming approach; also, it is academically frustrating in the sense that trained and committed development workers can be ignored and made obsolete by 'untrained' villagers; and it can be accused of being a more refined and deviously-exported version of western development. Tirmizion Diallo, an African anthropologist who represents the Gesellschaft für Technische Zusammenarbeit (GTZ) – the German equivalent to Britain's DFID – in Mozambique, works by maintaining open dialogue with the state, minority voices, and German projects. He works on form of more effective democratization programme, one in which 'to develop, is to discover and alter reality by unlocking indigenous potentiality' (VoD 1995).

At the end of *Living with the Unexpected*, Possekel (1999, pp. 229–40) reproduces a selection of scenarios and visions for Montserrat which the focus teams produced. One scenario worked with Montserrat as 'an integral part of the Mother Country' (UK) with 'Environmental laws designed along UK lines' and 'National parks, historic landmarks, national treasures well funded, protected, promoted' (p. 236). That was their vision for the environment on Montserrat. Another scenario was entitled 'Environmentally Sound Montserrat' and – consistent with other visions of Montserrat and notions of the environment concept – envisioned the following conservation headings:

> **Environment**
>
> Clean Air, Water, Seashore, Wind Generated Power, Geothermal Energy, Solar/Electric Cars, Hiking, Biking Trails Controlled, aesthetically pleasing development (p. 237)

When Possekel lists the main participants in her participatory work, those who came up with these scenarios, it is clear that she is tapping into the government and governing elite on the island: surveyors, directors, technical officers, President of the Montserrat National Trust, hotel managers and two high school students. As such, this sample is neither random nor representative of opinion or voices on Montserrat. As a sample, it is an example of skewed indigenous potentiality from those who have been markedly successful under colonial governance.

Conclusion

The United Nations has a Disaster Relief Coordinator. The United States has the Federal Emergency Management Agency (FEMA) which has been in existence since 1979, plus at least another 23 federal agencies charged with disaster responsibilities (White and Haas 1975) including the EPA mentioned above. As well as her British connections, Montserrat is a member of the Caribbean Disaster Emergency Response Agency (CDERA) which has been serving all CARICOM (Caribbean Community and Common Market) members since 1991 under the motto 'Managing Disasters with Preparedness'. And Britain recently established a Civil Contingencies Secretariat (CCS) in 2001 to prepare, prevent and cater for domestic disasters – to improve UK 'resilience'. The British disaster presence on Montserrat is now also served largely by the Montserrat Volcano Observatory which monitors, plans and pronounces upon the volcanic eruption and 'living with the unexpected' though now more anticipated. It would appear, then that (mother) countries are starting to learn from the disasters which have plagued them and their dependencies. They are putting into place organizations which are, at least, designed and dedicated to disaster planning. This is an improvement from the pre-eruption development structures and report-reading and filing practices.

Whilst the global development structures might be in place at last, the development practices and politics/political ecology of aid, environmental planning and social engineering remain controversial. The US government took advantage of hurricane San Ciriaco, using food appeals across the cities of the US to show Puerto Rico the benefits of US sovereignty (Schwartz 1992: 321), eventually restricting aid only to those who worked as 'a new Yankee version of the *libreta*' (p. 325), the Spanish work card scheme fixing labour and controlling labourers. One hundred and ten years later and, under the guise of Hurricane Hugo, the British government took greater control of the colony, substantially revising the island's constitution, and eventually introducing conditional development work tied to the ratification of political and economic conditions in inappropriate places on the island. Disasters continue to be in the making.

Figure 5.4 MVO scientist monitoring the volcano during a tourist visit (photo by author 2005)

Acknowledgements

I would like to thank the people and Government of Montserrat who assisted me with this research; Kay Milton for some pointers; and the ODI for inviting me to their workshops. The viewed expressed in this chapter, and any errors, are entirely my own responsibility.

References

Baldacchino, G. (1993), 'Bursting the Bubble: The Pseudo-Development Strategies of Microstates', *Development and Change*, 24, pp. 29–51.

Butler, R. (1993), 'Pre- and Post-impact Assessment of Tourism Development', in D. Pearce and R. Butler (eds), *Tourism Research: Critiques and Challenges*, London: Routledge, pp. 135–55.

Clay, E., Barrow, C., Benson, C., Dempster, J., Kokelaar, P., Pillai, N. and Seaman, J. (1999), *An Evaluation of HMG's Response to the Montserrat Volcanic Emergency – Volume 1*, London: Overseas Development Institute report for the Evaluation Department of DFID.

Cordeiro, F. (1900), 'Tropical Hurricanes', *Journal of the American Geographical Society of New York*, 32(3), pp. 249–59.

Davis, M. andSeitz, S. (1982), 'Disasters and Governments', *The Journal of Conflict Resolution*, 26(3), pp. 547–68.

de Kadt, E. (ed.) (1979), *Tourism: Passport to Development?*, Washington: George Washington University Press.

Doughty, P. (1999), 'Plan and Pattern in Reaction to Earthquake: Peru, 1970–1998', in A. Oliver-Smith and S. Hoffman (eds), *The Angry Earth: Disaster in Anthropological Perspective*, London: Routledge, pp. 234–56.

EPA (2004), *US Environmental Protection Agency*, <http://www.epa.gov>.

Fergus, H. (1994), *Montserrat: History of a Caribbean Colony*, London: Macmillan Caribbean.

Foster, D., Fluet, M. and Boose, E. (1999), 'Human or Natural Disturbance: Landscape-Scale Dynamics of the Tropical Forests of Puerto Rico', *Ecological Applications*, 9(2), pp. 555–72.

Gardner, K. and Lewis, D. (1996), *Anthropology, Development and the Post-modern challenge*, London: Pluto Press.

Geertz, C. (1973), *The Interpretation of Cultures*, New York: Basic Books.

GoM (2004), Ministry of Agriculture, <http://www.malhe.gov.ms>.

Hoffman, S. (2002), 'The Monster and the Mother: The Symbolism of Disaster', in A. Oliver-Smith and S. Hoffman (eds), *Catastrophe and Culture: The Anthropology of Disaster*, Oxford/Santa Fe: James Currey/School of American Research Press, pp. 113–42.

Holder, J. (1988), 'Tourism and Environmental Planning: An Irrevocable Commitment', *Caribiana*, Caribbean Conservation Association.

IDC (1998), *Montserrat – First Report*, House of Commons, London, The Stationery Office.

Ingold, T. (2000), *The Perception of the Environment: Essays in Livelihood, Dwelling and Skill*, London: Routledge.

Milton, K. (2002), *Loving Nature: Towards an Ecology of Nature*, London: Routledge.

MNT (2004), *Montserrat National Trust*, <http://www.montserratnationaltrust.com/museum.htm>.

Moseley, M. (1999), 'Convergent Catastrophe: Past Patterns and Future Implications of Collateral Natural Disasters in the Andes', in A. Oliver-Smith and S. Hoffman (eds), *The Angry Earth: Disaster in Anthropological Perspective*, London: Routledge, pp. 59–71.

Oliver-Smith, A. (1986), *The Martyred City: Death and Rebirth in the Andes*, Albuquerque: University of New Mexico Press.

Oliver-Smith, A. (1999a), '"What is a Disaster?": Anthropological Perspectives on a Persistent Question', in A. Oliver-Smith and S. Hoffman (eds), *The Angry Earth: Disaster in Anthropological Perspective*, London: Routledge, pp. 18–34.

Oliver-Smith, A. (1999b), 'Peru's Five-hundred-year Earthquake: Vulnerability in Historical Context', in A. Oliver-Smith and S. Hoffman (eds), *The Angry Earth: Disaster in Anthropological Perspective*, London: Routledge, pp. 74–88.

Oliver-Smith, A. (2002), 'Theorizing Disasters: Nature, Power, and Culture', in A. Oliver-Smith and S. Hoffman (eds), *Catastrophe and Culture: The Anthropology of Disaster*, Oxford/Santa Fe: James Currey/School of American Research Press, pp. 23–48.

Pattullo, P. (1996), *Last Resorts – The Cost of Tourism in the Caribbean*, London: Cassell and Latin American Bureau.

Pérez, L. (2001), *Winds of Change: Hurricanes and the Transformation of Nineteenth-Century Cuba*, Chapel Hill: University of North Carolina Press.

Possekel, A. (1999), *Living with the Unexpected: Linking Disaster Recovery to Sustainable Development on Montserrat*, London: Springer-Verlag.

Schwartz, S. (1992), 'The Hurricane of San Ciriaco: Disaster, Politics, and Society in Puerto Rico, 1899–1901', *The Hispanic American Historical Review*, 72 (3), pp. 303–34.

SDP (1998), 'Sustainable Development Plan 1998–2002: Montserrat Social and Economic Recovery Programme – a Path to Sustainable Development', Montserrat Development Unit, <http://www.devunit.gov.ms/sdp.htm>.

Skinner, J. (1996), 'Visions of Development: Haben oder Sein', *Anthropology Today*, 12 (1), pp. 24–25.

Skinner, J. (2000), 'The Eruption of Chances Peak, Montserrat, and the Narrative Containment of Risk', in P. Caplan (ed), *Risk Revisited*, London, Pluto Press, pp. 156–83.

Skinner, J. (2003), 'Anti-social "Social Development"? The DFID Approach and the 'Indigenous' of Montserrat', in J. Pottier, A. Bicker and P. Sillitoe (eds), *Negotiated Development: Power and Identity in Development*, London: Pluto Press, pp. 98–120.

Skinner, J. (2004), *Before the Volcano: Reverberations of Identity on Montserrat*, Kingston, Jamaica: Arawak Publications.

Steward, J. (1955), *Theory of Cultural Change: The Methodology of Multilinear Evolution*, Urbana, IL: University of Illinois Press.

Thin, N. (1996), 'Environment', in A. Barnard and J. Spencer (eds), *Encyclopaedia of Anthropology*, London: Routledge, pp. 185–88.

Turner, L. and Ash, J. (1976), *The Golden Hordes: International Tourism and the Pleasure Periphery*, New York: St Martin's Press.

Urry, J. (1990), *The Tourist Gaze: Leisure and Travel in Contemporary Societies*, Bristol/London: Sage Publication.

VoD (1995), 'Visions of Development', International Workshop held at the University of Tübingen, Germany.

Wadge, G. and Isaacs, M.C. (1988), 'Mapping the Volcanic Hazards from Soufriere Hills Volcano, Montserrat, West Indies using an Image Processor', *Journal of the Geological Society of London*, 145, pp. 541–51.

Wallace, A. (1956), *Tornado in Worcester*, Washington, DC: Committee on Disaster Studies,

National Academy of Sciences, National Research Council.
White, G. and Haas, J. (1975), *Assessment of Research on Natural Hazards*, Cambridge, MA: MIT Press.
Young, R. (1992), *White Mythologies: Writing History and the West*, London: Routledge.
Zaman, M. (1999), 'Vulnerability, Disaster, and Survival in Bangladesh: Three Case Studies', in A. Oliver-Smith and S. Hoffman (eds), *The Angry Earth: Disaster in Anthropological Perspective*, London: Routledge, pp. 192–212.

Chapter 6

Environmental Planning and Heritage Tourism in Cuba During the Special Period: Challenges and Opportunities

Joseph L. Scarpaci

Introduction

The planning literature is rife with research on the impacts that globalization is having on national, regional, and local economies and environments (Afshar and Pezzoli 2001; Dicken 2003; Klak 1998; Johnston et al. 1995). International tourism in developing countries, once considered a vice of underdevelopment, reflects the ways that globalization is moving through the world. Tourism has recently gained a new role in economic development because it affords relatively quick transfers of capital and draws on comparative advantages such as sun, surf, and interesting landscapes (Barberia 2000). Within the latter niche arises heritage tourism; the promotion of selling cultural and natural resources that offer alternatives to the steel-and-glass tropical landscapes of places like Cancun, Miami, and Acapulco (Scarpaci 1998; Jones and Bromley 1999; Jones and Varley 1999). These new heritage tourists, or 'a new class of tourist: trendies on the trail', as Mowforth and Munt (2003: ch. 4) call them, are scrambling for unique Third World destinations. In Latin America and the Caribbean, historic quarters of older cities have proven a powerful allure (Ward 1993; Coyula 2002; Portes et al. 1997), especially after UNESCO and national commissions bestow heritage status upon them (Rojas 1999; Scarpaci 2005).

One of the challenges that international tourism brings to these small heritage quarters is how to provide an array of basic tourist services (lodging, water, food, transportation) without homogenizing the landscape to the extent that it becomes unrecognizable, while accentuating the local conditions that make these spaces unique (Albrow 2000; Ashworth 2003; Gancedo and Gutiérrez 2002; Graham et al. 2000; Peters 2002; Robinson et al. 2002; Cosgrove 1985; 1987). Doing so, moreover, with an eye towards the environment is increasingly rising on domestic and international policy agendas. In the case of Cuba, a recent article about nature in the prestigious *Smithsonian* magazine champions the vast swamps and pristine rivers of the island, but avoids the polemic about whether these environmental enclaves are by design or default. The real question is whether these well-preserved wildlands can be sustained that way for long (Linden 2003: 94)?

Heritage tourism is full of debates on the collective memories that these landmarks represent (Barthell 1996; Brett 1996; Lowenthal 1985). Whose past is to be preserved and at what cost? In the Caribbean, such questions are key since slavery, exploitation, waves of ethnic immigration, and class differences all form current landscapes of these historic places (Richardson and Scarpaci 1994). If places become too contrived, they lose their appeal (Lash and Urry 1994; Rojeck and Urry 1997; Scarpaci 2003a). Furthermore, how can historic preservation be integrated sensitively into broader assessments of environmental impact and local economic development? Tung's study of 22 historic places around the globe shows that while each historic preservation site is fraught with tension and conflict about who benefits and who ultimately pays, in the long run, failure to entertain environmental sensitivity can spoil these heritage sites, even beyond repair (Tung 2001).

The Caribbean, and Cuba in particular, brings many of these issues to the forefront. Long endowed with architecture of world renown (*Carta Internacional* ..., Crain 1994), the Caribbean offers both a benign climate and landscapes that are windows to a complex colonial history (Amaral 1994; Fraser 1990, 2000; Hardoy 1983; Hardoy and Gutman 1992; Buisseret 1980). Cuba, for instance, affords the largest collection of colonial military architecture in the western hemisphere (Rigau 1994; Scarpaci et al. 2002; Marín 2002) while also promoting unique modern architecture (Rodríguez 2000). A literal 'tourist craze' for Cuba swept the global travel industry in the 1990s: 'Natives sense change in the air, but in the meantime this West Indies island nation that time forgot charms with its infectious music and funky fleet of classic cars' (Bowermaster 2004: 5). Cuba also displays many attributes that insulate it from the kinds of micro-state Caribbean vulnerabilities in an era of sweeping environmental change. These vulnerabilities include a lack of economic diversity, little regulation of foreign investment, predominantly rugged mountainous terrain, and a poorly educated labour force (Conway and Timms 2003). Accordingly, Cuba would seem to be in good standing to forge a sustainable environmental-development model based on heritage tourism. Or is it?

This chapter analyzes a portion of these selected environmental planning issues in the context of three Cuban cities: Havana, Trinidad, and Baracoa. I aim to highlight the major planning challenges affecting these cities, with a particular focus on fresh water and waste-removal concerns. The study sites span a variety of locations: a primate city, a medium-sized tourist pole on the south-central coast, and a small port town at the western edge of the island. Drawing on local financial models, I conclude with observations about financing civil engineering projects that are tied to the ebb and flow of heritage tourism in these Cuban cities, and the relationships among various planning entities.

Environmental Planning and Tourism

The historic quarters of Havana as well as other Cuban cities (Baracoa, Santiago, Camagüey and Trinidad) rely largely on early twentieth-century freshwater and waste-removal infrastructure. In Havana, for instance, the Albear water system of 1893 was geared for a city of 600,000. Civil engineers on the island speak often of the nearly '500 years of plumbing' that sustain many historic quarters, some of which have been become archeological and tourist sites in Habana Vieja (Figure 6.1). Metropolitan Havana currently discharges waste water off the Almendares River and just off Habana Vieja; both are pumped into the Florida Straits. The rise of international tourism compounds the problem of this waste removal.

The Laws of the Indies of 1494 and subsequent provisions laid out the design templates for Latin American plazas (Gade 1974; Guillén Martínez 1958; Griffin and Ford 1980; Hansen 1934). Understandably, colonial rulers never envisioned the kind of urbanization that took hold in the last century. Fortunately, many of the original 'shells' (*cascos*) of these historic places were preserved as the newer, modern Central Business District grew up adjacent to the colonial core (Stanislawski 1956; Theodorson 1982). Over time, a series of cisterns and primitive aquifers have been replaced by pipes from a central system. In addition, while waste removal in the form of latrines has become a relic of the past, modernity has, at best, been able only to pipe these contaminants into nearby streams, rivers, and oceans. Cuba, like other Latin American and Caribbean nations, has difficulty funding infrastructure enhancements due to competing demands for other social projects (Scarpaci and Irarrázaval 1994).

Cuba in the Special Period: 1989–2004

Since the demise of the Soviet Union and its trading bloc, Cuba has been forced to insert itself in the global economy. From 1959 until around 1989, the socialist government largely ignored tourism. Indeed, its ethos was one of a 'minimum of urbanism and a maximum of ruralism' (Eckstein 1997). Fidel Castro opposed a Caribbean development model that touted barmen and chambermaids as examples of gainful work; his vision of the island was that Cuba could be 'another America' (1996; Cordescu 1999). By the mid-1990s, the gross national product of the island had fallen by two-thirds from the 1989 level, and by 2003, it had not yet returned to the level of the 1980s. In 1990, tourism fetched a quarter of a billion dollars in gross revenues. By the decade's end, Cuba earned just over two billion dollars from tourism (Peters 2002: 3).

To be sure, environmental quality was nowhere near pristine condition at the time of the Revolution. Sugar production had exerted its toll on the environment. Forest clearing and railroad expansion moved in tandem and greatly modified the landscape as rail lines spread westward from Havana in the 1840s. Thousands of acres of precious woods were left to spoil in the process. A half century earlier, even Baron von Humboldt noticed that mahogany was used to fill the ruts in Habana Vieja (von Humboldt 2001). Forest clearings caused massive runoff during the rainy season, killing off aquatic life in many freshwater streams.

This post-Soviet period, called a 'special period in a time of peace', led to the legalization of the United States dollar in 1993. Drawing on a stock of architecturally rich neighborhoods, Cuba has been aggressively promoting urban heritage tourism

Figure 6.1 **Late sixteenth-century water pipe that drew water from the Almendares River, 9 km west, of Habana Vieja. This section was revealed during renovations near Plaza Vieja, in Habana Vieja in the mid-1990s. Photograph taken June 2004.**

(Leal 1996, 1999, 2002). On one hand, illicit activities such as black marketeering and prostitution have sprung up (Trumball 2001; Cornebise 2003; Elinson 1998). On the other hand, the government aggressively seeks foreign investors (Conas 1985), especially multinational tourist companies (Burr 1999; Jafari 2002). Rarely, however, are these facilities asked to improve existing waste-disposal practices. In fact, tourist waste is combined with domestic by-products, thereby worsening environmental quality (Díaz-Briquets and Pérez López 2000). Scarpaci et al. (2002) note one report done by Soviet advisors in the mid-1980s that estimated a need to invest US$15 billion to upgrade Havana's water and sewage. Fifteen years later, Scarpaci et al. (2002) revised that to fit a city of 2.2 million residents, and to reflect the impact of over a million tourists in the city annually. They concluded that it would likely require US$30 billion to upgrade water and sewage systems.

Environmental Planning and Tourism in Cuba

In December 1980, Law No. 33 was passed. This law, 'On the Protection of the Environment and the Rational Use of Natural Resources', came into effect in 1981. Chapter III of the law created the National System for the Protection of the Environment and the Rational Use of Natural Resources, or COMARNA (Díaz-Briquets and Pérez-López 2000: 50–52). Theoretically, it coordinates these disparate agencies into comprehensive environmental planning and ensures that the proper agency takes charge of specific areas (Table 6.1).

Several national, provincial, and city agencies manage matters that fall under the rubric of 'environmental planning'. Nationally, the Ministry of Science and Technology regulated industrial and energy production matters. The Ministry of Public Health monitors air and water pollution but usually at point-specific sites versus broad environmental protection. More evaluation that is ad hoc comes from the Ministry of Sugar (MINAZ). Resources are documented by the Institute of Physical Planning and their cartographic work aids in overall environmental planning. Locally, various agencies related to the above also take note of environmental matters. In all instances, however, Cuba's constitutional framework and public administration system allow the State Council – the maximum arbitrator – to overrule any fines, sanctions, and mandatory actions proposed by national or local-level authorities (Scarpaci 2002).

In the sections that follow, I identify environmental planning issues in three Cuban settings associated with heritage tourism.

Havana

The socialist nation's record of providing potable water is 100 per cent to the urban population, and 91 per cent to the rural population; only Barbados exceeded that regard (100 per cent) in the Latin American and Caribbean realm (PAHO 1994). This is good news for the largest city because population growth often exacerbates environmental quality. Along with this potable water standard are policies set forth by

Table 6.1 Environmental planning administered by Cuba's National System for the Protection of the Environment and the Rational Use of Natural Resources (COMARNA)

Environmental realm	Responsible government agency
Agriculture	Ministry of Agriculture with assistance from the Ministry of the Sugar Industry
Atmosphere	Ministry of Public Health
Fisheries	Ministry of Fisheries
Flora and Fauna	Ministry of Agriculture
Human settlements	Ministry of Public Health
Livestock	Ministry of Agriculture
Maritime shipping	Ministry of Transportation
Minerals	Ministry of Basic Industry
Soils	Ministry of Agriculture
Tourism	National Tourism Institute
Water	National Institute of Hydraulic Resources

Source: Modified after Díaz-Briquets and Pérez-López 2000: 55.

the socialist government to enhance the built environment of provincial cities, smaller towns, and rural hamlets (*bateyes*). As noted above, a deliberate anti-urban (or, more precisely, anti-Havana) strategy diverted a disproportionate amount of resources from the capital, primate city, of Havana. Indirectly, such efforts have curtailed the kind of 'hyper-urbanization' that afflicts the capitals of many developing nations. During the fiscally austere 'Special Period' (discussed below), Havana has been a primary destination for illegal migrants who move to Havana seeking work. All changes of residence must be sanctioned by the government and those in violation are forced to return to their former residences (*Entra en vigor* 1997).

Despite such an urban policy that attenuates environmental impact, Havana shows the strain of a weakened infrastructure. At least four major water and sewage problems exist.

Firstly, water is not available at all times of the day. Sections of the city are allocated water at various times; most often the shortages are announced, occasionally they are not.

Secondly, there is considerable leakage at: 1) the major water mains running from the major aqueducts; 2) secondary mains running through neighborhoods; 3) connecting pipes running from the streets to individual buildings; and 4) connections to roof-top cisterns. Although data are imprecise, it is common to hear from planners and civil engineers that, on average, 55 per cent of Havana's water is lost in delivery. Loss is attributed to the age of the system. The Canal de Vento aqueduct was built in the 1890s and the Cuenca Sur (Southern Watershed) and Marianao aqueducts were updated in the 1950s (Díaz-Briquets and Pérez-López 2000: 241). As a result, low pressure impedes effective delivery. Water trucks are ubiquitous and essential in topping off building cisterns due to low water pressure in the city's main lines (Figure 6.2). Fuel for trucks and electrical consumption for pumps in buildings also represent a consumption of fossil fuels that are largely purchased with scarce hard currency.

Thirdly, raw sewage drivels from street and curb sewer lines along city streets.

Figure 6.2 A water truck delivery in Cerro, Havana

Lastly, a more severe problem concerns the extraction of fresh water from the Vento and Sur aquifers. Located south of the capital, population and tourist growth over the past decades have required deeper drilling into the sedimentary rocks. Because of the narrow band of land separating the Atlantic Ocean (offshore from Havana) and the Caribbean Sea (just 75 km south), there is potential to draw in saltwater subterraneously in order to compensate for the pressure lost by the drawing of water to the surface (Scarpaci et al. 2002). Should salt-water intrusion become a severe problem, the city's freshwater source would be jeopardized, and the state would be forced to embark on a multi-million dollar project to extrude the salt water from the aquifer.

Metropolitan Havana's municipal government built a sewage system in 1913 that consists of two discharge pipes. One flows below Havana Bay and exits to the east of El Morro castle, just offshore in Playa del Chivo. For several years, however, this pipe, that runs in shallow water for a few hundred metres offshore, has been broken. It is commonplace to see amateur fishermen hovering in inner tubes just over the broken raw-sewage line, where fish feed at the break. A second discharge line flows under the Almendares River that separates Vedado from Miramar. Like the Playa del Chivo line, it carries the sewage just a few hundred metres offshore before it empties into the Florida Straits. On the one hand, the currents of the Florida Straits run strong and, for the most part, the sewage is carried out to the high seas. On the other hand, when the prevailing Northeast Trade Winds increase or when high-pressure systems from the north (*norteños*) move into the Caribbean (especially during the winter), some of these wastes wash ashore, compounding odors that come off Havana Bay and pass over the historic quarters of Habana Vieja. It is important to note that both the Playa del Chivo and Almendares discharge pipes were designed to accommodate a city of 600,000 residents. When they were built, Havana had half that many residents. Today, the lines must accommodate 2.1 million residents in addition to thousands of tourists in the city daily. While there are no major tourist beaches near these pipelines (cf. Playas del Este in the eastern side of the metropolitan area), many Cubans swim in these waters. Most tourists in Havana opt for the aquamarine waters of 22 km-long Varadero beach, just a two-hour ride to the east of Havana

Not all urbanization, agricultural, or industrial production has harmed the Havana environment during the Special Period. Cuba's agro-ecosystem necessarily changed between 1959 to 1989, from one that was heavy on mechanization and fossil-fuel inputs, to the advent of alternative agriculture. This alternative has necessarily entailed the use of organic inputs into rural and urban agriculture. Composting and animal waste today form a significant 'organic' input into national agriculture. By default, then, the economic crisis nationally revived widespread urban gardens and helped to 'green' the island's environmental policies. Metropolitan Havana is full of these organic gardens, called *organipónicos*. They aim to complement the rationed food system with food that is less reliant on agrochemicals and not part of the canned or frozen provisions given to 11 million Cubans. What were once empty lots of unused open spaces, have now become fresh-garden centers. Tomatoes, lettuce, cucumbers, and basil are common crops. Often, public housing complexes or factories work specific lots for fellow residents or co-workers (Uriarte 2002). In the latter, gardening is well suited to housewives and the retired. These lots are, on average, 1 ha. in size and produce 20 kg of vegetables per square metre annually (World Resources Institute 2002: 162). The externalities of having chemical fertilizers enter Havana's watershed have been reduced by using these organic production methods. Although the gardens are not part of the heritage tourism landscape, tourists cannot help but notice them in a city that is so cosmopolitan.

Habana Vieja

Havana Bay adjoins Habana Vieja on its eastern flank and, for centuries, has served as a depository for human and industrial sewage. Unfortunately, this bag-shaped bay – like many on the island – naturally cleanses itself slowly. While the narrow entrance to the bay protects ships from tropical storms and sea surges, it takes nine days or so to recycle water fully through the bay. This rate is too slow to accommodate the waste of the 85,000 residents of Habana Vieja (Díaz-Briquets and Pérez-López 2000: 245) as well as thousands more in Regla, Cerro, Casablanca, and others. The result is a highly polluted body of water for those who live in the old city. Water quality is further compounded by oil refineries in the back-bay section of Regla (south-southwest of Habana Vieja). Lezcano (1994) estimated that in the early years of the Special Period, nearly 300 tons of organic matter and 40 tons of oil products had entered the bay daily. Statistics such as these led a team of Soviet experts in 1982 to conclude that Havana Bay was 'practically dead' and that the bay's pollution spilled over into coastlines beyond its mouth (Hernández 1982: 29–30). With light winds prevailing on hot summer days, the combination of foul waters within crowded tenement houses can be especially unpleasant (Nickel 1990).

Despite historic preservation efforts to enhance the architectural beauty of the old city, sweeping civil engineering projects have not yet commenced. As noted above, sewage systems often back up. This is especially evident in Habana Vieja, and particularly during the weekend. It is common to see and smell raw sewage along the thoroughfares of the UNESCO World Heritage Site. Although a very successful historic preservation company (Habaguanex) is administered by the City Historian's Office in Habana Vieja, the vast majority of funds are directed to refurbishing hotels, museums, restaurants, and art galleries – residential housing needs are secondary (Segre and Baroni 1998; Scarpaci 2000).

Trinidad

Historic Trinidad

Trinidad (pop. 42,000) is a colonial jewel that sits at the foot of Escambray Mountains, on a narrow coastal plain fronting thc Caribbean Sea in south-central Cuba. One of seven original settlements (villas), the town prospered in the early nineteenth century because of slave-labour practices in the sugar industry. An exodus for French sugar cane planters from the Haitian slave revolt of 1791, coupled with more planters after the Louisiana Purchase of 1803, enticed French growers and investors to that part of Cuba. By the 1860s, however, rail lines elsewhere in Cuba, as well as new technology that used steam engines instead of animal and slave labour, severely undermined the economy of Trinidad (Zanetti and García 1998). The opulence that reflected the 50-year boom left an indelible mark on the small town, and heritage tourism is now the principal source of revenue in both Trinidad and the adjacent Sugar Mill Valley (Valle de los Ingenios) which houses several dozen former sugar-mill plantations (Marín 1945; Moreno Fraginals 1976; Núñez Jiménez et al. 1986). In 1988, UNESCO declared Trinidad and the valley a World Heritage Site. With the advent of the Special Period, economic development has been closely allied with heritage tourism.

Trinidad's historic district has no hotels. One facility built in 1958, Las Cuevas, sits on a hillside just north of the historic district. In the 1970s, the state built a hotel on the Ancón peninsula, just 11 km south of Trinidad. In the 1980s, a second hotel on the peninsula emerged. In 2000 a new resort, Trinidad del Mar, opened. The combined hotel bed count is about 700 on the peninsula and about 200 at Las Cuevas.

Self-employed workers have, since 1993 and the legalization of such trades and the US dollar, tapped into the tourist industry (Peters and Scarpaci 1998). Numerous home restaurants (*paladares*) sprang up in the 1990s as did bed-and-breakfast inns (B&Bs). However, by the late 1990s, both the rising costs of licenses and stricter regulation of restaurant and lodging norms forced dozens of these facilities to close. By 2004, just two home restaurants operated in Trinidad and only about a dozen B&Bs function. Nonetheless, perhaps as many as 100 illegal B&Bs operate within the historic district, as do scores of illegal restaurants (Personal communication, Restoration Office of rinidad, 28 May 2004).

Trinidad's model of financing historic preservation is novel and has been copied by Santiago de Cuba and Camagüey. It consists of levying a 2 per cent tax on all gross revenues earned by dollar-charging firms, and 1 per cent on firms working in pesos. Unlike the historic-development corporation in Habana Vieja (Habaguanex), the Trinidad Restoration Office does not run hotels, gift shops, art stores, general merchandise stores, or restaurants. Rather, it focuses exclusively on restoring private residences with the exceptions of a few public spaces and items such as town squares, public lighting, and sidewalks. Since 1999 – the year the national government approved this method of taxation for the Trinidad Restoration Office – about US$400,000 has annually employed over 300 workers and allows the office to focus on the 144 houses of the poorest neighborhood in Trinidad, Barrio Tres Cruces. As of mid-2004, the Trinidad Restoration Office, with the help of the Barcelona, Spainish NGO, Architects without Borders, has been able to rehabilitate about half of the Tres Cruces homes. The office has also held focus groups to gain input on how to redesign Calvary Square in the Tres Cruces. In short, Trinidad's financial model of development is tethered to the volume of tourism in Trinidad and its focus on poor residential housing maintains a social-justice perspective (Scarpaci 2003b).

Playa Ancón

A multi-purpose tourism destination, the Trinidad vicinity affords the heritage tourism of historic Trinidad as well as the amenities of Caribbean. Just 11 km south of the town is the Ancón Peninsula, which houses three hotels. The current planning dilemma that rests at the crux of this environmental and heritage-tourism debate is the national government's tendering of bids for an additional 4,000 beds along the peninsula. Nowhere in the Trinidad area is there a water treatment facility. Currently, all hotels discharge their wastes into the Caribbean. A fivefold increase in hotel beds poses two challenges. One is the treatment of wastewater and the other is the increased traffic in the UNESCO World Heritage site 11 km to the north. Beachcombers visit the historic core and additional foot traffic in the old city would bring many more buses to the edge of the historic quarters (which is gated and allows only service and residential vehicles to enter). With their air-conditioners on while they are parked, these buses would also add to noise pollution. As well, tourists would consume more water and use restroom facilities, which, in turn, would likely exacerbate the already fragile plumbing and sewage system. Unfortunately, the national government has not consulted with the local Restoration Office of Trinidad, which remains steadfastly opposed to the waterfront development proposal (Scarpaci 2003). If sustainable development, as Robert Dyck (1998) argues, must satisfy locals' needs and is to be part of integrated planning, then the implications here are obvious. More specifically, the Trinidad experience suggests that participatory democracy at the grassroots is not as prevalent has others have argued (Arnold 1999), and that there is need for improvement (Collado et al. 1996).

Topes de Collante and the Escambray Mountains.

In just a 30-minute drive from Trinidad, tourists can reach the top of the Escambray Mountains, where there is a maturely dissected plateau called Topes de Collante. In addition to a spectacular view of the coastal plain, Trinidad town, and the Sugar Mill Valley, a variety of eco-tourist activities exists there. Topes de Collante and the Escambray consist of a variety of tropical pines, eucalyptus, and spectacular ferns. There are several campsites and a variety of bird watching, horseback riding, and hiking opportunities. A two-hour walk brings hikers to the Caburní waterfalls. Less adventurous travelers can visit the Codina farm that displays a variety of medical plants, orchid and bamboo gardens, and caves. A large hotel built by the Batista government in the 1950s as a sanitarium serves as a conventional hotel. Travelers also have the options of returning to Trinidad or camping at Topes de Collante; a tourist allure of urban-cultural and rural-ecotourism can be experienced in a single day.

The Topes-Escambray tourist venues are handled by a single Cuban travel company: Gaviota. This firm is a spin-off of the Revolutionary Armed Forces of Cuba. Their expertise in working this area stems back to the counterinsurgency period between 1961–1965, when rebels hid out in the mountains during the early years of the Revolution. Later, Soviet advisors visited the area and the Cuban armed forces gained expertise in providing ancillary services such as lodging, food preparation, and related activities. With the demise of the Soviet Union, Gaviota has served as a dollar-generating enterprise for the armed forces (Rohter 1995). If little is known about the conventional tourist companies that report to the Ministry of Tourism, or the joint-venture operations between the Cuban government and European firms, then even less is known about this army-related enterprise. Like other tourist facilities discussed in this chapter, there are no wastewater treatment facilities at the Topes-Escambray sites. Rather, effluent is discharged in streams, septic tanks, or outhouses. Freshwater, however, is readily available on the north side of the Escambray Mountains owing to orographic participation induced by the Trade Winds.

Baracoa

Cuba's oldest city, Baracoa, means 'existence of the sea' in Arawak. Nestled in a small coastal plain in a remote corner of eastern Cuba, the city's various nicknames attest to the eco-tourism and environmental allures surrounding the city: 'City of Rain', 'City of Mountains', and 'City of Waters' are just some of Baracoa's nicknames. Fishing, tourism, coffee, and chocolate cultivation and production characterize the economy. The city and county hold just under 100,000 residents. These occupy just 5 per cent of the surface area that constitutes the coastal plain, while the remainder of the land is classified as mountainous. It was only in 1964 that Baracoa was connected with a modern, paved highway (La Farola) that linked it with Santiago de Cuba. Prior to that, air and maritime travel were the main ways that tourists reached this corner of the island. It serves as a departure point for excursions to explore a plethora of endemic flora and fauna in the adjacent valleys as well as virgin forests, especially the UNESCO Cuchillas del Toa Biosphere to the northwest of the city. The tightly folded mountains rising abruptly from the narrow coastal plain draw as much as 3000 millimetres of rainfall which, in turn, make the tropical rain forests surrounding Baracoa a major eco-tourism destination (Marrero 1983; Matos 2000).

Historic Baracoa

Despite its banner as the 'first city in Cuba', the town is distinctly not colonial in its architecture. Still, it does boast a variety of vernacular wooden buildings as well as Neo-Classical designs with French influences. Unlike Habana Vieja and Trinidad, it has no restoration office that manages an independent budget. In fact, several churches are being restored with the financial and technical help of Habaguanex in Habana Vieja. Heritage tourist sites within Baracoa's National Landmark district include the Fuerte Matachín (Matachín Fort), located on the town's seaside promenade, which, like Havana, is called the Malecón. The fort serves as the Municipal Museum. Its chief displays include pre-Columbian artifacts as well as paintings, items related to pirates and corsairs, and information on slavery and the plantation economy. Within walking distance, one finds the Casa de la Trova (local music shows), Fondo de Bienes Culturales (works of local craftsmen, sculptors, and painters), and the Casa del Chocolate (serving chocolate candies and beverages, a regional specialty).

Adjacent Forests, Beaches, and Parks

As the easternmost tourist pole in Cuba, Baracoa serves as a springboard to pristine forests and beaches. El Yunque Mountain, a limestone formation that rises 575 m, dominates the vicinity of Baracoa city. Its mountain slopes form part of the UNESCO biosphere that house unique flora and fauna such as two carnivorous plants, an endemic palm tree (*Cocothrinaz yuquensis*), and one of the rarest and oldest plant species in the world (*Popocarpus*). Animal life include the endangered caguero hawk (*Chondrobierax wilsonii*), the endangered royal woodpecker (*Campeophilus principalis*), and, allegedly, the smallest amphibian in the world (*Sminthillus limbatus*, measuring less 1 cm). Tourists can take river excursions along the Toa River that lead inland to the Parque Natural Río Toa. The park has several camping sites and refuges designed to lessen the impact on the local environment. The shoreline also affords swimming opportunities at Boca de Yumurí (the mouth of the Yumurí River) and Playa Maguaná. Southeast of Baracoa is a small village, Maisí, whose name is also given to a spectacular set of marine terraces at the eastern edge of Cuba. The terraces are remote and are not well developed in terms of roads, campsites, and related infrastructure. However, there is a national park there, Parque Natural Terrazas de Maisí, but it is often closed off to tourists because the adjacent Windward Passage has become a common drop-off point for drug shipments originating from South America. High-speed 'cigarette' boats pick up bails of marijuana and cocaine and shuttle the drugs northwestward along the Bahaman archipelago, and ultimately, to the United States. On clear days, Haiti is visible from several vantage points such as the village of Maisí and the nearby terraces.

Summary and Conclusions

This chapter has presented three case studies with different heritage tourism financing mechanisms and environmental planning challenges (Table 6.2). Havana's Habaguanex boasts an annual budget of hundreds of millions of dollars that are generated from the many facilities it operates. While some of the restored properties are residential, the bulk of its projects are focused on commercial ventures. Trinidad, on the other hand, pegs its annual restoration budget to the ebb and flow of the regional economy. The restoration office there works exclusively on residential housing. A pending policy outcome involves the national government's solicitation of joint-venture hotel operations at nearby Ancón peninsula. Doing so, it was argued, would increase foot traffic in the UNESCO World Heritage Site just 11 km away. Significantly, the national government has not consulted with the local restoration authority about increasing tourism. That national-level government agencies fail to consult local governments is not unique to Cuba (Scarpaci and Irarrázaval 1994). Rather, it undermines a long-standing problem in public administration, regardless of whether a particular locale operates in a market or centrally planned economy. Lastly, Baracoa serves as a springboard to an array of eco-tourist destinations and lacks a separate entity for financing heritage tourism.

Environmental planning and heritage tourism in Cuba will have to work in tandem to ensure that both the cultural and natural landscapes of the island remain both national patrimony and agents of sustainable economic development. Environmental pressure on these resources has been attenuated, in part, due to the four-decade long trade embargo and travel restrictions of the United States. This has been a mixed

Table 6.2 Heritage tourism financing mechanisms and environmental planning challenges

Location	Restoration agency	Heritage financing mechanism	Environmental planning challenges and opportunities
Habana Vieja	Habaguanex	Operates hotels, B&Bs, variety stores, art galleries, museums and other shops in hard currency	Focuses on architecturally significant structures and public spaces; incapable of financing waste-water treatment without national support; concern over fresh water availability from local aquifers
Trinidad	Restoration Office	Receives 2% and 1% tax from dollar and peso firms, respectively	Abating beachfront hotel construction; minimizing illegal B&Bs in historic district that tax water supplies; incapable of financing waste-water treatment without national support; abundant fresh water supply from Escambray Mountains
Baracoa	None	Reliant on provincial and national funds	Has low-level of tourism to date; incapable of financing waste-water treatment without national support; abundant fresh-water supply in adjacent watersheds

blessing. On the one hand, 'remote geography helps some high-scoring destinations stay unspoiled. Other places have learned how to cope with popularity' (Tourtellot 2004:62). Although the island is just 90 miles from the largest travel market in the world, the geopolitical constraints have tempered the flow of US tourists to the island; whilst attracting those from Canada and Europe. On the other hand, tourist revenues could provide much needed cash for infrastructural enhancements.

The condition of Cuba's national economy makes it unlikely that the water distribution networks will be upgraded soon. Political opposition by the United States makes low-cost loans from the Inter-American Development Bank, the World Bank, or commercial lenders an impossibility. In a different geo-political setting, Washington might consider massive aid from the United States' Agency for International Development. That does not preclude other support from agencies such as Oxfam or member states of the European Union (EU). Bilateral aid, however, tends to be of a smaller scale from the latter, and a chilled relationship has ensued between Cuba and the EU since Cuba handed out harsh sentences to about 70 dissidents in 2003. In post-Soviet Eastern Europe, nongovernmental (NGOs) agencies have filled an important void in spaces where the state and international capital have not ventured (Regulska 2000; Sheppard 2000). In Cuba, however, NGOs were brought in under tighter control in the mid-1990s, and the question as to whether they are seeds of civil society or puppets of the state, remains unanswered (Gunn 1995). Still, Cuban NGOs lack an autonomy to receive foreign aid and disburse funds without careful state oversight.

Currently, fresh water and wastewater civil engineering projects are woefully inadequate to accommodate heritage tourists and locals. It is apparent that more resources from the national treasury will be required to finance this infrastructure. Cuba is not unique in that its historic districts lack modern services (Gutiérrez 1990). Nonetheless, major capital and infrastructure projects and environmental planning in Cuba will require careful coordination among myriad agencies charged with safeguarding the island's resources.

References

Afshar, F. and Pezzoli, K. (2001), 'Globalization and Planning: Guest Editors' Introduction. Integrating Globalization and Planning', *Journal of Planning Education and Research*, 20, pp. 277–90.

Albrow, M. (2000), 'Travelling beyond Cultures', in F.J. Lechner and J. Boli (eds), *The Globalization Reader*, New York: Blackwell, pp. 118–25.

Amaral, A. (ed.) (1994), *Arqustiectura Neocolonial: América Latina, Caribe, Estados Unidos*, Mexico City: Fondo de Cultura Económica.

Arnold A. (1999), *Democracy in Cuba and the 1997-98 Elections*, Havana: Editorial José Martí.

Ashworth, G.J. (2003), 'Globalisation or Localization: Towards Convergence in the European City, paper presented at the meeting of the Association of American Geographers, New Orleans, March.

Barberia, L.G. (2002), 'The Caribbean: Tourism as Development or Development for Tourism?', *ReVista: Harvard Review of Latin America* (Winter), pp. 72–5.

Barthell, D. (1996), *Historic Preservation: Collective Memory and Historic Identity*, New Brunswick, NJ: Rutgers University Press.

Bowermaster, J. (2004), 'The Beat in Cuba', *National Geographic Traveler*, 21 (2) 5, pp. 96–106.

Brett, D. (1996), *The Construction of Heritage*, Cork: Cork University Press.

Buisseret, D. (1980), *Historic Architecture of the Caribbean*, London; Heinemann.

Burr, C. (1999), 'Capitalism: Cuban Style', *Fortune*, 1 March (International Edition), pp. 72–4.

Carta Internacional sobre la Conservación y la restauración de monumentos y sitios, issued by the '*Congreso Internacional de Arquitectura y Técnicos de Monumentos Históricos*', held in Venice in 1964: published in *Summa* No. 77, Buenos Aires.

Codrescu, A. (1999), *Ay, Cuba! A Socio-Erotic Journey,* New York: St Martin's Press.

Collado, R., Mauri, S. and Coipel, M. (1996), 'Revitalización urbana, desarrollo social y participación. La experiencia en el barrio San Isidro', in R. Dávalos and A. Vázquez (eds), *Participación social. Desarrollo urbano y comunitario*, Havana: Universidad de La Habana, pp. 106–18.

Conas (1995), *Foreign Investment Act of Cuba*, Havana: Conas.

Conway, D. and Timms, B. (2003), 'Where is the Environment in Caribbean Development Theory and Praxis?', *Global Development Studies* 3 (1–2), pp. 91–130.

Cornebise, M.W. (2003), 'The Social Construction of Tourism in Cuba: A Geographic Analysis on the Representations of Gender and Race during the Special Period', PhD dissertation, Department of Geography, The University of Tennessee, Knoxville, April, preliminary draft.

Cosgrove, D. (1985), *Social Formation and Symbolic Landscape*, London: Croom Helm.

Cosgrove, D. (1987), 'New Directions in Cultural Geography', *Area*, 19, pp. 95–101.

Coyula, M. (2002), 'City, Tourism, and Preservation. The Old Havana Way', *ReVista: Harvard Review of Latin America* (Winter), pp. 66–9.

Crain, J. (1994), *Historic Architecture in the Caribbean Islands*, Gainesville: University Press of Florida.

Díaz-Briquets, S. and Pérez-López, J. (2000), *Conquering Nature: The Environmental Legacy of Socialism in Cuba,* Pittsburgh: University of Pittsburgh Press.

Dicken, P. (2003), *Global Shift: Transforming the World Economy*, 4th edn, New York: Guilford.

Dyck, R. (1998), 'Integrated Planning and Sustainability Theory for Local Benefit', *Local Environments*, 3, pp. 27–41.

Eckstein, S. (1977), 'The Debourgeoisement of Cuban Cities', in I.L. Horowitz (ed.), *Cuban Communism*, New Brunswick, NJ: Transaction Books, pp. 443–74.

Edwards, M. (1999), *Future Positive: International Co-operation in the 21st Century*, London: Earthscan Publications Ltd.

Elinson, H. (1998), *Cuba's Jineteros: Youth Culture and Revolutionary Ideology*, Georgetown: Cuban Briefing Series No. 20, Center for Latin American Studies, Georgetown University.

Entra en vigor el decreto de migración en Cuba. El Nuevo Herald Digital (12 May).

Fraser, V. (1990), *The Architecture of Conquest*, New York: Cambridge University Press.

Fraser, V. (2000), *Building The New World: Studies in the Modern Architecture of Latin America, 1930–1965*, New York and London: Verso,

Gade, D. (1974), 'The Latin American Central Plaza as Functional Space', *Proceedings of the Conference of Latinamericanist Geographers*, 5, pp. 16–23.

Graham, B., Ashworth, G.J. and Turnbridge, J.E. (2000), *A Geography of Heritage: Power, Culture and Economy*, London: Arnold.

Griffin, E. and Ford, L. (1980), 'A Model of Latin American City Structure', *Geographical Review*, 37, pp. 397–422.

Guillén Martínez, F. (1958), *The Tower and the Town Square: An Essay on Interpreting America*, Madrid: Ediciones Cultura Hispánica.

Gunn, G. (1995), 'Cuba's NGOs: Government Puppets or Seeds of a Civil Society?', *Cuba Briefing Papers Series*, Washington, DC: Georgetown University.

Gutiérrez, R. (ed.) (1990), *Centros Históricos: América Latina*, Bogotá: Colleción SomoSur.

Gutiérrez, A. (n.d.), *Trinidad*, offset (ISBN 959-7064-02-2), Trinidad.

Gutiérrez, O. and Gancedo, N. (2002), 'Tourism Development: Locomotive for the Cuban Economy', *ReVista: Harvard Review of Latin America* (Winter), pp. 76–8.

Hansen, A.T. (1934), 'The Ecology of a Latin American City', in E.B. Reuter (ed.), *Race and Culture Contacts*, New York: McGraw Hill, pp. 124–42.

Hardoy, J.E. (1983), 'The Inhabitants of Historical Centres', *Habitat International*, 7, pp. 151–62.

Hardoy, J.E. and Gutman, M. (1992), *Impacto de la urbanización de Iberoamérica: tendencias y perspectivas*, Madrid: Mapfre

Hernández, G. (1982), 'Detener la contaminación de nuestras agues marinas', *Bohemia*, 74 (18) (30 April), pp. 28–31.

Humboldt, A. (2001), *The Island of Cuba*, Princeton: Markus Wiener Publishers.

Jackson, J.B. (1984), *Discovering the Vernacular Landscape*, New Haven: Yale University Press.

Jafari, J. (2002), 'Retracing and Mapping: Tourism's Landscape of Knowledge', *ReVista: Harvard Review of Latin America* (Winter), pp. 12–15.

Johnston, R., Taylor, P. and Watts, M. (eds) (1995), *Geographies of Global Change: Remapping the World in the late Twentieth Century*, Boston: Blackwell.

Jones, G.A. (1994), 'The Latin American City as Contested Space', *Bulletin of Latin American Research*, 13, pp. 1–12.

Jones, G.A. and Bromley, R.D.F. (1999), 'Investing in Conservation: The Historic Center in Latin America', *Built Environment*, 25, pp. 196–210.

Jones, G.A. and Varley, A. (1999), 'Conservation and Gentrification in the Developing World: Recapturing the City Center', *Environment and Planning A*, 31, pp. 1547–66.

Klak, T. (1998), *Globalization and Neoliberalism: the Caribbean Context*, Lanham, MD: Rowman and Littlefield.

Lash, S. and Urry, J. (1994), *Economies of Signs and Space*, London: Sage.

Leal, E. (1996), *Viaje en la memoria*, Havana: Oficina del Historiador de la Ciudad.

Leal, E. (1999), Opening remarks, plenary session, the Fourth International Conference on Cultural Heritage and Historic Preservation, Ministry of Culture, National Center for Restoration, Conservation and Museum Science (CENCREM), 12 October, Spanish language presentation audio-recorded and transcribed by and available from the author.

Leal, E. (2002), Plenary address delivered to the international meeting of the Association of Collegiate Schools of Architecture, Habana Vieja, Convento de San Francisco, Salón Blanco, 23 June.

Lezcano, J. (1994), 'Capital en ruinas', paper presented at the Congreso Internacional de Derechos Humanos, Miami: Florida International University.

Linden, E. (2003), 'The Nature of Cuba', *Smithsonian* (May), pp. 94–9.

Low. S.M. (2000), *On The Plaza: The Politics of Public Space and Culture*, Austin: University of Texas Press.

Lowenthal, D. (1985), *The Past is a Foreign Country*, Cambridge: Cambridge University Press.

Marín, F. (1945), *Historia de Trinidad*, Havana: Jesús Montero.

Marín, V. (2002), 'Cuba: The Preservation of Architecture as Seen as Saving a Legacy for humanity', in *Havana: Patrimony, Patience and Progress: Architecture, Urban Planning and Historic Preservation in Havana, Cuba*, published by The Vera List Center for Art and Politics at The New School and Heritage Trails Worldwide, New York: New School University.

Marrero, L. (1983), *Cuba: Economía y Sociedad*, Vol. 9. Madrid: Editorial Playor.

Matos, H. (2000), *Baracoa: Un Paraíso Cubano*, Barcelona: Reproduccions Gràfiques Montgròs.

McGregor, D.F., Barker, D. and Evans, S.L. (eds) (1998), *Resource Sustainability and Caribbean Development*, Kingston: University of West Indies.

Moreno Fraginals, M. (1976), *The Sugar Mill: The Socio-economic Complex of Sugar in Cuba, 1760–1860*, New York and London: Monthly Review Press.

Mowforth, M. and Munt, I. (2003), *Tourism and Sustainability: Development and New Tourism in the Third World*, 2nd edn, London and New York: Routledge.

Nickel, A. (1990), 'El casco histórico de La Habana: La situación de vivienda y los conceptos de renovación urbana en La Habana', *Revista Geográfica*, 112, pp. 75–90.

Núñez Jiménez, A., Zerquera, C. and de Lara, F. (1986), *Trinidad de Cuba: Monumento Nacional*, Havana: Instituto Nacional de Turismo.

PAHO (Pan American Health Organization) (1994), *Health Conditions in the Americas – 1994*, Vol. 1, Washington, DC: PAHO.

Patullo, P. (1996), *Last Resorts: The Cost of Tourism in the Caribbean*, London: Cassel Wellington House.

Peters, P. (2002), *International Tourism: The New Engine of the Cuban Economy*, Arlington, VA: Lexington Institute.

Peters, P. and Scarpaci, J.L. (1998), *Five Years of Small-scale Capitalism in Cuba*, Arlington, VA: Alexis de Tocqueville Institute.

Portes, A., Dore-Cabral, C. and Landolt, P. (eds) (1997), *The Urban Caribbean. Transition to the New Global Economy*, Baltimore and London: Johns Hopkins University Press.

Richardson, B. and Scarpaci, J.L. (2004), 'The Quality of Life in the 20th Century Caribbean', in B. Brereton (ed.), *The General History of the Caribbean*, Vol. 5, Hampshire, England: Macmillan Caribbean, pp. 627–66.

Regulska, J. (2000), 'The Emergence of Political and Civil Societies in Warsaw: Post-1989 Dilemmas', *Urban Geography*, 21 (8), pp. 701–23.

Rigau, J. (1994), 'No Longer Islands: Dissemination of Architecture Ideas in the Hispanic Caribbean, 1890–1930', *The Journal of Decorative and Propaganda Arts*, 20, pp. 237–25.

Robinson, M., Evans, N., Long, P., Sharpley, R. and Swarbrooke, J. (2002), *Tourism and Heritage Relationships: Global, National and Local Perspectives*, Sunderland, UK: The Teleport, Doxford International.

Rodríguez, E.L. (2000), *The Havana Guide: Modern Architecture 1925 – 1965*, New York: Princeton Architectural Press.

Rohter, R. (1995), 'In Cuba, Army Takes on Party Jobs, and May be the Only Thing that Works', *The New York Times*, 8 June, p. A-12.

Rojas, E. (1999), *Old Cities, New Assets*, Washington, DC: Inter-American Development Bank.

Rojeck, C. and Urry, J. (eds) (1997), *Touring Cultures*, London: Routledge.

Scarpaci, J.L. (1998), 'The Changing Face of Cuban Socialism: Tourism and Planning in the Post-socialist era', in D. Keeling and J. Wiley (eds), *CLAG Yearbook*, Austin: University of Texas Press, pp. 87–110.

Scarpaci, J.L. (2000a), 'Reshaping *Habana Vieja*: Revitalization, Historic Preservation, and Restructuring in the Socialist City', *Urban Geography*, Vol. 21, pp. 724–44.

Scarpaci, J.L. (2000b.), 'Winners and losers in restoring Old Havana', in J.P. López and J.F. Alonso (eds), *Cuba in Transition*, Vol. 10, Washington, DC: Association for the Study of the Cuban Economy, pp. 289–99.

Scarpaci, J.L. (2002), 'Havana: The Dynamics of Mayoral Executive Power in Havana', in D.J. Meyers and H. Dietz (eds), *Capital City Politics in Latin America: Democratization and Empowerment*, Boulder, CO: Lynne Reiner Publishers, pp. 163–92.

Scarpaci, J.L. (2003a), 'Architecture, Design, and Planning: Recent Scholarship on Modernity and Public Spaces in Latin America', *Latin American Research Review*, 38, pp. 236–50.

Scarpaci, J.L. (2003b), 'Heritage Planning in Trinidad, Cuba',, in J.P. López and J.F. Alonso (eds), *Cuba in Transition*, Vol. 13, Washington, DC: Association for the Study of the Cuban Economy.

Scarpaci, J.L. (2005), *Plazas and Barrios: Heritage Tourism and Globalization in the Latin American Centro Histórico*, Tucson: University of Arizona Press.

Scarpaci, J.L. and Irarrázaval, I. (1994), 'Decentralizing a Centralized State: Local Government Finances in Chile Within the Latin American Context', *Public Budgeting and Finance*, 14 (4), pp. 120–36.

Scarpaci, J.L., Segre, R. and Coyula, M. (2002), *Havana: Two Faces of the Antillean Metropolis*, Chapel Hill: University of North Carolina Press.

Segre, R. and Baroni, S. (1998), 'Cuba y La Habana. Historia, población y territorio', *Ciudad y Territorio* (Buenos Aires) 30 (116), pp. 351–79.

Sheppard, E. (2000), 'Socialist Cities?', *Urban Geography*, 21 (8), pp. 758–63.

Stanislawski, D. (1956), 'The Origin and Spread of the Grid-pattern Town', *Geographical Review*, 36, pp. 105–20.

Theodorson, G.A. (1982), *Urban Patterns: Studies in Human Ecology*, University Park: The Pennsylvania State University Press.

Tourtellot, J.B. (2004), 'Destination Scorecard', *National Geographic Traveler*, 21 (2), pp. 60–67.

Trumball, C. (2001), 'Prostitution and Sex Tourism in Cuba.', paper presented at the Association for the Study of the Cuban Economy (ASCE), Miami, FL, 3 August.

Tung, A. (2001), *Preserving the World's Great Cities: The Destruction and Renewal of the Historic Metropolis*, New York: Clarkson Potter Publishers.

Uriarte, M. (2002), *Cuba. Social Policy at the Crossroads: Maintaining Priorities, Transforming Practice*, An Oxfam America Report, Boston: Oxfam America.

Violetta, B. and Scarpaci, J.L. (1999), 'Havana Construction Boom in Old City', *CubaNews*, December, Washington, DC: Target Research Group, p. 4.

Ward, P. (1993), 'The Latin American inner city. Differences in Degree or Kind?', *Environment and Planning A*, 25, pp. 1131–60.

World Resources Institute (2002), *World Resources 2000–2001*, Washington, DC: World Resources Institute, pp. 159–62.

Zanetti, O. and García, A. (1998), *Sugar and Railroads: A Cuban History, 1837–1959*, Chapel Hill: University of North Carolina Press.

Chapter 7

'Nuff Respec'? Widening and Deepening Participation in Academic and Policy Research in Jamaica

David Dodman and Jane Dodman

Introduction: A Place for Participatory Research?

'Nuff respec' is a commonly used phrase in Jamaican patois. Literally meaning 'lots of respect', it is used as a phrase of greeting, thanks and appreciation. The central importance given to the concept of 'respect' in this context can also be understood as an authentic endogenous voice calling for active involvement in the formation and implementation of social and environmental plans. Environmental research and planning that includes a substantial component of community and individual participation is one way of responding to this call.

In this chapter we discuss the application of participatory methodologies in both academic- and policy-related research in Jamaica. We start by defining the concept of 'respect', and follow this with an examination of the ways in which participatory methodologies can be adapted for both academic- and policy-related research. This is facilitated through reference to specific case studies describing the use of participatory appraisal as part of community training and planning projects (such as those carried out by the Jamaica Social Investment Fund) and as a tool for understanding urban environmental problems in Kingston; the relevance of action research in integrating education, research, and social change in inner-city communities; and the use of visual methods to reduce the distorting effects of uneven power relations in exploring child-environment interactions. The lessons learned from these exercises in participatory research are then shown to be applicable both to academic research (such as the understanding of social change and human-environment interactions) and to environment and development policy.

Despite their increasingly widespread acceptance, there are no universally accepted definitions of 'participation' or 'participatory development'. Mohan (2002) suggests that the concept of participation is used either in an *instrumental* sense (meaning that it is used to increase the efficiency of formal development programmes) or a *transformative* sense (in which giving value to alternative voices enables meaningful social change to occur). Similar classification systems have been used elsewhere, for example by Pelling (1998) who contrasts *utilitarian* and *empowerment* approaches to participation, and Cleaver (2001) who conceives of *efficiency* benefits and *equity and empowerment* benefits. Participatory research also provides both these practical and ethical benefits: information gathered from the people who experience the conditions that are being researched are able to provide more in-depth information about this than 'experts' who are further removed from the issues; whilst there is a moral component involved in amplifying the voices of those whose opinions are seldom heard.

Caribbean Cultural Identity: The Importance of Respect

When conducting research in the Caribbean, it is important to recognize that many of the defining and classifying mechanisms used in academic thought are remnants of a totalizing colonial discourse. This has provoked a substantial backlash from some quarters, such as the Rastafarian movement in Jamaica. Indeed, the Rastafarian concept of 'Babylon', the 'oppressive social, political, economic and cultural realities of the Western world' (Murrell et al. 1998: 443) frequently identifies academic institutions as one of the major forces perpetuating the marginalization of oppressed peoples.[1]

Citizen action in the Third World has often been suggested as working towards the goals of 'liberty, equality and autonomy' (Haynes 1997: 5) and addressing issues of class, power, sexual/gender relationships and culture (Castells 1977; 1983). In Jamaica, these concerns tend to be subsumed under the discourse of 'respect' and 'justice'. Levy and Chevannes (1996) titled their influential report on urban violence and poverty in Jamaica *They Cry 'Respect'*, the Jamaican national anthem requests 'true respect for all' and Nettleford (2003: xix) explains that 'the word "respec" (for respect) is frequently intoned in the argot of Jamaican urban inner city and rural life; and any failure to observe that psychic space claimed by the individual Jamaican is regarded as an assault on one's cultural identity'. In his later work, Castells (1985) placed increasing importance on the role of cultural identity (although always alongside the goals of collective consumption and political self-management) as a motivating force for urban social change, and this motivation is of particular importance in the Caribbean context. For example, when faced by with the monotonous and degrading tasks required in poorly-paid jobs, Jamaicans have been found to engage in a 'collection of culturally encoded responses to economic and social inequality that is viewed by a community at large as necessary for the preservation of a certain sense of dignity and way of life' (Mullings 1999a: 293). This 'dignity' is seen to be of greater importance to the workers than the potential consequences of decreased earnings or dismissal.

The central importance accorded to the concepts of 'respect' and 'justice' in Jamaican patois can be interpreted as genuine calls for grassroots participation in all aspects of research, planning, and implementation of projects for social upliftment and environmental improvement. Failure to involve local people is not merely a passive oversight, but is actively 'dissing' (disrespecting) them. It also applies a useful corrective to the benevolent, but frequently misguided, application of western-developed participatory principles to other parts of the world.

Local Knowledges

The development of participatory research methodologies stemmed from a growing concern about the intrinsic biases of western-based research, and the privileged position given to academic knowledge. It draws on feminist-inspired practices, which although often defiantly non-relativist, maintain that partial, locatable, critical knowledge – 'situated' or 'local' knowledges – are indeed possible. These assert that 'knowledge is multiple and positional, that different groups perceive, interpret and represent things depending on their economic and social position, their culture, gender and their place in power relations' (Hamnett 2000: 65) and 'emphasise the contingency of knowledge claims and recognise the close relationship among language, power and knowledge' (Barnett 1998: 380). These theories are manifested in methodologies in which the researcher adopts the 'role of supplicant seeking reciprocal relations based in empathy with people having greater knowledge of the immediate question' (Peet 1998: 281). The interpretation of social meaning in this way can simultaneously have *explanatory* power for how and why things (such as environmental problems) have arisen and *predictory* power as to the best ways of addressing them.

However, it is necessary to remember that 'local' knowledge is also culturally, socially, and politically produced, and a forward-looking participatory methodology takes account of this. Although participation seeks to give control to local people, many of the processes affecting their lives are not readily tackled at the local scale (Mohan 2002), and participatory research can help to identify these problems and their solutions. Well-conducted participatory research also helps to eliminate the assumption that communities are homogeneous entities, and helps to include the viewpoints of individuals who suffer from any one of a variety of exclusions (Rose 1997a; Sharp et al. 2000). As the researcher exists in a privileged position which entails 'greater access both to material resources and to the power inherent in the production of knowledges about others' (Rose 1997b: 307), there is both an academic and a moral obligation to put local knowledges, no matter how limited, specific and partial they may be, to the forefront wherever and whenever possible. Indeed, 'only local stakeholders, with their years of experience in a particular situation, have sufficient information and knowledge about the situation to design effective social change processes' (Greenwood and Levin 2000: 96). The incorporation of local knowledges can therefore lend legitimacy to projects, increase the likely effectiveness of any future communication with local communities, and create cognitive gains for policymaking (Irwin et al. 1999).

Yet the participation of local people in research and planning is not, in itself, sufficient. Rather, the methods used must be tailored to the interests and abilities of the participants. This is important not only for improving the quality of data, but also for ensuring that the participants themselves can gain from taking part. Formal interviews and questionnaires are frequently associated with government or market researchers and may increase suspicion of the researcher and her/his motives. They are also more likely to lead to normative responses, in which the respondent constructs the persona or answers what they feel the researcher would like to hear, rather than the most honest answer. Indeed:

> The defining characteristic of participatory research is not so much the methods and techniques employed, but the degree of engagement of participants within and beyond the research encounter. Participatory approaches did not originate as a methodology for research, but as a process by which communities can work towards change. When employed or adapted as a means of research, many would point to the importance of retaining this fundamental principle. (Pain and Francis 2003: 46)

These objectives can be achieved by the use of novel methodologies which reduce the role played by language and formal structures. They are frequently qualitative rather than quantitative in nature, and rather than seeking to explain social phenomena, aim to understand and interpret them. In practice, this approach recognizes that 'local people, whether they can read or not, can map, diagram, list, estimate, rank, construct and score matrices, and in other visual ways present and analyze their complex realities' (Chambers 1998a: 108). In the remainder of this chapter, we report on some of the specific methodologies that can be used in the processes of participatory research and planning in the Caribbean.

These local knowledges must also be seen in conjunction with the positionality of the researcher. For example, Mullings (1999b: 341) explores the dynamic of 'the complexities of [her] own attributes' positioning her as an insider or outsider in conducting research with managers and workers in information processing companies in Jamaica. The positionality of the researcher is becoming increasingly recognized as an important factor in analysing social data, as individuals cannot objectively observe phenomena, but rather assess them on the basis of prior experiences. In truly participatory research, this must be taken one step further. The researcher must not only be aware of these individual complexities, but must also make a significant effort to share these with the participants who, after all, are exposing their own particularities to the research process. This is of particular importance in cross-cultural settings, although it also applies in the case of researchers operating within their own societies. The discussion firstly turns to the methodology of 'participatory appraisal'.

Participatory Appraisal

Participatory appraisal is one possible method with the potential to link research and action within a participatory framework. The history of participatory appraisal is inextricably linked with the writing and work of the Brazilian educator, Paulo Freire. Current writers on participation and empowerment often refer back to Freire and his influence on their thinking and writing. Crawley (1998: 24), writing about the empowerment claim of participatory appraisal, argues that the 'concept of participation as "empowerment" is closely linked to the ideas of Paulo Freire', and Eade (1997: 10) argues that thinking about capacity-building was influenced by earlier ideas about participation, empowerment, civil society and social movements which were in turn 'significantly shaped by the work of Paulo Freire, and the impact of Liberation Theology'. Robert Chambers, who has been one of the most influential proponents of participatory appraisal and similar participatory methodologies, acknowledges the role of Freire: 'Participatory action-reflection which seeks to empower owes much to the work and inspiration of Paulo Freire, to his books *Pedagogy of the Oppressed* (1970) and *Education for Critical Consciousness* (1974), and to the practice and experience of conscientization in Latin America' (Chambers 1997: 106).

Many different strains of participatory appraisal have been conceptualized and utilized, including participatory rural appraisal, participatory urban appraisal, and participatory rapid appraisal. Rather than being strictly defined methodologies, these all rest on foundational concepts which are then applied in a contextually specific system. Three of the core principles are:

1 poor people are creative and capable, and can and should do much of their own investigation, analysis and planning;
2 outsiders have roles as convenors, catalysts and facilitators;
3 the weak and marginalized can and should be empowered (Chambers 1998b: 135).

Participatory appraisal methods have increasingly been adopted by non-governmental organizations (NGOs), community-based organizations (CBOs), government departments, training institutes and universities, and have a great deal of potential in linking academic research with practical intervention and the pursuit of social justice.

Community development programmes in Jamaica in the 1980s were influenced by the animation work which was being undertaken by Roman Catholic priests in Haiti. Animation programmes, drawing on the principles behind animation in cartoons, sought to bring people and communities to life as they worked together to pool ideas and resources for community action and transformation. Whereas animation had its origins in NGOs which were church and/or community based and was introduced to Jamaica by community development practitioners and funded by organizations like OXFAM, participatory appraisal was introduced to Jamaica through the World Bank and the University of the West Indies.

Participatory appraisal first came to the attention of the NGO community in Jamaica through a study of local perceptions of urban poverty and violence, which was initiated jointly by the World Bank and the Centre for Population, Community and Social Change at the University of the West Indies (UWI). Both institutions produced reports: the World Bank's target audience was policy makers, and the UWI report, *They Cry 'Respect': Urban Violence and Poverty in Jamaica* (Levy and Chevannes 1996), was intended primarily for researchers and NGOs. These studies brought to the attention of NGOs ways in which participatory appraisal could be used for community training and empowerment. Since this initial study, the Jamaica Social Investment Fund (JSIF), the Social Development Commission (SDC) (an agency of the Jamaican government) and a range of NGOs and CBOs have used these methodologies in community programmes.

Methods based on the principles of participatory appraisal are relevant in both rural and urban settings. Whereas research into urban environmental problems has frequently ascribed greater importance to technical measurements than to the lived experience of the city's inhabitants, participatory appraisal methods have been used to illuminate environmental problems in Kingston from the perspective of those who are most acutely affected by them (Dodman 2004). In this case, the methods included the construction of Venn diagrams (colloquially referred to as 'dumpling diagrams'[2]) and various forms of matrix ranking. This research showed how the frequency and severity of environmental problems vary socio-spatially across the city and showed the different motivations and abilities of different groups of people to respond to these. Rather than solely documenting problems, participatory appraisal methods can show the potential of individuals and communities to respond to them. The discussion next turns to another methodology for participatory planning, 'action research'.

Action Research

Action research has become a popular research tool for persons interested in using research data to effect change. Rapoport (1970) states that 'action research aims to contribute both to the practical concerns of people in an immediate problematic situation and to the goals of social science by joint collaboration within a mutually acceptable ethical framework' (cited in McKernan 1991: 4). The researcher begins with an idea that change is desirable in a social situation and seeks to improve practice through a series of small achievable steps. Although there is nothing inherently emancipatory about action research, some researchers root it in these terms (see, for example, Carr and Kemmis 1986). They see that action research has the potential to result in greater empowerment, equity and justice in the places where it is conducted and in the wider society. Although action research is sometimes criticized for being weak on the generation of theory, its proponents argue that its prime purpose is to improve practice rather than to generate knowledge or find universal or particular truths.

The development of action research is generally attributed to the social psychologist Kurt Lewin, who coined the phrase 'action research' in his social experiments and human relations training in the 1940s (see Carr and Kemmis 1986; Elliott 1991; Elliott 1993; Hopkins 1993; McKernan 1991). However, some writers trace action research's epistemological concerns back to Aristotle, whilst others recognize the contribution of cultures which Eurocentric scholarship overlooks. They also acknowledge the contribution of Marx and Freire, as well as practices like participatory appraisal, perspectives on gender and race, experiential learning and psychotherapy, and some spiritual practices.

Action research extends the boundaries of participation as it is also concerned about 'voice' and the ways in which the voice of practitioners and participants can be heard. For example, educational action research may be initiated by academics or other 'outsiders', but it is often conducted by classroom teachers. When practitioners and outsiders work together their research becomes a discourse which is grounded in the study of practice. Elliott (1993: 42) contends that the 'dialectical relation between theory and practice can only be maintained if these two dimensions of practical discourse are sustained'. Sometimes the outsider plays the role of critical friend, who is 'a person or group who is trusted, who understands the school's context and purposes, who wishes it to be successful and who, because of these things, can be constructively critical' (Halsall 1998: 48).

There are links between participatory research and action research. The participatory methods used above rest on the premise of researchers 'finding out', whilst action research seeks to facilitate change at the same time. Some writers prefer to use the term 'participatory action research' as a way of recognizing the convergence of two intellectual and practical traditions, 'that of "action research" (in the Lewinian tradition) and that of "participatory research" which has its origins in community development movements in the Third World' (McTaggart 1994: 314). For Hall (2001: 171), participatory research is 'an integrated three-pronged process of social investigation, education and action designed to support those with less power in their organizational or community settings'. He argues that much of this research has arisen from NGOs, CBOs and civil society. McTaggart (1994: 318) goes on to suggest that 'participatory action research is concerned simultaneously with changing *individuals*, on the one hand, and, on the other, the *culture* of the groups, institutions and societies to which they belong'.

The action research process involves a series of steps or a spiral, where the first action step produces data. This enables the researcher to describe and evaluate the effects of the data and to implement a further action step. The action research process involves four moments (plan, act, observe, reflect), which are repeated until the completion of the research. The analysis primarily takes place through the self-reflective enquiry of the researcher. However, the analysis is not a separate stage in the research, as it begins with the practical deliberation, the first steps in the research process and continues through the collection of data and until the writing has been completed.

The second author has been engaged in an action research project in an inner-city school in Kingston for the past three years. She is a member of the organization that operates the school and has been involved with it since its inception. Her role was as research initiator, facilitator and critical friend. The teachers worked as action researchers in their classrooms. They were not traditional researchers, as most of them were in the process of completing their own teacher education and had not previously been exposed to research in theory or practice. The objective of the research was to plan and implement small achievable steps which sought to make the school motto come alive in the lives of the children. Each teacher selected one aspect of the school motto, which spoke to self-esteem, love, industry, community and excellence. They conducted the research by initiating discussions and new activities, like drama, art and craft and group work. One teacher used the experience of the children's lives in the community to try to change their taken for granted assumptions about people who were different, yet belonged to their community. The primary aim of the research was to impact the school and the children. In reality it also impacted the teachers, for example in their relationship to their home community, in their realization that they too had the potential to excel. The action research changed the way the teachers understood their role in a particular inner-city context and extended the school's mission of offering more than the basic academic curriculum. The research effected a change from a teacher-directed focus to a learning school, where the children and teachers learnt from each other. Action research was seen as an appropriate model, as the aim of the research was to effect change in practice in a particular context.

The practice of action research has traditionally been limited to institutional settings such as schools and hospitals. However, there is great potential for the principles of action research to be applied in communities in the Caribbean seeking to address social and environmental problems. The combination of research, social action, and environmental improvement represents a participatory methodology with the potential to make substantial changes to deprived urban and rural communities in the region and elsewhere.

Visual Methods

One of the major changes in social science research over the last decade has been a 'shift towards qualitative, discursive forms of inquiry where the aim is to engage people in extended conversation so as to better understand the nature of argument and evidence they draw upon to make sense of the world' (Burgess 1999: 142). However, the use of the word 'conversation' already hints that this has frequently depended on the use of verbal communication. The ways in which language is used can constrain rather than liberate qualitative enquiry, and verbal methods can perpetuate and exaggerate a wide variety of social inequities. Combating this is of particular relevance in the Caribbean context, in which particular forms of language are associated with particular socio-economic, and thus power-related, positions. As Evans states with reference to Jamaica:

> Jamaica has a Creole language derived from the languages of the colonizer and the colonized and the language of the former colonizers is more extensively accepted. Because the standard language, in this case Standard Jamaican English (SJE), is closely associated with the dominant social and economic classes, it has more prestige and status and its use is mandatory for certain social and public situations. The Creole language, in contrast, is low in status and prestige, derived as it is from oppressed slave societies and the poor marginalized groups in Jamaica. (Evans 2001: 105)

One way in which the pitfalls associated with the use of verbal communication can be addressed is through the acknowledgement that many different modes of expression can be used as texts through which to understand the world (Barnes and Duncan 1992). Cultural productions in the forms of art, literature, and music can provide a rich vein of historical and contemporary information about social processes. Indeed, the use of visual imagery and stories can provide integrative insights into the separate realities of diverse groups of people, based on the situated interpretations of both 'narrators' and 'readers' (Rocheleau 1995).

Rather than merely interpreting these, a participatory approach can also involve non-traditional or marginalized groups in producing these representations. One possible means of facilitating this is through self-directed photography, in which individuals take photographs exploring a certain theme and in which 'understanding is facilitated through observation of what the other selectively attends in the environment' (Ziller 1990: 10). In one such project, one of the authors (David Dodman) issued single-use (disposable) cameras to high school students from a variety of social backgrounds in Kingston, in order for them to record their own impressions and interpretations of their surroundings (Dodman 2003). This combination of an unusual methodology with a high level of youth participation provided a unique insight into the human-environment interactions taking place in the city and revealed a variety of information about the ways in which social class, age and gender influence perceptions of, and relationships with, the urban environment. Rather than merely providing data for academic analysis, this method is also directly empowering, as the act of photographing means 'putting oneself into a certain relation to the world that feels like knowledge – and, therefore, like power' (Sontag 1973: 4).

The methodologies used when dealing with groups such as children or young people are also frequently inappropriate, when in fact 'our ways of knowing how different children characterize their environment should be sensitive to the contexts of their daily lives, using methods which facilitate environmental competence and personal identity' (Aitken and Wingate 1993: 66). Photographs facilitate this, as they are able to 'engage thought, extend the imagination, and to undermine the implicit authority of the written word' (Walker 1993: 73). In general, visual methods help to avoid one of the common problems involved in doing research with children and young people, in which children tell people in authority (including researchers) what they think they want to hear. In contrast, visual methods help to distinguish between 'normative statements and those that are closer to children's feelings and experiences' (Johnson 1996: 34).

Another way of enabling children's participation in research is to ask them to draw pictures related to a research theme. In the action research referred to above, one of the teachers asked her children to draw pictures illustrating their understanding of love. The pictures were interesting both for what they depicted and what they did not depict. Some of the children drew pictures of families, either the nuclear family or a child with mother or father. It was clear that some of the pictures represented a perceived reality about love and family and not the children's actual reality. For example, one boy drew both his mother and father, but later related that he lived only with his mother. There were no pictures of grandparents, but grandmothers in particular are often the key and stabilizing influence in the children's lives, as some of the children live with grandparents, not their parents.

At Christmas, the same teacher asked her children to draw pictures about Christmas and love. They included some images which depicted their reality, for example ice cream, balloons and going out for 'fast food'. The big houses, Father Christmas' sleigh, the snow, chimneys and smoke were, in contrast, images from television, and perhaps books. These drawings raised issues of the children's identity and values and the extent to which they thought these were the essential ingredients for a 'Happy Christmas'.

Many of these children have difficulty writing and expressing themselves verbally. The pictures themselves tell a story and may provide a prompt for shyer pupils to express their emotions through the picture itself and through subsequent discussion with the teacher and other children. The pictures depict relationships with other people, interactions with their surroundings and ideas about their community and how they would like it to be. Moreover, in a context in which children are bombarded with conflicting images about their self-worth, their drawings reflect some of these complexities of identity and sense of self.

Value in Academic Research

The use of participatory research methods helps to liberate academic enquiry from the positivist, euro-centric worldview with which it has frequently been associated in the past. Social scientists have far too frequently treated the real world as merely a source of examples with which to validate their theories. In contrast, participatory research re-centres the research process on the lived experiences of individuals in a variety of settings. Like qualitative research, participatory researchers 'study things in their natural settings, attempting to make sense of, or interpret, phenomena in terms of the meanings people bring to them' (Denzin and Lincoln 1994: 2).

These methods are of particular value when combined with a grounded theory approach to the creation of academic knowledge (Strauss and Corbin 1994, Bailey et al. 1999):

> In grounded theory, research design and analysis are cyclical. Through research activities ... the researcher develops tentative explanations or propositions. These are then 'tested' and revised to guide a fresh collection of data, to review the original data and literature, to appraise new literature and to form new explanations ... This process, whilst being systematic and 'scientific', nevertheless remains open to unexpected paths of questioning and discovery ... Creativity, intuition and, to some extent, curiosity guide the planning of the research process, which in *itself* leads the researcher critically to examine and reflect upon this research process. (Bailey et al. 1999: 173, emphasis in original)

Participatory research can therefore be used within a rigorous intellectual framework of enquiry, without falling prey to the restrictions of quantifiable predictions. Various participatory research methods have proven themselves in the field as being able to produce robust, good quality data in an ethical way in a variety of settings (Kesby 2000, Young and Barrett 2001, Pain and Francis 2003). Quantitative methods have been shown to have limited validity in the understanding of many of the problems facing the Caribbean – for example, Lundy (1996; 1999) shows how these can underestimate the environmental and health problems caused by structural adjustment. In contrast, the use of qualitative participatory research methods at the micro-level helps to ascertain the effects of global processes at the grassroots level.

Participatory academic research can also play an important role in enhancing social capital in the communities in which it is practised. Thomas-Hope and Spence (2003, and also in their contribution to this volume) show how a participatory research project into people, land management and environmental change enabled a transition from superficial social networks to the generation of social capital among small farmers in Portland, Jamaica. In this case, the participatory nature of the research ensured that a deeper sharing of information and knowledge was obtained than if the research outcomes had been presented by experts at the end of the process.

Yet perhaps the most difficult objective for participatory academic research is to allow a participatory determination of the research objectives themselves. The challenge for participatory researchers working from within the academy is not just to encourage the participation of local people in pre-determined projects, but to allow these people to identify priorities and to shape the direction of future research.

Application to Policy

In recent years, policymakers in Jamaica and the rest of the Caribbean have adopted participatory research methods in order to respond better to community needs and community demand. Participatory Learning and Action (PLA) techniques are used with community organizations which are seeking to identify and prioritize community needs and to solve problems. Informed thinking and community consensus allow for funding proposals to be written and submitted which speak to real needs.

An early use of participatory methodologies in policy research in Jamaica in 1995 resulted in the report entitled *They Cry Respect*, discussed above. This study had the objective of providing 'a critical basis for the Social Investment Fund (SIF) being established by the Government with the assistance of the World Bank and other international agencies' (Levy and Chevannes 1996: 1). Social Investment Funds are quasi-financial intermediaries that channel resources, according to pre-determined eligibility criteria, to small-scale sub-projects for poor and vulnerable groups. Around sixty SIFs exist around the world, formed in response to the recognition that the structural adjustment programmes imposed by the International Monetary Fund (IMF) and World Bank were producing a wide variety of negative social and environmental effects.

The Jamaica Social Investment Fund (JSIF) was launched in 1996 with a US$20 million loan from the World Bank, with the specific aim of funding sub-projects in social infrastructure (such as schools and health centres), economic infrastructure (such as roads and water supplies), social services (such as parenting education), and organizational strengthening. Other contributors to the fund are the Inter-American Development Bank, the European Union, and local counterpart funds. JSIF has been the prime mechanism for funding small-scale community projects in Jamaican in recent years, and has its very genesis in a process of participatory appraisal and research.

The ways in which JSIF funds are utilized at the micro-scale of the community are also determined by participatory methodologies. These can include priority ranking, voting, matrix scoring, and pairwise ranking. The variety of participatory methodologies engages participants in different ways in the process of identifying community priorities. At the same time, participatory facilitators are training community residents in participatory methodologies that can then be used in a variety of local decision-making processes (Dodman 2002). Beneficiary assessment and project monitoring and evaluation for JSIF projects are also conducted using participatory appraisal methods. In participatory monitoring and evaluation, the process is planned and managed by local people, project staff, and other stakeholders rather than by senior managers or outside experts; and the beneficiaries themselves collect and analyse data.

Participatory methodologies are also being used to reshape the Jamaican local government system. This is in keeping with a broader shift from government to governance, and a recognition that 'the central issues for environmental justice are community empowerment and access to the resources necessary for an active role in decisions affecting people's lives' (Heiman 1996: 119). The Jamaican Government's Social Development Commission (SDC), influenced by international guidelines for sustainable development planning, has facilitated the formation of Community Development Committees (CDCs) comprised of the leadership of recognized community-based organizations in communities throughout the country. These feed into Parish Development Committees (PDCs), which are 'participatory mechanisms that involve the State, private sector, community leaders and other members of civil society in the process of local governance' (Ministry of Local Government 2002: 33). These PDCs are responsible for the preparation of long-term strategic plans for sustainable development. In Kingston, for example, this has resulted in the preparation of a sustainable development plan based on processes of consultation and participation, which will become the guiding vision for the development of the city (Kingston and St Andrew Parish Development Committee 2001, 2005).

Participatory appraisal and research methods have therefore been used to direct policy in several ways: through determining priorities for action (at the macro- and micro-levels); identifying funding needs and priorities; and monitoring and evaluating projects. They can also lead to the formation of partnerships for more effective environmental management. Participatory researchers involved in partnerships with urban authorities and civil society can assume important additional roles beyond those of research. These may include: 'advocacy and awareness creation for environmental and social concerns; planning and monitoring; and capacity-building and training of local researchers, civil servants and civil society leaders' (Wacker et al. 1999: 123). The partnerships formed by participatory research can result in researchers having a much broader role to play in the implementation of local environmental management systems such as those promoted by Agenda 21.

Conclusions

Participatory research methods can yield detailed, high-quality information from a different perspective than that of the researcher. However, these methods are not unproblematic. Precisely because participation is generally associated with moral or desirable goals it is seldom thought that it may harbour evil or malicious purposes (Rahnema 1992). Further, 'while participatory thinkers do admit that all knowledge systems carry a number of values and biases, they seem to exclude the possibility that, as products of a certain knowledge born out of the economic/developmental age, they could be, themselves, the carriers of very questionable values and biases' (Rahnema 1992: 122). The inclusion of local knowledges within an externally defined participatory framework may also do no more than filter the dominant discourses of more powerful actors through the allegedly participatory process (Kothari 2001).

There must therefore be a constant awareness of the power relations between the researcher and the other people involved in the research in order to limit the normative aspects of responses which are always likely to be biased as a result of perceptions of what the listener expects to hear. There are also ethical issues related to the use of other people's knowledges in a programme of academic research – on the simplest level, care must be taken not to waste participants' time or effort for something which may not provide them with any clear benefits. Despite the best intentions of many of its protagonists, 'participatory research methods tend to reinscribe relations of authority between the outside facilitator and the grassroots' (Mohan 2001: 153).

However, as shown above, the principles of 'justice' and 'respect' can operate as useful correctives to these potentially damaging effects of participatory discourse. These endogenous appeals can lead to participatory research and planning moving beyond a patronizing relationship into one with broader benefits for all those involved. McGranahan et al. (2001) stress the role of participatory collective action in organizing environmental improvements in deprived neighbourhoods, whilst in the context of Kingston, Figueroa (1998) has shown the potential of community participation in the effective management of solid waste. Participatory researchers must seek to include themselves within these partnerships, rather than solely seeking the involvement of communities in their own pre-conceived agendas.

Participatory researchers therefore find themselves in close spatial and social proximity to the problems that they seek to study and address. The participatory researcher ought then to find her/himself playing the role of a bridge between ostensibly objective and disinterested management systems and local knowledges that fail to take account of larger issues. Researchers who participate actively in both of these fora can greatly further the potential for effective environmental planning. Participatory research can then be a part of linking what David Harvey (1996) terms 'militant particularisms' together, and a means of expanding the efficacy of grassroots activities to a wider scale. Harvey (2001) argues that left to their own devices, collective movements tend to be conservative and to preclude rather than promote the search for alternatives. Participatory research which interacts at a meaningful level with different militant particularisms can be a part of the process that links these separate entities together to provide a potent force for social and environmental improvement.

Robert Chambers (1998b: 145) gives a specific mandate to teachers in universities, training institutes and colleges 'to go ourselves and with our students to local people to learn, to revise our curricula, rewrite our textbooks, to lecture less and more to help others learn'. This involves not only a widening of participation in research, but also a deepening of the level of engagement by researchers in local communities. By conducting participatory research along these lines, and by incorporating locally generated calls for 'justice' and 'respect', participatory research in Jamaica and the Caribbean will be better able to provide a basis for participatory environmental planning and action.

Notes

1 To this end, witness Peter Tosh's lyrics 'wi sick an wi tired wid di isms, schisms' (Get Up, Stand Up: 1973) or Bob Marley's 'building church and university, deceiving the people continually' (Babylon System: 1979).

2 Circular boiled or fried dumplings made primarily of flour are essential components of the diet for many Jamaicans. When similar exercises have been used in Trinidad, the Venn diagrams are referred to as 'roti diagrams' after the flat round bread commonly eaten there.

References

Aitken, S. and Wingate, J. (1993). 'A Preliminary Study of the Self-directed Photography of Middle-class, Homeless, and Mobility-impaired Children', *Professional Geographer*, 45 (1), pp. 65–72.

Bailey, C., White, C. and Pain, R. (1999), 'Evaluating Qualitative Research: Dealing with the Tension between "Science" and "Creativity"', *Area*, 31 (2), pp. 169–83.

Barnes, T. and Duncan, J.S. (1992), *Writing Worlds: Discourse, Text and Metaphor in the Representation of Landscape*, London: Routledge.

Barnett, C. (1998), 'The Cultural Turn: Fashion or Progress in Human Geography', *Antipode*, 30 (4), pp. 379–94.

Burgess, J. (1999), 'Environmental Knowledges and Environmentalism', in P. Cloke, P. Crang and M. Goodwin (eds), *Introducing Human Geographies*, London: Arnold.

Carr, W. and Kemmis, S. (1986). *Becoming Critical: Education, Knowledge and Action Research*, London: Falmer.

Castells, M. (1977), *The Urban Question: A Marxist Approach*, London: Edward Arnold. [originally published in French in 1972].

Castells, M. (1983), *The City and the Grassroots: A Cross-cultural Theory of Urban Social Movements*, London: Edward Arnold.

Castells, M. (1985), *From the Urban Question to the City and the Grassroots*, Urban and Regional Studies, University of Sussex, Working Paper 47.

Chambers, R. (1997), *Whose Reality Counts? Putting the First Last*, London: Intermediate Technology.

Chambers, R. (1998a), 'Beyond "Whose Reality Counts"? New Methods We Now Need', in O. Fals Borda (ed.), *People's Participation: Challenges Ahead*, New York: Apex Press/ Intermediate Technology Publications.

Chambers, R. (1998b), 'Us and Them: Finding a New Paradigm for Professionals in Sustainable Development', in D. Warburton (ed), *Community and Sustainable Development: Participation in the Future*, London: Earthscan.

Cleaver, F. (2001), 'Institutions, Agency and the Limitations of Participatory Approaches to Development', in B. Cooke and U. Kothari (eds), *Participation: The New Tyranny?*, London: Zed Books.

Crawley, H. (1998), 'Living up to the Empowerment Claim? The Potential of PRA', in I. Guijt and M. Shah (eds), *The Myth of Community: Gender Issues in Participatory Development*, London: Intermediate Technology, pp. 24–34.

Denzin, N. and Lincoln, Y. (1994), 'Introduction: Entering the Field of Qualitative Research', in N. Denzin and Y. Lincoln (eds), *Handbook of Qualitative Research*, London: Sage.

Dodman, D. (2003). 'Shooting in the City: An Autophotographic Exploration of the Urban Environment in Kingston, Jamaica', *Area*, 35 (3), pp. 293–304.

Dodman, D. (2004), 'Community Perspectives on Urban Environmental Problems in Kingston, Jamaica', *Social and Economic Studies*, 53 (3), pp. 31–59.

Dodman, J. (2002), 'Determining Priorities in Rural Communities in Jamaica', *PLA Notes*, 43, pp. 53–6.

Eade, D. (1997), *Capacity-Building: An Approach to People-centred Development*, Oxford: Oxfam.

Elliott, J. (1991), *Action Research for Educational Change*, Buckingham: Open University.

Elliott, J. (1993), 'Professional development in a land of choice and diversity', in D. Bridges and T. Kerry (eds), *Developing Teachers Professionally: Reflections for Initial and In-service Training*, London: Routledge, pp. 23–50.

Evans, H. (2001), *Inside Jamaican Schools*, Kingston: UWI Press.

Figueroa, M. (1998), 'The Community as a Resource for Solid Waste Management', in E. Thomas-Hope (ed.), *Solid Waste Management: Critical Issues for Developing Countries*, Kingston: UWI Press.

Greenwood, D. and Levin, M. (2000), 'Reconstructing the Relationships between Universities and Society through Action Research', in N. Denzin and Y. Lincoln (eds), *Handbook of Qualitative Research*, 2nd edn, Thousand Oaks, CA: Sage.

Hall, B. (2001), 'I Wish This Were a Poem of Practices of Participatory Research', in P. Reason and H. Bradbury (eds), *Handbook of Action Research: Participative Inquiry and Practice*, London: Sage, pp. 171–8.

Halsall, R. (1998), 'School Improvement: An Overview of Key Findings and Messages', in R. Halsall (ed.), *Teacher Research and School Improvement*, Buckingham: Open University, pp. 28–53.

Hamnett, C. (2000), 'The Emperor's New Theoretical Clothes, or Geography without Origami', in G. Philo and D. Miller (eds), *Market Killing: What the Free Market Does and What Social Scientists Can Do about It*, Harlow: Longman.

Harvey, D. (1996), *Justice, Nature and the Geography of Difference*, Oxford: Blackwell.

Harvey, D. (2001), *Spaces of Capital: Towards a Critical Geography*, Edinburgh: Edinburgh University Press.

Haynes, J. (1997), *Democracy and Civil Society in the Third World*, Cambridge: Polity Press.

Heiman, M.K. (1996), 'Race, Waste, and Class: New Perspectives on Environmental Justice', *Antipode*, 28 (2), pp. 111–21.
Hopkins, D. (1993), *A Teacher's Guide to Classroom Research*, 2nd edn, Buckingham: Open University.
Irwin, A., Simmons, P. and Walker, G. (1999), 'Faulty Environments and Risk Reasoning: The Local Understanding of Industrial Hazards', *Environment and Planning A*, 31, pp. 1311–26.
Johnson, V. (1996), 'Starting a Dialogue on Children's Participation', *PLA Notes*, 25, pp. 30–37.
Kesby, M. (2000), 'Participatory Diagramming: Deploying Qualitative Methods through an Action Research Epistemology', *Area*, 32, pp. 423–35.
Kingston and St Andrew Parish Development Committee (KSAPDC) (2001), *Dreams in Action from the Mountains to the Sea: The Kingston and St Andrew sustainable development plan*, proposal submitted to *Cities Alliance*, 7 November.
Kingston and St Andrew Parish Development Committee (KSAPDC) (2005), *Kingston and St Andrew Sustainable Development Plan* (draft).
Kothari, U. (2001), 'Power, Knowledge and Social Control in Participatory Development', in B. Cooke and U. Kothari (eds), *Participation: The New Tyranny?*, London: Zed Books.
Levy, H. and Chevannes, B. (1996), *They Cry Respect: Urban Violence and Poverty in Jamaica*, Department of Sociology and Social Work, University of the West Indies.
Lundy, P. (1996), 'Limitations of Quantitative Research in the Study of Structural Adjustment', *Social Science and Medicine*, 42 (3), pp. 313–24.
Lundy, P. (1999), *Debt and Adjustment: Social and Environmental Consequences in Jamaica*, Aldershot: Ashgate.
McGranahan, G., Jacobi, P. Songsore, J., Surjadi, C. and Kjellén, M. (2001), *The Citizens at Risk: From Urban Sanitation to Sustainable Cities*, London: Earthscan.
McKernan, J. (1991), *Curriculum Action Research: A Handbook of Methods and Resources for the Reflective Practitioner*, London: Kogan Page.
McTaggart, R. (1994), 'Participatory Action Research: Issues in Theory and Practice', *Educational Action Research*, 2 (3), pp. 313–37.
Ministry of Local Government and Community Development (MLGCD) (2002), *Report on Local Government Reform*, Kingston: Government of Jamaica.
Mohan, G. (2001), 'Beyond Participation: Strategies for Deeper Empowerment', in B. Cooke and U. Kothari (eds), *Participation: The New Tyranny?*, London: Zed Books.
Mohan, G. (2002), 'Participatory Development', in V. Desai and R. Potter (eds), *The Companion to Development Studies*, London: Edward Arnold.
Mullings, B. (1999a), 'Sides of the Same Coin?: Coping and Resistance among Jamaican Data-entry Operators', *Annals of the Association of American Geographers*, 89 (2), pp. 290–311.
Mullings, B. (1999b), 'Insider or Outsider, Both or Neither: Some Dilemmas of Interviewing in a Cross-cultural Setting', *Geoforum*, 30, pp. 337–50.
Murrell, N., Spencer, W. and McFarlane, A. (eds) (1998), *Chanting Down Babylon: The Rastafari Reader*, Philadelphia: Temple University Press.
Nettleford, R. (2003), *Caribbean Cultural Identity: The Case of Jamaica*, Kingston: Ian Randle [second edition with new introduction; first published 1978]
Pain, R. and Francis, P. (2003), 'Reflections on Participatory Research', *Area*, 35 (1), pp. 46–54.

Peet, R. (1998), *Modern Geographical Thought*, Oxford: Blackwell.

Pelling, M. (1998), 'Participation, Social Capital and Vulnerability to Urban Flooding in Guyana', *Journal of International Development*, 10, pp. 469–86.

Rahnema, M. (1992), 'Participation', in W. Sachs (ed.), *The Development Dictionary: A Guide to Knowledge as Power*, London: Zed Books.

Rapoport, R.N. (1970), 'Three Dilemmas in Action Research', *Human Relations*, 23 (4), pp. 499–513.

Rocheleau, D. (1995), 'Maps, Numbers, Text and Context: Mixing Methods in Feminist Political Ecology', *Professional Geographer*, 47 (4), pp. 458–66.

Rose, G. (1997a), 'Performing Inoperative Community', in S. Pile and M. Keith (eds), *Geographies of Resistance*, London: Routledge.

Rose, G. (1997b), 'Situating Knowledges: Positionality, Reflexivities and Other Tactics', *Progress in Human Geography*, 21 (3), pp. 305–20.

Sharp, J., Routledge, P., Philo, C. and Paddison, R. (2000), 'Entanglements of Power: Geographies of Domination/Resistance', in J. Sharp, P. Routledge, C. Philo and R. Paddison (eds), *Entanglements of Power: Geographies of Domination/Resistance*, London: Routledge.

Sontag, S. (1973), *On Photography*, New York: Farrar, Straus and Giroux.

Strauss, A. and Corbin, J. (1994), 'Grounded Theory Methodology: An Overview', in N. Denzin and Y. Lincoln (eds), *Handbook of Qualitative Research*, London: Sage.

Thomas-Hope, E. and Spence, B. (2003), 'Jamaica', in H. Brookfield, H. Parsons and M. Brookfield (eds), *Agrodiversity: Learning from Farmers across the World*, Tokyo: UNU Press, pp. 270–92.

Wacker, C., Viaro, A. and Wolf, M. (1999), 'Partnerships for Urban Environmental Management: The Roles of Urban Authorities, Researchers and Civil Society', *Environment and Urbanization*, 11 (2), pp. 113–25.

Walker, R. (1993), 'Finding a Silent Voice for the Researcher: Using Photographs in Evaluation and Research', in M. Schratz (ed.), *Qualitative Voices in Educational Research*, London: Falmer Press.

Young, L. and Barrett, H. (2001), 'Adapting Visual Methods: Action Research with Kampala Street Children', *Area*, 33, pp. 141–52.

Ziller, R. (1990), *Photographing the Self: Methods for Observing Personal Orientations*, London: Sage.

Chapter 8

Corporate Environmental Sustainability: Sandals Resorts International in Jamaica

Paul Kingsbury

Introduction

Despite a lack of conceptual consensus on tourism, researchers agree that international tourism is empirically related to two ideal types: on the one hand, 'mass tourism' is commercial, seasonal and typically located along coastal areas; it involves a high volume of tourists who generally adhere to their own cultural norms; and it relies upon high-density and standardized accommodation to produce a homogenized product and experience. On the other hand, is the post-1980s growth in 'alternative tourism', a term that encompasses a range of planning strategies (e.g., ecological, culturally responsible, or sustainable) that purport to offer benign alternatives to the political economic, cultural and environmental problems associated with mass tourism.

While these categories are significant characteristics of tourism, some researchers have observed the beginnings of a convergence between mass tourism and alternative tourism (Mowforth and Munt 2003). First, increases in the volume of alternative tourists, together with pressures to achieve scale economies, have meant that many alternative tourism developments share some of the characteristics of mass tourism. Second, practices of sustainability, usually associated with alternative tourism, do not necessarily involve deviations from mass tourism if they are managed in appropriate ways (Murphy 1998; Weaver and Lawton 2002; Weaver 2001a). The growth in international environmental monitoring and management programmes in the tourism industry, such as the Green Globe 21 Standard scheme established after the United Nations Rio Earth Summit in 1992 and launched in 1994 by the World Travel and Tourism Council (WTTC), is indicative of a growing corporate interest in issues of sustainability (see also Pugh 2001). These programmes provide hotels with an environmental management framework to improve the environmental aspects of operations, including management of energy and water resources, waste disposal and recycling and storage and use of hazardous materials. The political economic, cultural and environmental impacts of mass tourism are complex, presenting tourism corporations with significant challenges should they elect to and attempt to become sustainable.

Described as a new 'paradigm for the 21st Century' (Ayala 1996a: 46), one of the most recent and important transformations in Caribbean tourism concerns the adoption and adaptation of 'alternative tourism' planning policies and practices by conventional 'mass tourism' corporations to create new forms of 'mass ecotourism' or 'resort ecotourism' (Ayala 1996a, b; Ayala 1997; Haywood and Jayawardena 2004; Milne and Ewing 2004; Weaver 2001b). Given the novelty of mass ecotourism, its prevalence in the global south and uncertainty over its very possibility, there is a notable lack of studies evaluating corporate sustainability. Though international tourism monitoring agencies have developed a checklist approach for their certifications of sustainability, researchers have questioned whether corporate environmental strategy 'is genuine and effective or whether it is an attempt to display a corporate conscience for the sake of its public image' (Mowforth and Munt 2003: 196).

Clearly, the adoption of sustainable practices can be both a rational business strategy that enhances efficiency and a 'green' marketing tool designed to compete with the rapidly growing numbers of alternative tourists. Yet, how mass tourism corporations define sustainability, implement management strategies and evaluate programmes is poorly understood by researchers (Mowforth and Munt 2003; Pearce and Butler 1999; Wilkinson 1997). The literature's traditional theorization of detrimental mass tourism *versus* benign alternative tourism has meant that empirical research into sustainable tourism has been historically confined to small and isolated alternative tourism projects, while mass tourism has been usually regarded as inherently unsustainable (Fennell 1999; Harrison 2001; Weiler and Hall 1992).

Sandals Resorts International (Sandals), headquartered in Jamaica, is a company at the forefront of such transformations in international tourism. Sandals is the largest and most successful mass tourism company in the Caribbean that specializes in couples-only 'all-inclusive' vacations whereby the cost of accommodation, dining, amenities and airport transfers are prepaid and included in the total cost of the vacation. Researchers have noted, however, that large purpose-built self-contained complexes such as Sandals usually produce numerous socio-economic and environmental problems for local communities (Freitag 1994; Swarbrooke 1999: 330–33). In 1998 the hotel Sandals Negril Beach Resort and Spa (Sandals Negril) became the first all-inclusive hotel in the world to be certified to the Green Globe 21 Standard for its environmental policies and management. Sandals Negril has become an internationally recognized model of the opportunities posed by the convergence of alternative tourism and mass tourism. Sandals Negril boasts a revamped environmental management system (EMS), environmental training programmes for both employees and visitors and locally sensitive economic and cultural development initiatives.

Between June and August 2002, I conducted an organizational ethnography of Sandals that included participant observation, archival research and structured and semi-structured interviews that ranged from the highest levels of corporate management in Montego Bay to waste management workers in the Sandals Negril facility. This method of organizational ethnography involved immersion into the structure, culture, social relations and operations of Sandals. It required lengthy engagement with key personnel in the organization, during which both formal and informal interviewing took place.

A comprehensive critical evaluation of the authenticity or genuineness of Sandals Negril's sustainability is beyond the scope of this chapter. Rather, this chapter seeks to address the dearth of discussion on mass ecotourism and corporate environmental sustainability in the Caribbean by addressing three main questions: first, why did Sandals, which was already enjoying a 90 per cent occupancy rate at its Negril facility, choose to refashion its resort in this way? Second, how was this managerial initiative undertaken? Third, what were the main difficulties Sandals Negril faced in implementing its policies and practices of sustainability?

This chapter addresses these questions in four main sections: first I briefly review the tourism research literature on issues of environmental sustainability that pertain to the Caribbean. Second, I situate Sandals and Sandals Negril in the context of Caribbean and Jamaican tourism. Third, drawing on structured interviews with managers and directors, I illustrate the main decisions behind Sandals' move to 'mass ecotourism' that reveal how the corporation planned, developed and implemented its programmes of sustainability. I also describe how Sandals' labour management strategies played a crucial role in Sandals Negril's ability to acquire the Green Globe certificate. I conclude by suggesting directions for future research into corporate environmental sustainability.

Caribbean Tourism and Environmental Sustainability

Understanding the relations between tourism, development and environmental sustainability has long been an important area of discussion among Caribbean tourism researchers (Duval and Wilkinson 2004). While the role of tourism in preserving fragile and unique environments in the Caribbean has been documented, environmental conflicts and exploitation of resources, when coupled with pressures for profits, an inadequacy of local expertise and a lack of planning regulations, has become an important focus of research (Duval 2004a; Pattullo 1996; Wilkinson 1997). Concern over the detrimental effects of mass tourism on the natural environment in the Caribbean first appeared in the 1970s (Cohen 1978) and it further intensified in the 1980s under the influence of the 'green paradigm' (Holder 1988).

Environmental degradation associated with mass tourism development typically includes soil erosion, water and air pollution, loss of biodiversity, detrimental visual impacts and overloading of key infrastructure (Weaver 2001b). Much of alternative tourism aims to overcome mass tourism's environmental problems by actively ensuring the conservation of the natural environment through the acquisition and management of protected areas and the promotion of environmental education for tourists and local residents (Weaver 1993). Researchers, however, have observed that despite fewer tourists and commitments to environmental sustainability, alternative tourism's often remote, sprawling and dispersed development inflicts more damage on the environment than concentrated and isolated forms of mass tourism (Butler 1990; Mowforth and Munt 2003; Weaver 1998). While tourism-related ecological problems are not restricted to the Caribbean region, evidence indicates that they are often more severe because of their inherent vulnerability (e.g., reefs, rainforests, marine life, closed ecosystems, limited resources and fragile coastal areas) to tourist development (Conway 2002, 2004; Tewarie 2002).

The assessment and implementation of sustainable tourism is difficult because it is defined by future outcomes and tourism-environment relationships that vary geographically within and between the Caribbean and the global south (Duval 2004b). Three main planning approaches have been adopted to evaluate the environmental sustainability of both alternative tourism and mass tourism development: carrying capacity calculations, limits of acceptable change and environmental impact assessments (EIAs) (Mowforth and Munt 2003). EIAs (legally required by many development agencies such as the World Bank) are the most common approach in the Caribbean and among the foremost tools available to national decision makers in their efforts to prevent environmental deterioration. Fraught with political and definitional controversies, sustainable tourism may simply imply sustaining tourism itself regardless of the impacts on the physical environment (Duval and Wilkinson 2004; Place 1995). Given the conflicting interpretations of sustainability and the complex dialectical relationship between tourism and the environment, literature on the corporate interest and adoption of environmentally sustainable policies has yet to go beyond diverse speculation and calls for more research (Mowforth and Munt 2003; Pearce and Butler 1999). Furthermore, the literature on corporate environmental sustainability predominantly focuses on geographical contexts and case studies in the global north (e.g., see Dunphy, Griffiths and Benn 2003; Sharma and Starick 2003).

Caribbean Tourism, Sandals and Sandals Negril

Located in a transnational tourism region called the 'pleasure periphery' (Turner and Ash 1975), the Caribbean tourism product is renowned not only for its tropical islands of 'sun, sand, and sea' but also its resorts of 'sex, security, and subservience' that are synonymous with crime, drugs and harassment (e.g., see de Albuquerque and McElroy 1999; Duval 2004a; Gmelch 2003; Kingsbury 2005; Mullings 1999, 2000; Pattullo 1996; Sheller 2003). The Caribbean is the most dependent and competitive tourism region in the world. The Caribbean tourism industry provides at least a quarter of the region's GDP and total jobs (Momsen 2004). According to the World Tourism Organization (WTO), in 2003, the Caribbean attracted 12 million visitors from cruise ship visitors (10 per cent more than 2002) and 17.3 million stopover arrivals (8 per cent more than 2002) (WTO 2004). Yet, given the Caribbean's high dependency on tourists travelling from North America and Europe, many Caribbean island economies are still recovering from the events of September 11 that caused tourist arrivals to decline by 16 per cent in the last quarter of 2001 (Momsen 2004; Pantojas-García and Klak 2004).

The political economic, cultural and environmental problems associated with tourism development in the global south are the most spatially concentrated in the Caribbean. Caribbean islands often juxtapose relatively wealthy coastal resorts and cruise ship port towns with poor interior labour-supplying rural villages. As noted above, many Caribbean islands are not only environmentally unique but their island ecosystems are extremely delicate and vulnerable to the detrimental effects of both mass and alternative forms of tourism. It is now increasingly recognized that the future of international tourism in the Caribbean depends on the development of appropriate and sustainable forms of tourism, the success and availability of which will become a major determinant of visitor destinations (Duval 2004).

Following the Caribbean Tourism Organization's (CTO) recommendation that the region should develop an overall environmental convention that protects its ecological and social resources, governments throughout the region are now engaged in formulating sustainable tourism planning policies for the entire industry (Ayala 1996a, 1996b; Milne and Ewing 2004; Pearce 1992). In August 2000, for example, Jamaica's 'Master Plan' was completed by the Ministry of Tourism and Sport and key members in Jamaica's tourist industry. The document (based on principles of sustainable development) aimed to increase persons employed in tourism from 75,000 to 130,000, increase the sector's contribution to GDP from 8 per cent to 15 per cent and increase visitor spending from US$1.4 billion to US$2.9 billion. According to the CTO, in 2003, Jamaica attracted an unprecedented 1.3 million stop-over tourists (almost 7 per cent more than 2002) and 1.3 million cruise tourists (31 per cent more than 2002) making it the fifth most popular tourist destination in the Caribbean (CTO 2004). 2004 is set to be another record-breaking year for Jamaican tourism further bolstering its position as the country's primary foreign exchange earner and sector for employment.

Sandals Resorts International has played a profound and historic role in shaping and contributing to the magnitude of Jamaica's tourism product. During the early 1980s, in response to widespread civil unrest in Jamaica, Sandals and its competitor Super Clubs invented and refined the concept of the all-inclusive hotel. These guarded enclave-like resorts were extremely successful because they provided visitors with both a sense of security and luxury (George 1987; Hudson 1987; Kingsbury 2004). Described as 'the most important innovation in the Caribbean hotel sector during the last decade' (Curtin and Poon 1988) the all-inclusive vacation is now emulated throughout the Caribbean and the world.

Sandals is a privately owned company headquartered in Montego Bay, Jamaica. Sandals was founded and is currently owned by its Jamaican-born Chairman, Gordon 'Butch' Stewart – one of the most influential leaders in Caribbean tourism and owner of numerous Jamaican companies such as Air Jamaica. Sandals consists of 11 beachside Sandals resorts on the islands of the Jamaica, Bahamas, Antigua and St. Lucia. In addition, Sandals comprises four Beaches 'family resorts' on the islands of Jamaica and the Turks and Caicos. In 2002, Sandals had a total of 2,292 rooms and suites in Jamaica, approximately 7,000 employees distributed across the Caribbean and an operating budget in excess of US$300 million. In the 1990s, Sandals provided Jamaica with 10 per cent of its hard currency (1996: 22) and regularly attracts between 450,000 and 500,000 people each year. With year-round occupancy rates of nearly 90 per cent and a repeat-guest factor of 40 per cent, Sandals is considered one of the most successful companies in the highly competitive Caribbean all-inclusive market. In addition, Sandals has been voted the 'world's leading all-inclusive company' by travel agencies worldwide for an unprecedented ninth year in a row between 1994 and 2002.

According to its corporate mission statement, Sandals aims to 'offer the ultimate Caribbean vacation experience by innovatively, reliably and consistently providing the safest and highest quality services and facilities to guests, while attaching a premium to our human resources and being amongst the most environmentally responsible and community friendly groups in the hospitality industry'. Described by Butch Stewart as a 'straight case of niche marketing', Sandals markets itself as an 'ultra-inclusive', whereby guests staying at one resort get full access and privileges to all the others. Sandals, a place where 'all you need is love, and everything else is included', however, only caters for heterosexual couples.

Sandals' annual marketing budget, approximately US$15 million (exceeding the Jamaican Tourist Board's budget), is managed by Unique Vacations, Inc. based in Miami, Florida. Sandals has extensive international marketing networks with offices in the United States, Cuba, Canada, Italy, Frankfurt, United Kingdom and Germany. Sandals entices guests with 'WeddingMoon' packages that enable them to get married and honeymoon on its properties. Sandals' online representations endeavour to define its unique position in the all-inclusive market, portray its resorts as white sand and azure sea fringed paradises and depict figures of happy arm-linked pampered couples.

Despite its status as a mass tourism firm, Sandals has demonstrated a commitment to investing in alternative tourism projects in Jamaica. In 1999, for example, Sandals established a partnership with a small, alternative tourism style corporation, Countrystyle, which specializes in 'community tourism' and is headquartered in Mandeville. Sandals and Countrystyle are developing a US$55 million all-inclusive resort near the town of Whitehouse, on Jamaica's south coast. This development is noteworthy for the fact that it involves corporations with distinctly different approaches to the industry and because it will be the first all-inclusive style facility on Jamaica's south coast, an area heretofore dotted only with small, independent, alternative tourism style developments. The most concrete example of Sandals' allegiances with the values of alternative tourism is the hotel Sandals Negril.

Described as 'Jamaica's ultimate beach resort', Sandals Negril was opened in 1988. The hotel is located in Hanover Parish on a 21-acre site with a quarter mile beachfront described by its brochure as a 'seventh heaven along seven miles of splendor'. Sandals Negril consists of 227 rooms and suites in eight categories. The property features a suite concierge centre, gift shop, meeting facilities and four specialty restaurants Bayside (International), The 4Cs (Light Spa Cuisine), The Sundowner (Jamaican) and Komonos (Oriental). With regular rates that range from US$4,235 to US$2,205 for a seven-night stay, Sandals Negril offers couples two swimming pools, two whirlpools, four bars, suite concierge service, scuba diving, water skiing, sailing, canoeing, snorkelling, saunas and steam rooms, tennis courts, a fitness centre and a conference room for business travellers. Sandals Negril employs approximately 376 non-unionized workers who are organized into departments composed of a 'team leader' who supervises 'team members'. Sandals Negril's departments include the Grounds, Dining Room, Bar, Watersports, Housekeeping, Security, Maintenance, Stewarding, Kitchen, Front Office, Accounting and Entertainment.

What is different about Sandals Negril? First, to a greater degree than any other Sandals property, Sandals Negril has an explicit economic development programme that provides financial and managerial support for a variety of local businesses and community-based organizations; it operates Whitehall Basic, a local elementary school, and it offers a range of scholarships for local students; it provides seeds and technical support for local farmers and it purchases their products at guaranteed market-value prices; and it incorporates local produce, meats and seafood into each of its menus. Culturally, Sandals Negril encourages its visitors to establish off-property contacts with local people; it hires local entertainers and guides for a variety of cultural and educational programmes for its visitors; it provides space for local craftspeople to display and sell their merchandise on the property; and, perhaps most interestingly, it integrates local community-based organizations into the corporation's decision-making. Environmentally, Sandals has implemented a multi-pronged programme that conforms to the Green Globe 21 Standard for energy consumption, water use, air pollution, waste disposal, etc. Much of the facility was retrofitted to comply with these standards. In addition, it has an extensive environmental educational programme for both employees and visitors. It is to explicating why and how Sandals Negril became certified by the Green Globe that I now turn.

Sandals Negril's 'Green Light All the Way'

Implementation

Sandals Negril's acquisition of the Green Globe certificate did not involve a sudden or dramatic transformation in terms of its environmental policies and practices. Although Sandals Negril underwent a renovation project in 1996 that enabled it to become certified to the Green Globe 21 Standard at the World Travel Mart in 1998, the hotel already had a history of implementing environmental management, social and cultural development activities since it was opened in 1988. The effect of the Green Globe programme required that Sandals Negril formalize and in some cases intensify its operations.

In May 1998, Sandals Negril began developing a property-wide EMS to 'improve the organization, execution and evaluation of its efforts to minimize the impact of our operations on both the physical and social environment and, where possible, seeking to improve the environmental conditions in the surrounding area' (Sandals 2001: n.p.). Sandals Negril hired the London-based 'PA Consulting Group' (PA), a leading management, systems and technology consulting firm to provide environmental management services leading to Green Globe certification. PA began with a detailed five-day audit of the property that identified over 125 specific recommendations that have yielded annual savings of over $150,000. The result was the formalization of the hotel's EMS and a 'Sandals Negril Beach Resort and Spa Environmental Policy' document.

In addition to both established and innovative environmental practices (e.g. shredding waste office paper for donation to a nearby morgue to pad coffins) that distinguish Sandals Negril from other Sandals resorts, Sandals Negril is the most active hotel that promotes the social, cultural and economic welfare of its local communities. Several managerial staff of Sandals Negril are actively involved on the committees of local organizations, such as the Negril Chamber of Commerce, Jamaica Hotel and Tourism Association (JHTA), Negril Environmental Protection Trust, Negril Coral Reef Protection Society, Negril Resort Board, Whitehall Basic School, Negril Craft Vendors Association and Rutland Point Craft Vendors Association. According to Burchell Henry, Sandals Negril's Public Relations Manager:

> the whole community knows about Sandals Negril's efforts in the community. We're heavily involved in the greening of Negril and several managers, myself included, sit on all the boards of the various environmental agencies in the area so we are on top of what is happening in that regards we know the projects coming up, we share ideas, we share thoughts, we share some of our experiences, it's a green light all the way. To use that pun it's a green light all the way.

Henry emphasized that Sandals Negril had always embodied and continues to pursue a 'green light' of sustainability. Sandals Negril, through its role in the JHTA Negril Chapter, Environmental Committee, has assisted with the organization of other hotels' sustainability programmes in Negril such as encouraging suppliers to re-collect reusable containers. Although the WTTC established the Green Globe Standard programme as early as 1994, I asked Henry why Sandals Negril became certified in 1998. Henry pointed out that:

> I think it happened by accident you know. In going to a lot of these tourism forums, these sales conventions, and tradeshows, you would pick up that the traveling public would be asking about that. And as innovative in the industry, we said, 'yes! This is another way where we have to go'. This is another thing that we have to implement into our whole programme here, and the corporate office just took the decision.

Richard May, Sandals Group Environmental Manager, revealed that Mr Wayne Cummings was the resident manager at Sandals Negril who, in 1997, attended the Green Globe Standard conference in Port Antonio and 'returned back to his hotel and was gung ho! about it. He thought it would work and he decided along with his general manager and his management team that they wanted to take first shot at it'. According to May, one of the main reasons Sandals Negril was in the position to become the first all-inclusive hotel in the world to be Green Globe certified was because the WTTC and Green Globe International selected Jamaica as one of the pilot destinations to launch the Green Globe programme. This initiative was funded by the United States Agency for International Development and the Environmental Audits for Sustainable Tourism and implemented by the Jamaica Hotel and Tourist Association.

Reasons

May described how Sandals Negril already had a number of environmental programmes and practices established prior to certification because the hotel was located in the Negril Environment Protected Area (declared a natural reserve by the Government of Jamaica) and the Negril Preservation Area. Consisting of several marine parks and environmental sanctuaries, May argued that Negril was 'always considered one of the greener areas of Jamaica' and 'had at the time the best non-governmental operating environmental organization'. May revealed that Butch Stewart decided it was in Sandals' interest to eventually certify all of its hotels because 'there were already quite a lot of practices regarding efficiency in place' throughout all its properties.

A significant factor behind Sandals' decision to pursue certification was the financial incentives of maximizing cost efficiency and increasing control over resort operations. Between 2000 and 2002, Sandals had implemented a central purchasing system that enabled the firm to purchase 'environmentally friendly' products for its entire hotel chain. Anthony Morris, Sandals Negril's Purchasing Manager, noted that 'savings were considerable, and that 80 to 90 per cent of Sandals' products were Jamaican'. Sandals makes it policy to refuse to import anything that is produced or grown in Jamaica, as long as these local products meet the Sandals standards and specifications.

The marketing potential for an environmentally friendly resort was another important reason. Leo Lambert, Director for Corporate and Community Communications, noted that Sandals' customers were becoming increasingly concerned with environmental issues: 'the fact of the matter is that next to the gay lobby, the environmental lobby is one of the most powerful in the world'. Lambert also stated that Sandals was often under considerable pressure from European tour groups to have an environmental programme or face the possibility of not being marketed. For Lambert, Sandals had to respond to these 'global realities … in terms of how we implemented the programme and how fast we activated it'. Another significant 'reality' Sandals faced were the challenges associated with financial investment and the difficulties of training its employees in the practices of sustainability.

Challenges

While Sandals Negril had numerous environmental programmes in place, the initial challenge of adopting an EMS was a financial one. According to Henry, 'the only large transformation was money' spent on purchasing new products such as biodegradable chemicals and low-wattage light bulbs. Asked how Sandals was able to maintain its economic competitiveness in the tourism industry, Sandals managers (Henry and Lambert) concurred that it was because Sandals' 'business was doing well', and Sandals was 'investing more in product upgrading than perhaps any of our competitors', 'equipped with the most powerful marketing machine that you will find in an organization in these parts', 'continuously improving', 'maintaining competitive prices' and 'getting repeat visitors back'. Lambert proudly asserted that Sandals':

service is impeccable, the surroundings are clean … the security is smiling at guests – all the things that they would need when they travel away: great service, smiles, attention to details … anticipate their needs and they'll keep coming back so your occupancies will be at a high.

Asked how Sandals determined the amount of resources that would be allocated to local communities, Lambert explained that such decisions were primarily in the hands of resort managers. Sandals, he told me, does not have a formal policy that determines how much money should be allocated to community outreach programmes. While Sandals is a privately owned company that relies on making a profit, Sandals' re-distributions of its surpluses into communities (e.g., money, materials, labour power) is to some extent complicit with non-capitalist or de-centred capitalist processes of accumulation (see Gibson-Graham 1996). According to Henry, one such process involves how:

barter arrangements come into play to offset what financially we may not be able to do. But like any company, you know, we have to do well, we have to make a profit but we have great sponsoring partners that admire our work that do similar things and wouldn't mind making contributions. There are always ways and means. I mean we are the innovators, we are the creators, and we will always find ways to make sure that our community programmes never fall by the wayside and we help as much as we can. Clearly, we can't do everything but we go as far as possible. If it's giving one chicken to a church barbecue then we will do it … We never normally have much of a problem. We hardly give cash; even when we give cash we are very careful about what is given out. Over the years we have been very comfortable with our efforts, really, we have been.

Interviews revealed that Sandals had very few organizational links or interactions with the Jamaican government and other state-led entities. Given Butch Stewart's pivotal role in rescuing the Jamaican dollar from collapse during the early 1990s (see 1996: 22), the scope of Sandals' independence from the state is exemplified by articles in Jamaica's national newspapers where Stewart advises and often criticizes the government's tourism policies. According to Lambert, Sandals' independence from entities such as the state not only permits innovation but also facilitates the extent to which Sandals could invest in the local communities. Lambert stated that:

one of the good things about Sandals is that it doesn't have a lot of bureaucracy … Mr Stewart who is a Jamaican, understands our culture and knows the 'ins and outs' of his countrymen. Now, what he tries to do, or what his policy is towards community outreaches, is to do as much as you can, whenever you can. If a product comes up, if a need is there, and we can assist, we will assist. That's how we operate. So the whole point is that we never see it in terms of how much we spend of our budget, we always see it in terms of what we can do.

Despite an ostensible lack of bureaucracy and an established history of pursuing environmentally sound practices, Lambert suggested that Green Globe certification still posed major challenges in terms of the 'changing habits' established over nearly a decade. 'From a corporate perspective', Lambert continued, 'the response to such a radical departure from old habits has been tremendous'. Henry noted that Sandals Negril's Green Globe certification posed major difficulties for management to familiarize its employees with standardized environmentally friendly practices and procedures. Henry stated that this meant 'employees being disciplined, being mature enough to ensure that the consistency is there to ensure that there was no breakup'. For May, the greatest difficulty that Sandals had to overcome was not an initial financial investment, but the 'whole issue of staff awareness, by far, that was at least 75 per cent of the implementation process'. May noted that:

> when you come to a point of looking at the environment and telling them [staff] this is for your own good, you can't just say we are going to do this for the environment you have to explain to them how what we are doing affects the environment ... you have to put it on a level so that that person can understand it.

Practices associated with employee training and labour management presented the main challenges for Sandals Negril's attainment of the Green Globe certification. Sandals Negril was thus able to achieve Green Globe status not only because of its pre-existing environmental practices and policies but also the extent to which it had already invested in and established employee training and labour management programmes.

Human Resources and Environmental Awareness

Sandals overcame the challenge of familiarizing its employees with environmental sustainability through the Sandals Training and Development Institute (STDI) which is charged with training employees. Sandals Resorts International has one of the most comprehensive human resource development programmes of any corporate entity in the Caribbean. Between 1997 and 2002, the company invested US$25 million in employee training programmes. Organized by the STDI, the company has forged partnerships with some thirty local and international training institutions. Over five hundred Sandals employees are enrolled in diploma, bachelors, masters and doctoral programmes. All of its employees are required to complete a minimum of 120 hours of training related to their particular job function every year. Under the Sandals Quality Advantage Programme, supervisors and managers are required to allocate 15 minutes of each working day to discussing one of the Sandals customer service basics with their staff.

According to the Sandals/Beaches Team Members Handbook, the goal of STDI is to ensure that its 'current and future workforce has skills, knowledge and attitudes to provide internationally competitive service. Systems (e.g. standards, training and certification) are in place to support job creation, career development and lifelong learning' (Sandals, n.d.: 3). Sandals states that it invests in human resources because the 'reasons are simple: a thoroughly professional Sandals workforce will ensure quality service delivery and therefore satisfied guests at our hotels. This in turn will mean a healthier Sandals' (ibid.: 24). The corporate rationale for a well-managed workforce, then, coincides with its reasons for pursuing environmental sustainability practices.

In addition, Sandals Negril was the hotel in which various environmental programmes and practices could be tested and refined so that they could be effectively incorporated into Sandals' other hotels. These programmes include an environmental awareness programme, staff orientations, an annual 'Environment Day', environmental lectures with local NGOs, nature attractions, area environmental programmes, water conservation and management, acceptable practices in the Negril Environmental Protection Area and an environmental reference centre (e.g., copies of reports, magazines and newsletters on environmental management in hotels). Sandals Negril also encourages members of its 'Green Team' (see below) to attend short courses in environmental management offered by the University of the West Indies, JHTA, Caribbean Action for Sustainable Tourism and others.

A key strategy in which Sandals Negril familiarized and trained its employees in sustainable practices prior to the acquisition of the Green Globe certificate was through the creation of Sandals Negril Green Team. Established in 1997, by Richard May, the Green Team produced a 16-page booklet entitled 'Sandals Negril Beach Resort and Spa, Guide to Green Thinking: The Employee Handbook' and was responsible for coordinating stronger links with local environmental organizations and promoting environmental practices and awareness for employees, guests and local residents. The Green Team enabled Sandals Negril to foster a corporate culture whereby employees are encouraged to participate in the hotel's EMS through incentive schemes. Throughout its entire hotel chain, Sandals employees are invited to take part in environmental programmes and recognition is given to every department that meets or exceeds its annual EMS targets. Funding is assigned to special projects suggested by the winning department. Sandals awards suggestions or ideas that a staff member gives to his or her department representative on the Green Team that is eventually adopted as a 'best environmental management practice'. Sandals Negril allocates approximately US$200,000 as part of its 'Staff Awards'. These awards include the 'most environmentally aware' employee, Green Team member and department for each quarter and year. Awards are received during Sandals Negril's monthly 'staff birthday meetings' where presentations and prizes such as baskets of groceries are also given to the employee 'who is best able to answer the questions asked at the party about the environmental management system at Sandals Negril' (Sandals 2001: n.p.). The Green Globe's requirement that hotels not only invest in environmental sustainability but also in social and cultural development programmes, echoes the way in which the Green Globe certification required that Sandals Negril's management not only invest in environmental policies but also strategies (e.g., staff award and recognition schemes) that bolstered the sustainability of its own corporate culture.

Conclusions

This chapter illustrated how and why Sandals Negril became the first all-inclusive hotel in the world to obtain the Green Globe certificate. Sandals Negril is at the forefront of 'mass ecotourism', a significant but under-researched transformation in Caribbean and international tourism. Caribbean tourism researchers, governments, tourism agencies and industry representatives have argued that mass ecotourism is crucial for the future development of the tourism industry and therefore the livelihoods of millions of people in the region.

Sandals, one the most important tourism companies in the Caribbean, is actively pursuing mass ecotourism and sustainability via Green Globe certification. Sandals Negril was able to gain the award because of Sandals' financial strength, cooperation with an international consultancy firm, ties with local environmental agencies in the Negril area and an established labour management programme. The main reasons Sandals pursued certification was because of its prior environmental practices, cost efficiency, growing customer concerns about environmental issues and European travel agencies' demands for environmental accountability. The challenges for certifying Sandals Negril to the Green Globe scheme initially concerned financial investment and then later the familiarization of its workers with practices of sustainability.

This chapter endeavours to initiate a much-needed discussion about corporate environmental sustainability in the Caribbean for tourist and non-tourist companies. Much of the above analysis, however, examined interviews with upper level management. Elsewhere, I have focused on the views of hotel workers, local residents and tourists on Sandals Negril's Green Globe certification (Kingsbury 2003). Here, I have explicated more fully the ways in which Sandals managers attempted to convince, train and educate its employees about the virtues of 'green' and 'environmentally friendly' policies. I argued that the hotel's labour practices and representations of sustainability formed what the psychoanalyst Jacques Lacan calls a 'university discourse' which emphasizes social bonds underpinned by enjoyment, education, indoctrination and learning (see also Kingsbury and Brunn 2004).

Now, most discussions on corporate environmental sustainability in tourism have argued that transformations such as Sandals Negril's are fully compliant with the extension and deepening of the capitalist expansion in the international tourism industry (Mowforth and Munt 2003). These critical investigations into the status of corporate sustainability in the global south advocate research that inquires into who decides what sustainability means for whom (Mowforth and Munt 2003). Researchers normally answer such questions by assuming that corporate sustainability should be measured in terms of the extent to which it is inauthentic. As a result, the value of these questions, which assert the class-based, discursive and contested dimensions of sustainability, is often eclipsed by a stubborn adherence to conceptualizing the corporation as invariably and singularly governed by unsustainable capitalist profit motives.

While the political economic conflicts and contradictions of tourism in the global south are irrefutable, these often 'capitalocentric' (Gibson-Graham 2002) analyses not only risk simplifying issues of class, power, exploitation, labour practices, management and consumption that are central to corporate activities, they also risk ignoring the complexities of the political economic *forms* of tourism. Political economic understandings of tourism in the global south have been constrained by a routine reduction of tourism's 'innocent fun' (its manifest elements) to its 'dirty failures and dark secrets' (the latent oppressive capitalist commodification, sickly aestheticization of poverty etc.) (Kingsbury 2005). Future research, then, can alert researchers about the full significance of the call to study the 'coalface of tourism: the relationship between tourists and those they are visiting' (Mowforth and Munt 2003: 70) by asserting how enjoyment is a political factor in tourism and tourism corporations like Sandals (see Kingsbury and Klak 2005). In short, we need to understand why and how tourism's enjoyed impacts, fascinations and expressions are not only relevant for tourists, but also for workers and managers.

Acknowledgements

I would like to acknowledge the support of Dr John Paul Jones III, Sandals Resorts International, the Department of Geography at the University of Kentucky and the Department of Geography at Miami University. The research reported in this paper was primarily funded by the National Science Foundation (Award No. 0202061).

References

de Albuquerque, K., and McElroy, J.L. (1999), 'Tourism and Crime in the Caribbean', *Annals of Tourism Research*, 26 (4), pp. 968–84.

Ayala, H. (1996a), Resort Ecotourism: A Paradigm for the 21st Century', *The Cornell Hotel and Restaurant Administration Quarterly*, 37 (5), pp. 46–53.

Ayala, H. (1996b), 'Resort Ecotourism: A Master Plan for Experience Management/A Paradigm for the 21st Century', *The Cornell Hotel and Restaurant Administration Quarterly*, 37 (5), pp. 54–61.

Ayala, H. (1997), 'Resort Ecotourism: A Catalyst for National and Regional Partnerships', *The Cornell Hotel and Restaurant Administration Quarterly*, 38 (4), pp. 34–45.

Butler, R.W. (1990), 'Alternative Tourism: Pious Hope or Trojan Horse?', *Journal of Travel Research*, 28 (3), pp. 40–45.

Caribbean Tourism Organization (2004), '*Caribbean Tourism Statistical Report (2003–2004 Edition)*, St Michael, Barbados: Caribbean Tourism Organization.

Cohen, E. (1978), 'The Impact of Tourism on the Physical Environment', *Annals of Tourism Research* , 5 (2), pp. 215–37.

Conway, D. (2002), 'Tourism, Agriculture, and the Sustainability of Terrestial Ecosystems in Small Islands', in Y. Apostolopoulos and D.J. Gayle (eds), *Island Tourism and Sustainable Development: Caribbean, Pacific and Mediterranean Examples*, Westport: Praeger, pp. 113–29.

Conway, D. (2004), 'Tourism, the Environment and Local Agriculture', in D.T. Duval (ed.), *Tourism in the Caribbean: Trends, Development, Prospects*, New York: Routledge, pp. 187–204.

Curtin, V. and Poon, A. (1988), *Tourist Accommodation in the Caribbean*, Barbados: Caribbean Tourism Research and Development Centre.

Dunphy, D., Griffiths, A. and Benn, S. (2003), *Organizational Change for Corporate Sustainability: Understanding Organizational Change*, New York: Routledge.

Duval, D.T. (ed.) (2004a), *Tourism in the Caribbean: Trends, Development, Prospects*, New York: Routledge.

Duval, D.T. (2004b), 'Trends and Circumstances in Caribbean Tourism', in D.T. Duval (ed.), *Tourism in the Caribbean: Trends, Development, Prospects*, New York: Routledge, pp. 3–22.

Duval, D.T. and Wilkinson, P.F. (2004), 'Tourism Development in the Caribbean: Meaning and Influences', in D.T. Duval (ed.), *Tourism in the Caribbean: Trends, Development, Prospects*, New York: Routledge, pp. 59–80.

Fennell, D. (1999), *Ecotourism: An Introduction*, New York: Routledge.

Freitag, T.G. (1994), 'Enclave Tourism Development: For Whom the Benefits Roll?', *Annals of Tourism Research*, 21 (3), pp. 538–54.

George, V. (1987), 'Tourism on Jamaica's North Coast: A Geographer's View', in S. Britton and W.C. Clarke (eds), *Ambiguous Alternative: Tourism in Small Developing Countries*, Suva, Fiji: University of the South Pacific, pp. 61–77.

Gibson-Graham, J.K. (1996), *The End of Capitalism (As We Knew It): A Feminist Critique of Political Economy*, New York: Blackwell.

Gibson-Graham, J.K. (2002), 'Beyond Global vs. Local: Economic Politics Outside the Binary Frame', in A. Herod and M. Wright (eds), *Geographies of Power: Placing Scale*, New York: Blackwell, pp. 25–60.

Gmelch, G. (2003), *Behind the Smile: The Working Lives of Caribbean Tourism*, Bloomington: Indiana University Press.

Harrison, D. (2001), *Tourism and the Less Developed World: Issues and Case Studies*, Wallingford, UK: CABI Publishing.

Haywood, K.M. and Jayawardena, C. (2004), 'Tourism Business in the Caribbean: Operating Realities', in D.T. Duval (ed.), *Tourism in the Caribbean: Trends, Development, Prospects*, New York: Routledge, pp. 218–34.

Holder, J.S. (1988), 'Pattern and Impact of Tourism on the Environment of the Caribbean', *Tourism Management*, 9 (2), pp. 119–27.

Hudson, B. (1987), 'Tourism and Landscape in Jamaica and Grenada', in S. Britton and W.C. Clarke (eds), *Ambiguous Alternative: Tourism in Small Developing Countries*, Suva, Fiji: University of the South Pacific, pp. 46–60.

Kingsbury, P. (2003), 'Transforming Corporate Mass Tourism: Sandals Resorts International in Jamaica and the Politics of Enjoyment', PhD thesis, University of Kentucky.

Kingsbury, P. (2005), 'Jamaican Tourism and the Politics of Enjoyment', *Geoforum*, 36 (1), pp. 113–32.

Kingsbury, P. and Brunn, S.D. (2004), 'Freud, Tourism, and Terror: Traversing the Fantasies of Post-september 11 Travel Magazines', in M.C. Hall, D.J. Timothy and D.T. Duval (eds), *Safety and Security in Tourism: Relationships, Management, and Marketing*, New York: Haworth Press, pp. 39–61.

Kingsbury, P. and Klak, T. (2005), 'Ridims of the Streets, Beaches, and Bureaucracies: Situating Fieldwork in the Caribbean', *The Southeastern Georgrapher*, 45 (2), pp. 251–73.

Milne, S. and Ewing, G. (2004), 'Community Participation in Caribbean Tourism: Problems and Prospects', in D.T. Duval (ed.), *Tourism in the Caribbean: Trends, Development, Prospects*, New York: Routledge, pp. 203–17.

Momsen, J.H. (2004), 'Post-colonial Markets: New Geographical Spaces for Tourism', in D.T. Duval (ed.), *Tourism in the Caribbean: Trends, Development, Prospects*, New York: Routledge, pp. 273–86.

Mowforth, M. and Munt, I. (2003), *Tourism and Sustainability: New Tourism in the Third World*, New York: Routledge.

Mullings, B. (1999), 'Globalization, Flexible Tourism and the International Sex Trade in Jamaica', in K. Kempadoo (ed.), *Sun, Sex and Gold: Tourism and Sex Work in the Caribbean.* Lanham, MD: Rowman and Littlefield, pp. 55–80.

Mullings, B. (2000), 'Fantasy Tours: Exploring the Global Consumption of Caribbean Sex Tourisms', in M. Gottdiener (ed.), *New Forms of Consumption: Consumers, Culture, and Commodification*, Lanham, MD: Rowman and Littlefield, pp. 227–50.

Murphy, P. (1998), 'Tourism and Sustainable Development', in W. Theobold (ed.), *Global Tourism: The Next Decade*, Oxford: Butterworth-Heinemann, pp. 173–90.

Pantojas-García, E. and Klak, T. (2004), 'Globalization and Economic Vulnerability: The Caribbean and the "Post-9/11 Shift"', in I.L. Griffith (ed.), *Caribbean Security in the Age of Terror: Challenge and Change*, Kingston, Jamaica: Ian Randle Press, pp. 176–98.

Pattullo, P. (1996), *Last Resorts: The Cost of Tourism in the Caribbean*, New York: Monthly Review Press.

Pearce, D.G. and Butler, R.W. (eds) (1999), *Contemporary Issues in Tourism Development*, New York: Routledge.

Place, S. (1995), 'Ecotourism for Sustainable Development: Oxymoron or Plausible Strategy?', *GeoJournal*, 35 (2), pp. 161–73.

Pugh, J. (2001), 'Local Agenda 21 and the Third World', in V. Desai and R.B. Potter (eds), *The Arnold Companion to Development Studies*, London: Arnold, pp. 289–93.

Sandals Resorts International (2001), *Corporate Environmental Program.*

Sandals Resorts International (n.d.), *Sandals/Beaches Team Members Handbook.*

Sharma, S. and Starick, S. (eds) (2003), *Research in Corporate Sustainability: The Evolving Theory and Practice of Organizations in the Natural Environment*, Northampton, MA: Edward Elgar.

Sheller, M. (2003), *Consuming the Caribbean: From Arawaks to Zombies*, New York: Routledge.

Swarbrooke, J. (1999), *Sustainable Tourism Management*, New York: CABI Publishing.

Tewarie, B. (2002), 'The Development of a Sustainable Tourism Sector in the Caribbean', in Y. Apostolopoulos and D.J. Gayle (eds), *Island Tourism and Sustainable Development: Caribbean, Pacific and Mediterranean Examples*, Westport: Praeger, pp. 35–47.

Turner, L. and Ash, J. (1975), *The Golden Hordes: International Tourism and Pleasure Periphery*, London: Constable.

Weaver, D.B. (1993), 'Ecotourism in the Small Island Caribbean', *Geojournal*, 31 (4), pp. 457–65.

Weaver, D.B. (1998), *Ecotourism in the Less Developed World*, New York: CABI Publishing.

Weaver, D.B. (2001a), 'Ecotourism as Mass Tourism? Contradiction or Reality', *Cornell Restaurant and Hotel Administration Quarterly*, 42 (2), pp. 104–12.

Weaver, D.B. (2001b), 'Mass Tourism and Alternative Tourism in the Caribbean', in D. Harrison (ed.), *Tourism and the Less Developed World: Issues and Case Studies*, New York: CABI Publishing, pp. 161–74.

Weaver, D.B. and Lawton, L. (2002), *Tourism Management*, 2nd edn, Milton, Australia: John Wiley and Sons.

Weiler B. and Hall, C.M. (eds) (1992), *Special Interest Tourism*, London: Belhaven Press.

Wilkinson, P. (1997), *Tourism Policy and Planning: Case Studies from the Commonwealth of the Caribbean*, New York: Cognizant Communication Corporation.

World Tourism Organization (2004), *WTO World Tourism Barometer*, Vol. 2, No. 2, January 2004, Madrid, Spain: World Tourism Organization. Available from <http://www.world-tourism.org/market_research/facts/barometer/WTOBarom04_1_en.pdf> [accessed 9 May 2004].

Chapter 9

Conservation and Recreation Planning on the Caribbean Coast: Cahuita, Costa Rica

Galen Martin

Among the plethora of models and theories addressing the relationships between biodiversity conservation and economic development, Biot et al. (1995) recognize three dominant conservation paradigms: 1) the classic approach with strict separation of humans and nature; 2) the populist approach stressing the virtues and wisdom of local and community-based management; and 3) the neo-liberal approach advocating economic solutions and proper valuation of natural resources. All three approaches have been advocated by various stakeholders in Costa Rica at the national scale and in Cahuita at the local level. While many organizational and project policies are a combination of such approaches, these three categories serve as a useful point of departure for a discussion of the various interest groups involved in the development of Cahuita and the management of Cahuita National Park (CNP). The park was established under the assumptions of the first paradigm, and continues to draw support as conservation space protecting biodiversity. At the same time, CNP is rationalized at the national and international level under paradigm 3 whereby the Cahuita area is commodified as ecotourism space generating income for local development, the national economy and the protection of nature. Finally, residents of the area, increasingly aware of the openings implied by the participatory conservation rhetoric of international organizations and their own government, struggle to interject their often-disparate voices through collective and individual actions. They remind all parties that the Cahuita area was, and continues to be, community space supporting the livelihood activities of local residents. This history of the park reflects the changing dominance of the different planning paradigms.

Conservation, Community and Conflict in Cahuita

In 1994, the Kelly Creek (Río Suarez) entrance to Cahuita National Park (CNP) (Figure 9.1) was the site of a community-wide protest, an action that literally drove park officials from the north side of the peninsula. In September of that year, the newly elected PLN (Partido Liberación Nacional) administration of José María Figueres raised all national park entry fees for foreigners from 200 to 2,400 *colones* (the exchange rate was 160 *colones*: US$1) in an effort to make the parks self-supporting and pay off the US$15 million owed to former owners of park land. Cognizant that most tourists came to Cahuita to enjoy the white sand beach and would be driven

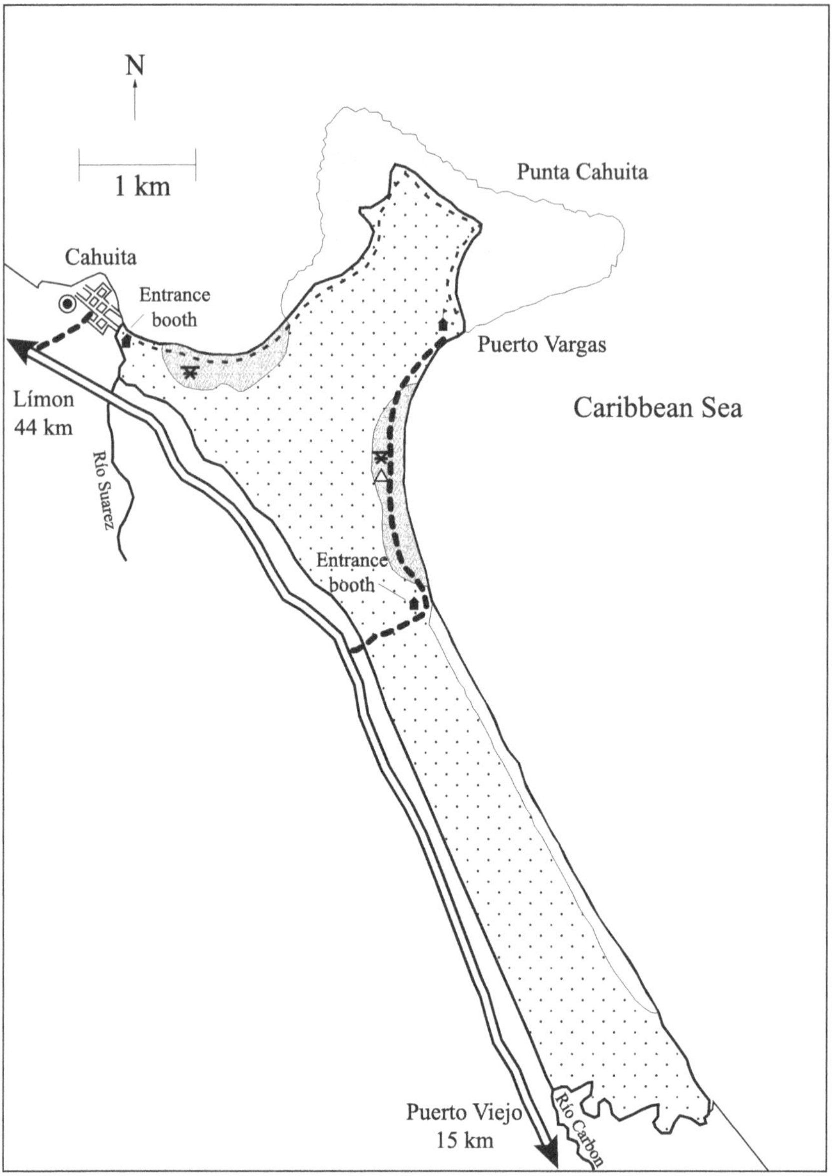

Figure 9.1 Cahuita National Park

Source: Franke 1993.

away by excessive fees, Cahuitans occupied the guard station and granted free entry to visitors. Their action was also fueled by the perception that park fees were channeled directly to San José and did nothing for Cahuita or the CNP. Certainly the fees had not been used to compensate Cahuitans for the loss of their land, many of whom had been dispossessed of their holdings with the establishment of CNP two decades earlier. The Minister of Natural Resources, principal promoter of the rate hike, responded to the protest by sending in a squadron of armed police to reclaim the entrance.[1] At the same time, a group of Cahuita businesses filed a motion with the Constitutional Chamber of the Supreme Court (Sala IV) challenging the right of any agency to collect fees for public access areas as defined by the 1977 Maritime Zone Law (Ley sobre la Zona Marítimo Terrestre y su Reglamento).[2] Although the Court did not rule in favour of the businesses, the protest and the legal action discouraged park officials from returning to the Kelley Creek entrance station. The citizens of Cahuita effectively, though still not legally, regained control of Playa Blanca, the primary recreation area of the CNP.

For the first two years, management consisted of a few clean-up days and a general strategy of non-intervention. Trails began to deteriorate, interpretive signs disappeared and security issues escalated. The partially-burned guard station at Kelley Creek stood as a reminder of both community action and inaction. Motivated in part by growing security concerns, several guides and community leaders opened a dialogue with the new Park Director, an Afro-Caribbean woman from the nearby town of Puerto Limón, transferred to CNP in early 1995 to replace the confrontational Hispanic director who had been in charge in September of 1994. Since 1996, representatives from two community organizations – the Chamber of Tourism (La Cámara de Turismo) and the Community Development Association (La Asociación de Desarrollo) – have worked with park officials to develop a management strategy that involves the community but does not violate the intents and purposes of the park.

Today, Playa Blanca visitors pay a donation to support the local guides and guards who patrol this section of the park. Thus this small park is effectively bifurcated into two management zones (one on the edge of Cahuita, one on the other side of Punta Cahuita). These reflect some, but by no means all, of the diverse vested interests in the area. This experimental management arrangement, unique in Costa Rica, emerged after three decades of miscommunication, distrust, cynicism and long periods of silence between the community and government conservation officials. A review of the fluctuating planning and management strategies for CNP over the past 30 years demonstrates missed opportunities for gaining local support for the park, ongoing tension between recreation (tourism) and conservation objectives, and the possibility of creative compromises.

Conservation and Community Challenges

The area that is now Cahuita National Park (CNP) was established as a National Monument by Executive Decree No. 1236-A in 1970. According to the IUCN categories of protected areas at the time, the purpose of a Category III Natural Monument was 'to protect and preserve nationally significant natural features because of their special interest or unique characteristics' (McNeely and Miller 1984). In 1978, the area was granted national park status (Executive Decree No. 8489-A), managed in order 'to protect natural and scenic areas of national or international significance for scientific, educational, and recreational use'. The main feature of this small marine park is 600 ha. of fringing coral reef, the most extensive formation in the country. The park also includes 1,068 ha. of adjoining land and an additional 22,400 ha. of marine area. By designating this area for conservation, officials hoped to restore marine life of economic importance, maintain the biotic diversity of the reef, and restore the adjoining tropical humid forest (Kutay 1991; Boza, conversation, February 1998; Wallace 1992). CNP was valued as a vital component of a comprehensive strategy to conserve representative samples of Costa Rica's great range of biological diversity (Boza and Cevo 1998). The park can be divided into four major ecological zones: alluvial coastal plain, lowland swamp forest, beach and lagoon, and coral reef.

As a conservation area, CNP faces a number of challenges:

1. human/nature issues are amplified because of the park's proximity to Cahuita village and its history as a site of extensive human economic activity;
2. failure on the part of the government to compensate Cahuitans for lost land in a timely manner has served as a hindrance to community support for the park and relations with park administrators;
3. while CNP generates significant revenue from entry fees as one of Costa Rica's more popular parks, it has been severely understaffed and underfunded. In addition, park neighbors complain that money flows out to government accounts in San José but little is returned to the park or the community;
4. when the park was established, there were no working models for the creation and management of marine parks. Though the IUCN and a plethora of international organizations emphasize the need for coral reef conservation throughout the world, this global effort has had little direct effect on CNP to date;
5. CNP's small size, elongated shape and isolation from other protected areas minimize its effectiveness as a conservation area;[3]
6. regional activities, most notably banana production and deforestation, had negatively affected the condition of the reef before the establishment of CNP and continue to threaten its vitality;
7. the park was established in large part to protect the coral reef. However, there is little baseline data and few ongoing studies to assess the actual condition of the reef over time. The same is true for turtles and terrestrial flora and fauna;
8. CNP was established as a recreation area but managed as a biological reserve. While these two goals may be compatible (Budowski 1977; Boza 1993) taken together they can lead to miscommunication and inconsistencies in management.

In addition to the park's unique compilation of biological diversity, the area's value as a potential centre of recreation and tourism activities was also instrumental in its establishment. One of the documents that served as a basis for the park's beginnings (Lemieux 1969), while outlining the biological and landscape features of the area, was essentially an assessment of tourism and recreation potential. Lemieux recognized the need for a comprehensive conservation strategy to preserve the features that attract visitors and suggested two alternative plans (discussed below). He also concluded that:

> tourism does not present any prejudicial utilization conflict with the other regional economic activities but does, in fact, constitute a complement, instead of an alternative, in the development of the region (Lemieux 1969: 188).

The concern was not so much the potential conflict between conservation and tourism but between tourism and existing livelihood activities. This was also one of the leading concerns of the Cahuita community members when they first engaged in conversation with national officials (Wallace 1992; Palmer 1993). However, the central tension that quickly emerged with the establishment of the park involved the relationship between conservation management and livelihood. At the time, the area's population consisted primarily of English-speaking Black Afro-Caribbean people of West Indian descent scattered in small subsistence agricultural settlements along the coast. With one Chinese-owned hotel and no continuous road connecting the southern coast to the regional centre of Limón, the village of Cahuita maintained only tenuous economic, political and cultural ties to the rest of the nation (Wallace 1992; Palmer 1993; Purcell 1993). The Monument's implications for local residents were not immediately clear: in sporadic public meetings from 1970 to 1977, the farmers and fishermen heard many differing versions of the regulations that applied to the area (Stone 1992; Palmer 1993; Wallace 1992; field interviews 1998). Management problems were exacerbated by confusion on the part of Costa Rican officials regarding 'natural' and agricultural – assumed to be cleared – landscapes (Stone 1992; Wallace 1992). Cahuitans were practicing what would later be called agro-forestry, planting coconut walks on the beaches and cacao in the forest. The most convincing argument on the part of the government was that a park was the only alternative to an invasion by tourism interests (Cahn 1984; Wallace 1993).

Ironically, by the late 1970s, tourism proved to be one of the few viable economic options for Cahuita residents after the devastating fungus known as moniliales pod rot (*Monilia roreri*) destroyed 95 per cent of cocoa production.[4] As they had done for almost a century, local residents supplemented diets and reduced incomes, by harvesting and hunting now protected flora and fauna within park boundaries (monkey, spiny lobster, iguana and turtles and turtle eggs) (Kutay 1991; Stone 1992). Thus, from the outset, park officials came to view local residents as antithetical to sound park management. In turn, local residents viewed the conservation area as a threat to traditional livelihood activities.

Despite these contentious beginnings, tourism development eventually evolved as a means for creating a symbiotic relationship between transformed livelihood activities and a fluctuating, often ill-defined conservation agenda. Over the past three decades, the Cahuita community has come to appreciate, support, and value the park. Nevertheless, significant tensions between resource exploitation, tourism development and biodiversity conservation persist. The practice of conservation in and around the park has been influenced more by politics and economic concerns than by a science-based agenda.

All of Costa Rica's national parks have been subject to a number of comprehensive management strategies that, due to changing administrations, top-down implementation, and lack of resources, have often had little impact on the day-to-day care of individual park units. Despite the many sophisticated and cutting edge proposals that have been articulated at the international and national levels promoting integrative strategies and participatory models, most Costa Rican parks, including CNP, have been managed according to the classic model that attempts to physically separate humans and nature. A model of environmental management that effectively disenfranchises the local people from land and aquatic resources that they once exploited has never proven effective or realistic for reasons outlined below. Cahuita National Park is an important case study for contextualizing debates about acceptable levels and types of human activity within conservation areas.

For each of the past three decades, we can examine different strategies and management plans for Cahuita National Park: Lemieux for initial rationale and groundwork, community-government negotiations and contestations in the 1970s, Kutay in the 1980s and most recently, the evolving co-management arrangement with its roots in the 1990s. The plans, more often implicate than explicate, reflect the character and potential of the landscape under study and serve as a window into trends and concerns of both the local community and of conservation planners.

Initial Proposals for a Protected Area

The Lemieux (1969) study and proposal provides baseline information for what became CNP and the surrounding south Caribbean (Atlantic) region. At the park's inception, the landscape had already witnessed extensive alteration by local residents and regional economic undertakings, most notably banana production. The alluvial plains had been converted to agro-forestry production of cacao, laurel, and cultivated root crops. Beach area vegetation was dominated by coconut palm, the source of early management conflicts (Wallace 1992; Palmer 1993). A human occupation map constructed by Lemieux indicates only a small portion of the area designated as 'natural forest'. Roads provided access from the main highway to Puerto Vargas (as it does today) and south along the beach to what is now the southern reach of the park. However, in 1969 the main highway originated just a few miles north of Cahuita at Penshurst. The highway connecting Penshurst to Limón City would not be completed until 1976. Until then travel was by the banana train or by boat. The western fringe of what was to become the designated conservation area was cleared for pasture. The landing strip constructed by the Belcher Company is clearly visible. Belcher also constructed buildings at Puerto Vargas to serve as its centre of operations for forest product extraction. The only other edifices on the point were five remaining houses near the site of the original village of Cahuita.[5] The final piece of construction, remnants of which can still be seen today, was the pier that was built in the 1930s.

One vital category of information that was not included in Lemieux's study was the extent and nature of private land holdings within the suggested park boundaries. The problem was compounded by the fact that many of the local farmers did not hold official title to the land they utilized. Because of its size and official claims to the land, Belcher was paid while locals who had occupied the area for several generations were not. The unresolved issue of ownership and compensation, as evident in field interviews, continues to shape park-community relations to this day.[6]

Lemieux clearly made no pretence that this was a pristine area, an image often associated with national parks. Even in the late 1960s, Cahuita was more of a restoration than a preservation challenge. Lemieux's realistic and practical assessment of the situation is most apparent in the first of his two proposed management outlines. The first called for the establishment of a national monument limited to the peninsula and the coral reef area.

The monument proposal had several noteworthy features. It called for forest restoration (Zone D) but the southwest boundary excluded areas cleared for pasture and intensive cacao production. The plan clearly envisioned the monument primarily as a recreation site. In the broader regional proposal, Lemieux cited the following as recreational activities appropriate to this area: sunbathing, fishing, boating, hiking, wildlife viewing, diving, and camping. Several aspects of the plan coincide with current practices. The reef was designated for swimming and diving. Area 1, the white sand 'Playa Cahuita' (now called Playa Blanca) is a feature area. Puerto Vargas now serves as the park headquarters and visitor centre. The hiking trail connecting Cahuita village and Puerto Vargas via the point is extant. Other aspects have never been developed: the marine station, the shipwreck site and the boat dock at Río del Perezosa. In addition, camping and concessions have never been permitted for Playa Blanca. The plan, as presented in map form, does not make recommendations regarding the five 'rustic' houses at Monkey Bay. However, the text suggests that they could serve as examples of environmentally unobtrusive forms of architecture ('… que podrían servir de modelo pués no alteran el ambiente de las playas') (Lemieux 1969: 111).

Lemieux's study predates the popular use of the buffer zone concept, but he realized that this small area could not stand alone as a biological unit.[7] The monument proposal suggests that the adjacent land area receive some type of protected status but neither the extent nor type of the protection for this secondary area is defined. In the national park proposal (Figure 9.5) the extent of the protected area was designated using the Río Tuba to the north and the Río Carbón to the south to partially define the boundaries. The most significant difference between the two proposals was that expanded boundaries would have included Cahuita village and a significant agricultural area (Zone D). Had this model been adopted, park administrators may have been compelled to create an innovative management model that integrated conservation and human settlement appropriate for IUCN Category V. The nascent Costa Rican park system, however, was quickly being constructed around the internationally dominant nature/not nature

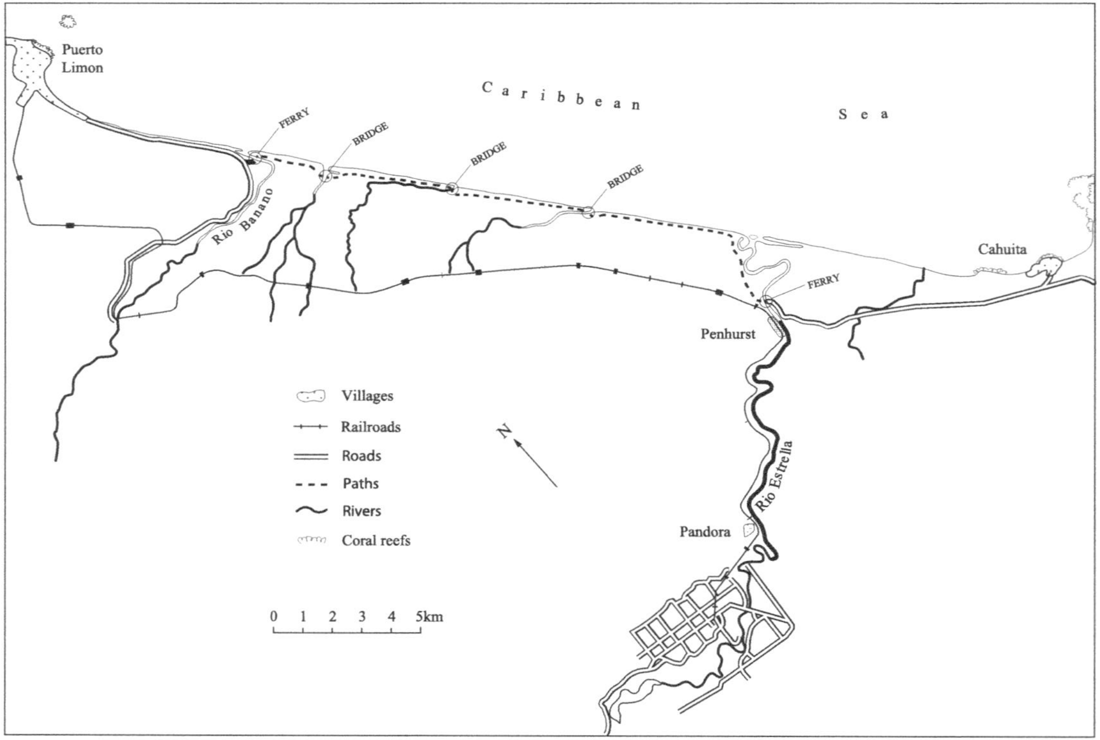

Figure 9.2 Regional transportation map

Source: adapted from Lemieux 1969, revised and edited by the editor and Michael Engelmann.

Figure 9.3 Cahuita Point aerial photo, 1968

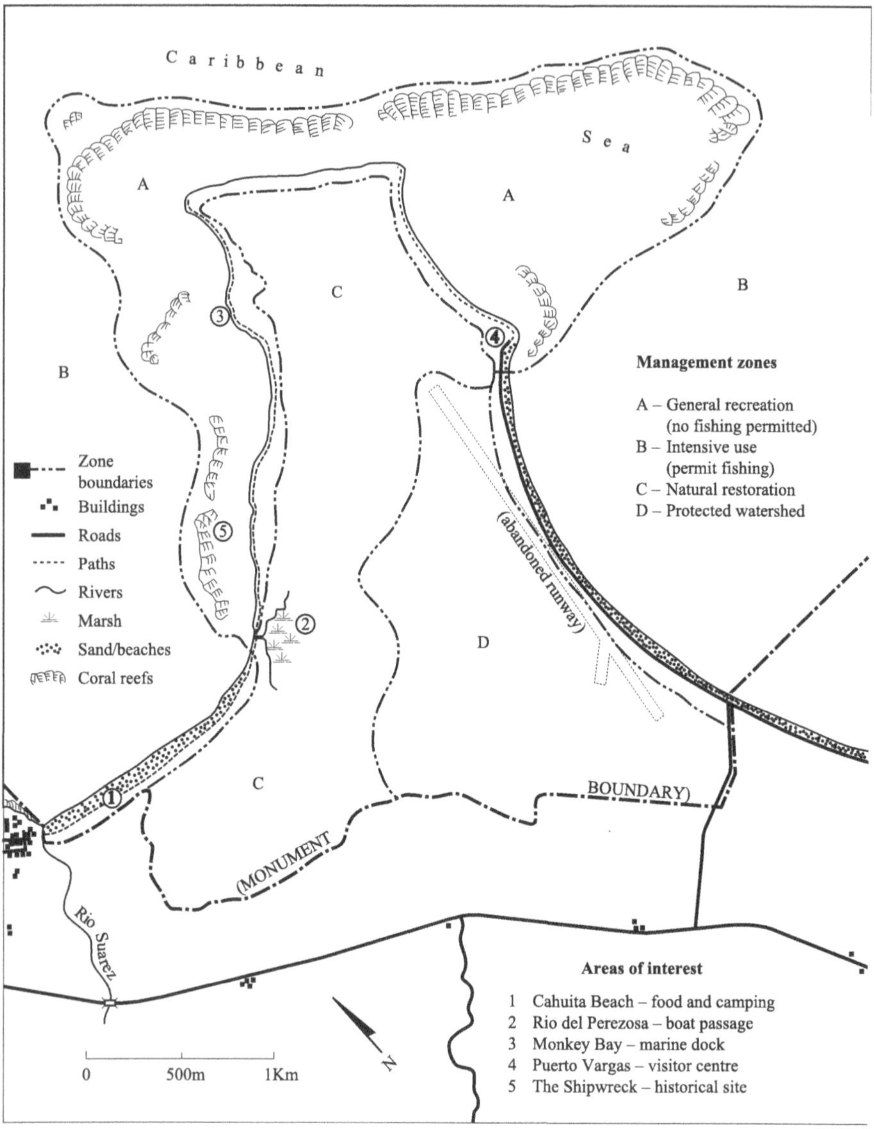

Figure 9.4 Coral National Monument proposal

Source: adapted from Lemieux 1969, revised and edited by the editor and Michael Engelmann.

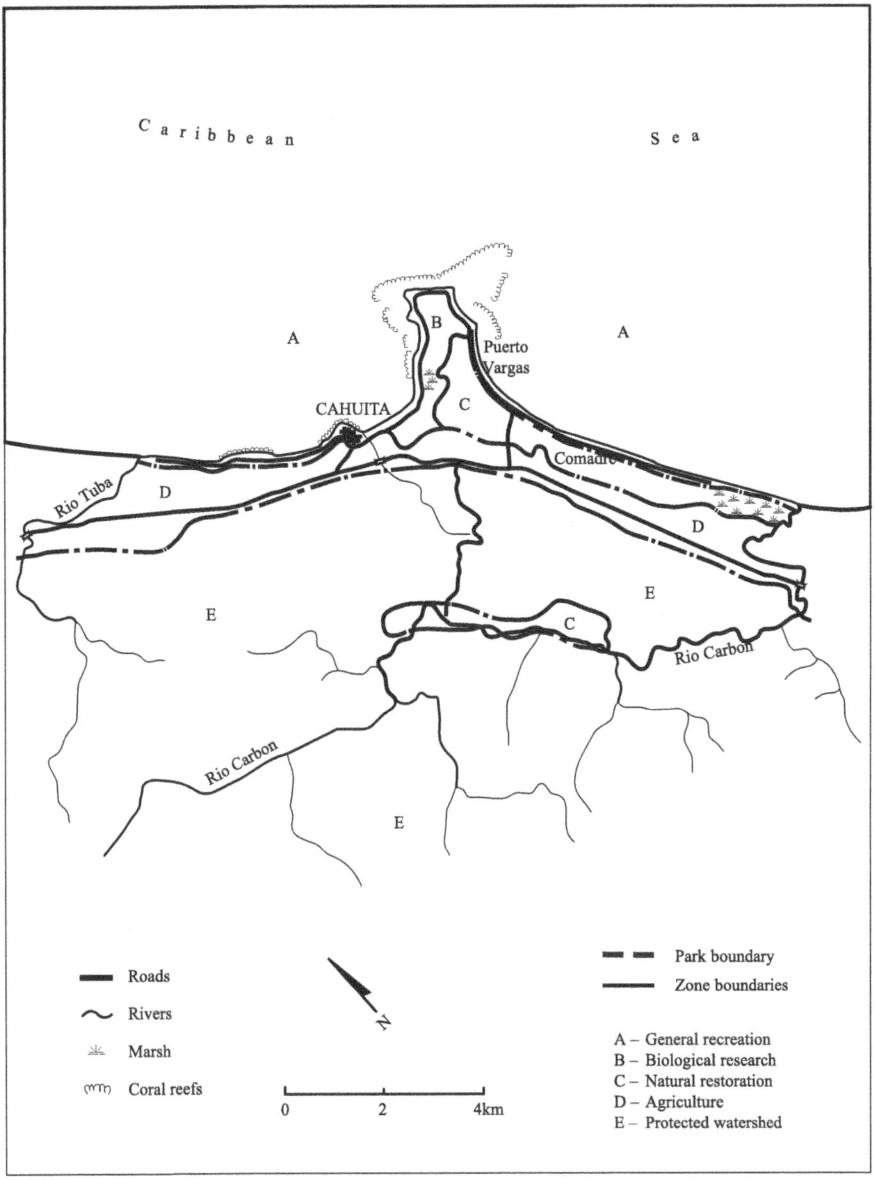

Figure 9.5 Lemieux's National Marine Park Proposal

Source: adapted from Lemieux 1969, revised and edited by the editor and Michael Engelmann.

paradigm. While the Yellowstone model could accommodate visitors, recreation and scientific activities, it drew the line at cultivation and permanent human populations. The final boundaries of Cahuita National Marine Monument and later Cahuita National Park were a compromise between the two proposals. The watershed or buffer zone concept was never adopted and the village was excluded. The area designated for protection, as defined in the Executive Decree, included all of the area of the monument proposal plus a strip of land stretching south to the Río Carbón bounded by the sea and the highway (Figure 9.4).

The 1970s – from Monument to National Park

The executive decree establishing Cahuita Marine Monument brought the national government into negotiation with a segment of the country's population with which it had little experience in order to preserve a natural landscape which had been little studied. While IUCN guidelines for Natural Monuments allowed for human activities, the initial restrictions of the executive decree went beyond those suggested by Lemieux. The decree restricted commercial fishing while forbidding forestry activities, commercial agriculture, hunting, trapping, turtle hunting and egg gathering. As mentioned, plans for the area's management became quite confused as jurisdiction over the Monument passed from the Park Service to the Junta de Administración Portuaria y de Desarrollo Económico de la Vertiente Atlántica (JAPDEVA) (Atlantic Zone Port Authority) and back to the Park Service in a period of five years. According to Palmer (1993), farmers and fishermen heard many different versions of regulations that, in turn, were only sporadically enforced:

> First they were told they could continue to catch fish for local consumption; then they were told spear guns were prohibited on the reef. How can one dive for lobster among barracuda and sharks without a spear gun?, they asked. Coconut cultivators were told once to stop chopping the underbrush in their coconut walks; later they were reprimanded for failing to keep the area clean. (235)

By 1974 the growing confusion was heightened by discussion of changing the status of the reserve to that of a national park. Government officials and community leaders established an ad hoc commission to review the community's needs. In his articulation of many resident people's position on the National Park at the time, Alphaeus Buchanan expressed a populist perspective on park management:

> If the government is really concerned about protecting the area, there is nobody more capable of preserving and protecting it than those who preserved and protected it for more than a hundred years. They can come and enjoy it as long as they respect our rights and our property...If they are intelligent they would realize that you can't function a park in an area where people are going to be hostile. If they take away our rights, the people are going to be hostile, and the tourists are not going to want to come, and the park is not going to be effective. (quoted in Palmer 1993: 236)

Clearly many locals did not envision what was to follow, especially given the outcome of three years of negotiation – a dialogue with the government that appeared to pre-empt a hard line exclusionary model for the park. Residents made it clear that they wanted to preserve their traditions tied to the sea and the land. They wanted to continue their livelihood activities, undertakings that they did not consider as a threat to the aesthetic and biological integrity of the conservation area. Support for the park idea stemmed largely from the notion that this was the best way to preserve their culture, enhance their prosperity, and keep their land out of the hands of foreigners. In a community meeting in 1970, Alvaro Ugalde, one of Costa Rica's national park system founders, suggested that park status would effectively hamper uncontrolled tourism development and land grabbing. This proved to be a compelling argument at the time. While Ugalde's agenda was clearly nature conservation, for the community this was secondary to cultural preservation.

During these negotiations government officials appeared sympathetic to a limited but multiple use model for the park. In a 1977 interview with Palmer, Guillermo Canessa, then administrator of Cahuita National Monument, expressed a vision of a park that accommodated at least some specific local needs, a vision mirroring Lemieux's original proposal for the area. In this proposal, the government would curtail many traditional economic activities in the park while providing employment opportunities through tourism infrastructure development:

> There is not just one reason for the Park in Cahuita; there are many reasons. The coral reef is the best in Costa Rica. This will be our only marine park and will offer students an opportunity to learn about marine biology and ecology. The beaches provide a natural recreation area. The animal and plant life of the area deserve study and protection. And there is historical significance in the area as well, the shipwrecks on the reef for example.
>
> The cocoa farms and coconut walks in the Park area don't harm the reef in any way, but other activities do. We'll need to protect the land area because anything that drains from these lands goes through the rivers and creeks to the sea and affects the life in the sea. Cattle pastures, for instance, must be limited in the area for this reason and the wildlife must be protected from hunters.
>
> We want to provide a park for education and recreation. We want to build a museum where students from all over the country can come and study exhibits, watch films and slides, so that they can appreciate what they see in the Park. Throughout the area we'll have signs pointing out everything of biological or historical interest. What we hope to provide is an open-air classroom.
>
> At the entrance to the Park in Cahuita, we'll have concessions for refreshments and souvenirs. People in Cahuita will have the opportunity to manage these concessions, so it will be a benefit to the local economy. Men who are fishermen now will be able to take Park visitors out to see the reef on guided tours. They'll be able to fish for local consumption, but to protect the reef we will have to prohibit commercial fishing.
>
> The main recreation area will be Puerto Vargas where we're starting to set up camping and trailer facilities. We'll be able to accommodate large and small groups with sanitation facilities and drinking water, and somebody from Cahuita will get a concession to operate a grocery store for the campers.

> The Park can serve the community of Cahuita in many ways. We can participate in any kind of community improvement project, like waste disposal, for instance. We can work with committees to improve all the social services. The Park will be a great educational benefit to the school children, too. (quoted in Palmer 1993: 237–8)

During the same year Canessa articulated this vision for community-–park relations (1977), the ad hoc commission of community representatives and park officials presented its report and recommendations to President Obuder. The agreement between the community of Cahuita and the government stated that local people were a 'favourable factor' in the conservation of nature and culture. Residence and subsistence activities should be allowed, 'as long as they do not extend beyond their currently occupied areas nor change their traditional methods of work' (translation from Weitzner and Fonseca Borrás 1999). The commission provided an outline and initiative for what would have been an innovative integrated conservation and development plan (ICDP), though granted the conservation aspect was not well developed.

In the final outcome the commission's work was ignored and the actual legislation establishing Cahuita National Park in 1978 made no reference to the proposed amendments (Kutay 1991; Wallace 1992; Weitzner and Fonseca Borrás 1999). Those few residing within park boundaries were forced to relocate and coconut growers and cacao farmers were asked to curtail their activities. The government offered to compensate landholders for their losses, but in most cases failed to do so. Moreover, the government supported very little of the infrastructure development suggested by Canessa and Lemieux as an impetus for tourism and recreation development.

Atrophy in the 1980s

Defining a park's boundaries, of course is only the beginning. Lines on a map, no matter how well grounded, do not assure that conservation practices are taking place. Moreover, the practice of creating parks by executive decree meant that the establishment of conservation areas and procurement of funding for operation were separate processes. In the 1970s and 1980s, it became common practice for outgoing national presidents to establish new parks and leave the funding issues to the next administration, in every case the opposition party. Ugalde, in 1981, acknowledged the problem:

> The government has had no doubts or qualms in establishing the present system, but it has not been able or willing to provide the funds necessary for land acquisition … It is very easy to pass a law, to freeze the land, to say, 'That's a park', and for us to send a few rangers to take care of the land. But then what? (in Wallace 1992: 102)

Costa Rica's parks, while better staffed and funded than many of the 'paper parks' throughout the world, have, from the beginning, suffered from understaffing and underfunding. CNP has been no exception. Lacking funds and personnel for proactive programs, the early management of the park concentrated on regulating human activity within park boundaries. Park administration focused on accommodating the growing number of visitors from outside the area while limiting livelihood activities – fishing, hunting, and cultivation – of the local populace. Livelihood activities were never completely banned in practice but the nature and extent of restrictions was an immediate source of conflict between locals and park officials. The situation was exacerbated by rapid turnover of park personnel at the local level, jurisdiction transference of administration at the regional level and contradictory mandates issued at the national level. At the same time, more and more was expected from protected areas as they became integrated into the emerging discourse regarding sustainable development at both the local and national levels (Gámez and Ugalde 1988).

Kutay's criteria for assessing the status of the park during this period reflected this emerging paradigm calling for the integration of conservation, social and economic agenda. He concluded that after a decade-and-a-half, CNP was failing to live up to its potential both as a conservation area and as a sustainable resource for local residents. He found that:

> resource conflicts have intensified to the point that a working relationship between park authorities and local people has completely broken down. Not only is the ecological integrity of the park in jeopardy, but many of the basic needs of local people remain unmet. (Kutay 1995: 119)

The destruction of the community's principal cash crop, cacao, with the onset of the Monilla blight in 1978 curtailed one of the most visible economic activities within the park's boundaries and diminished the market value of agriculturally productive property. At the same time, the elimination of the community's main cash crop made the issue of alternative and traditional livelihood activities within the park a more pressing issue. Activities such as hunting, fishing, coconut harvest, turtle hunting and egg gathering, and herb gathering intensified. Kutay found that park administrators had reached an agreement with the community that allowed for some livelihood activities within the park, mainly fishing. However, none of the agreements or rights of the traditional users were guaranteed by law. Residents admittedly violated the agreements while an ever-changing cadre of park rangers and administrators, most unfamiliar with the area's unique history and culture, enforced the agreements arbitrarily and inconsistently. Always looming in the background was the fact that nearly 90 per cent of the land within the park was still under private ownership though the functional meaning of ownership was unclear in these circumstances.

It is difficult to assess the specific degree of the environmental impact of human exploitation of terrestrial or marine resources in CNP – there is little baseline data from which to work. Further, it is difficult to compare local versus regional impacts on the state of the park, especially the marine area. Oral history tells us that previous generations of Cahuitans caught numerous and abundant species of fish as well as spiny lobster.[8] At the time of Kutay's study, local fishermen were in agreement that catches were decreasing in size. They did not, however, necessarily conclude that over-fishing was the main culprit. They were aware of other regional sources of environmental alteration. A limited number of scientific studies of the reef area produced evidence that the declining state of the reef in the 1970s and 1980s was to a large extent associated with regional deforestation and resulting high turbidity levels (Cortés and Risk 1985). In addition pesticide-laden run-off from up-current banana plantations in the Estrella Valley damaged coral and fish populations. The flow included hundreds of thousands of blue plastic bags used in banana production that snagged on the coral, shielding it from vital solar energy.

Regardless of the source of their diminishing numbers, Kutay (1991) surmised 'all marine species that are currently exploited in the park by the local population are in a state of decline' (119). Of specific concern was the demise of three species of sea turtles (green, hawksbill and leatherback) that migrate through or nest in the area. Turtle shells, meat and eggs had been an abundant and prized resource that originally drew Afro-Caribbeans to the area. By the mid-1980s, sea turtles were becoming an international *cause célèbre.* The turtles were protected by international treaties, Costa Rican law, and local agreements. In the Caribbean region turtle conservation was spearheaded by Archie Carr who, working out of Turtuguero on the north Caribbean coast of the country, founded the Caribbean Conservation Corps. In a pioneering effort in community based conservation, Carr was successful in convincing local residents of his area that conserving turtles could prove more beneficial than exploiting them directly (Carr 1956; Wallace 1992). The turtles nesting on the beaches of CNP, however, had no such champion and locals continued to consume and sell a shrinking supply of turtle meat, eggs and shells.

Despite the apparent links between human exploitation of natural resources and the declining state of the national park, Kutay focused his sharpest critique not on the local residents pursuing basic livelihood activities, but rather on the failure of the park administration to creatively and constructively respond to the tension between conservation and development goals in this specific site. Despite the emerging discourse and literature regarding parks as a basis for sustainable development at the local level, the CNP authorities had yet to explore these avenues. Kutay (1991: 128–9) opined:

> Not involving the community has been the greatest failure of the park staff....Regrettably, there seems to be a tendency among park planners and managers to maintain the view that human exploitation or residence in national parks is *a priori* incompatible with conservation objectives. On the contrary, national park criteria do permit limited human use of the protected area wherever it has been determined that such uses will not conflict with the essential purpose and objectives of biological conservation. The future challenge is to develop an awareness among park professionals of cultural values and methods for integrating them in planning and management.

In an attempt to address the needs of both the park and the community, Kutay proposed that the park be zoned for different levels of activities, an approach similar to Lemieux's original proposal. As indicated in Figure 9.6, the proposal includes:

- *primitive zone* of strict protection to maintain the natural state for scientific purposes:

- *extensive use zone* where the goal is to minimize the impact of permitted uses: recreation, environmental education and 'traditional resources use';
- *cultural history zone* where objectives are to 'restore and preserve the artifacts and history of Afro-Caribbean culture';
- *intensive use zone* for concentrated recreation and tourism activities;
- *rehabilitation zone* where exotic plants and species are to be replaced with local species;
- *special use zone* devoted to infrastructure for park administration.

Kutay's plan called for integration of strict conservation goals with recreation activities and the interests of the community. Of his own management proposal, he writes:

> The final test of this plan is not simply whether it successfully protects the ecological values within the park while permitting human use of its resources. Rather, it is a question of securing national conservation objectives within a management regime that promotes the cultural heritage of the region and the socioeconomic status of its people. (Kutay 1991: 128)

Kutay's study and proposal reflected the cutting-edge participatory conservation literature of the late 1980s, models and proposals that were guardedly optimistic that conservation areas could simultaneously meet the needs of a wide range of stakeholders and interest groups. His recommendations, however well articulated, appear to have generated little momentum for a more integrative management style. The community's reconnection with CNP (as an institution) after the initial period of exclusion and alienation was very gradual. It coincided with the transformation, by default, of the local economy from an agrarian to a tourism base during the 1980s. During this same period, the Talamanca region was increasingly integrated into the national sphere of influence through improvements in transportation and communication, and the growing population of Hispanics in the area.

As Costa Rica struggled with the international debt crisis and structural adjustment, it looked to tourism development as a key economic strategy to right the ship. The state continued to increase the scope of protected areas but given the financial difficulties of the national economy, little money garnered from the fees was invested in park improvements and staffing. Even as Cahuitans began to view CNP through the tourism lens, they questioned whether the real purpose of the park was not primarily to serve as a source of revenue for the national government. This perspective was amplified by the fact that the government had not been forthcoming with the land payments it had promised. Meanwhile park management, out of financial necessity and an assumption that simply minimizing economic activities protects nature within designated boundaries, was characterized by a 'let it be' approach. The conservation area's status did succeed in shielding the terrestrial portion of the park from the rapid rates of deforestation that characterized nearly all of Costa Rica's unprotected areas during the 1980s. By the end of the decade, CNP stood out on vegetation maps as an isolated strip of green. As for the status of the reef, what little scientific evidence we

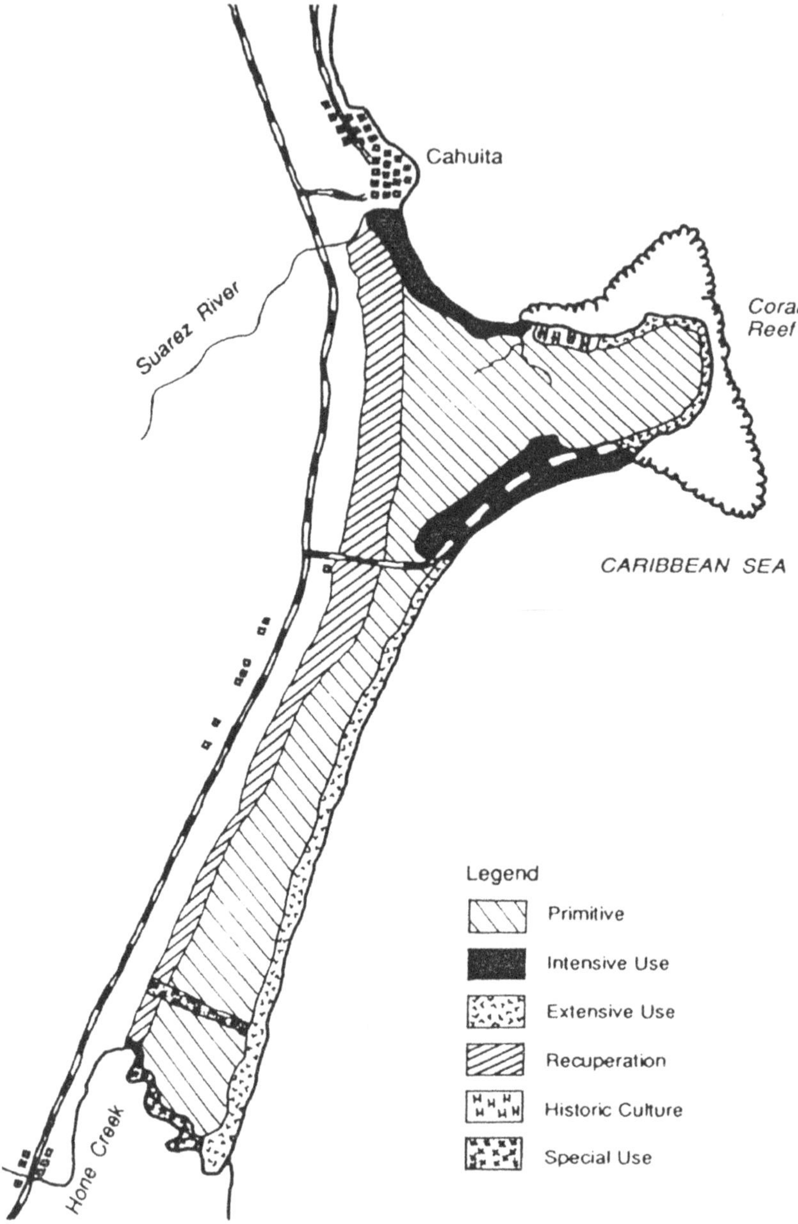

Figure 9.6 Kutay's (1991) management proposal

have suggests that the condition of the reef continued to deteriorate for the reasons stated above (Hands, French and O'Neill 1993).

Current Practices

In April 1991, the condition of the reef was further obscured when Limón Province experienced an earthquake measuring 7.2 on the Richter Scale. Much of the Caribbean coast was thrust up over one meter, a tectonic event that had an immediate and profound impact on the coral reef. The brown, dead coral now protruding along the shores of the Cahuita area serves as a reminder of the event. On the human side, the event isolated the entire Talamanca region for weeks, depriving the area of tourism revenue (except for the tourists who could not leave). Many of the resident informants for this study look back on the event as one of the few times in recent history when the community came together to confront a challenge. The only other single event that elicits memories of a unified community was the response to the park fee increase, events outlined above. This political event, sparked by the national government's need for greater revenue, served as the impetus for the novel management plan for CNP culminating in Executive Decree 26 929 in May 1998.

In the interim period between the 1994 takeover of the Kelly Creek entrance and the 1998 agreement, the community became increasingly involved in the upkeep of Playa Blanca moving from a complete 'let it be (natural)' approach to the organization of volunteers to maintain trails, pick up garbage, and increase the level of security. During this time a Dutch Bilateral Aid Agency funded the construction of a bridge across Kelly Creek, latrines, changing stations and a new information booth to replace the one partially burned in the 1994 unrest. The same agency funded the new entrance facilities at Puerto Vargas giving equal treatment to both parties in the community–park service split. In 1997 Cahuita received the Bandera Azul (blue flag) for exceptionally clean water, an award that the community interpreted as an affirmation of their management (Weir 1998).

With the change of administration at the national level in 1994, the main protagonists on the government side were replaced by administrators less alienated from the community. Intense and drawn out negotiations opened between the community intent on maintaining free access to Playa Blanca and the government, represented by MINAE (Ministry of the Environment and Energy), wishing to reassert its control over CNP. The community leveraged its position by initially insisting on complete control of the park and timely compensation for the land of which they had now been deprived for over twenty years. Community representatives also argued that they should have free access to the reef that they believed they had the capacity to manage. In response to the latter claim, the government hired a biologist whose report asserted otherwise (A. Buchanan, conversation, May 1998; Weitzner and Fonseca Borrás 1999).

On 13 February 1997, the first formal agreement to emerge from the negotiations was signed.[9] The agreement prohibited fees at the Kelly Creek entrance, called on the government to follow through with funds for expropriated lands and established a service committee for co-administration of the park. The transformation of the relationship between the community and conservation administrators is reflected in the community committee names: the original Committee of Struggle (*Comité de Lucha*) became the Services Committee that in turn gained legal recognition as the Management Committee (1998). The Management Committee was charged not just with the administration of Playa Blanca, the original site of contention, but also with the entire park. MINAE's (1998) outline of rules embodied in the executive decree described the functions of the Management Committee:

> to ensure the adequate functioning and quality of services offered in Cahuita National Park; to establish fees for these services; to take the administrative measures necessary to ensure that the park is functioning well; to ensure the fulfillment of the public use rules outlined in the document, as well as those entrenched in Costa Rican environmental law; and to modify the rules of use as stipulated in the executive decree. (Translation in Weitzner and Fonseca Borrás 1999)

Clearly the legal establishment of the Management Committee, comprised of community representatives and park administrators, represented a step forward in the involvement of civil society in the care of the park.[10] What remains less clear is to what extent this involvement will contribute to enhancement of the park's biological community. What does it mean to ensure that 'the park is functioning well'? Is this largely from an administrative perspective or does it include an assessment of the park's ecosystems? While the executive decree describes public use and subsistence fishing rules, the primary emphasis is on the provision of services to visitors and management of CNP as a recreation area. Moreover, the community members of the Management Committee represent development interests – the Chamber of Commerce and the Development Association. Resource users and guides who frequent the park and have insights regarding its ecosystems were not included. This fact was not overlooked. One community representative on the Management Committee stated:

> We need a biologist, a good biologist to start with … from the community, we need various people, the fishers and the divers, for example, in order to maintain the reef. In other words, we need to involve the people that really live from the resources...They have lots of knowledge, because they have spent many years living with the reef and in the water (quoted in Weitzner and Fonseca Borrás 1999).

In most cases the tour guides and the fishermen are the same small group of people. There is an Association of Guides but it has little if any communication with the Management Committee and the Association itself is not inclusive of all. Often the same guides compete for clients in their capacity as guides and as fishermen attempting to harvest diminishing aquatic resources.

The surveys carried out for this study in 1998 indicated that the community of Cahuita was generally pleased with the new formal arrangement between the community and the park administration. Of the 86 respondents, 80 per cent said they were satisfied with the new arrangement. At the same time, it was clear that most respondents knew little of the details of the agreement or the composition of the Management Committee.[11] The overriding perception was that the community had 'won' in 1994 and was now officially in charge of Playa Blanca. Resident's suggestions for improving management were similar for Playa Blanca and Puerto Vargas – better garbage and litter cleanup, more guides and interpretive signs, and better security.

Interviews with park personnel, including the director, indicated that those working out of Puerto Vargas offered some perspectives in contrast to the community on the purpose of the park and the new management arrangement. In most cases (seven of nine) the park personnel also approved of the new arrangement, but not without suggestions or qualified statements. They stated that the management agreement helped share the burden of day-to-day upkeep and sense of responsibility for the general (aesthetic) condition of the park. Several park employees suggested that the Playa Blanca regulations and enforcement of rules were too lax regarding dogs and litter. They wanted more of a national park employee presence on the Cahuita side and more inquiries from the management committee. In other words, they wanted Playa Blanca run more like Puerto Vargas. One guard's complaint was that at Playa Blanca, 'They just don't do much'.

Survey and interview responses regarding the purpose of the park also indicate different understanding of the park. Both residents and park personnel overwhelmingly agreed that CNP was a strong asset for the community because it was a magnet for tourism. However, in response to questions regarding the purpose of the park, residents split their responses between conservation and tourism/recreation (Figure 9.7). There was also a marked difference in the perception of male and female respondents with women more focused on tourism. Park employees' responses, with the exception of one reference to sustainable development, focused on conservation including protection of the reef, land, forest and fauna.

Despite the increased involvement of the community in park affairs, from the perspective of the park personnel the bigger challenges facing the park still involve the enforcement (or lack thereof) of rules regulating resource exploitation. Though the number of Cahuitans who hunt and fish within park boundaries is small, disputes continue, sometimes on a personal level between a park guard and a fisher. Guards, for example, complain that divers are taking spiny lobsters that are below minimum size, an accusation that was corroborated by several divers. Another concern on a larger scale was the taking of leatherback turtle eggs, and the exploitation of green turtles for meat and eggs. (These products are readily available in markets in Limón on a seasonal basis.) In the Cahuita area, but not in Cahuita village to my knowledge, eggs were served as *bocas* (appetizers) in bars during nesting season. Turtle nesting, and therefore poaching, within the park takes place in the southern arm, an area seldom explored by park visitors and rarely patrolled by park personnel. One guard stated that months go by without checking this or other remote sections of the park. The nature guides in Cahuita, however, became aware of the value of turtle nesting as a tourist attraction. In 1998, local guides, community volunteers, and park personnel organized turtle patrols several nights a week during peak nesting season. Park guards, who lack

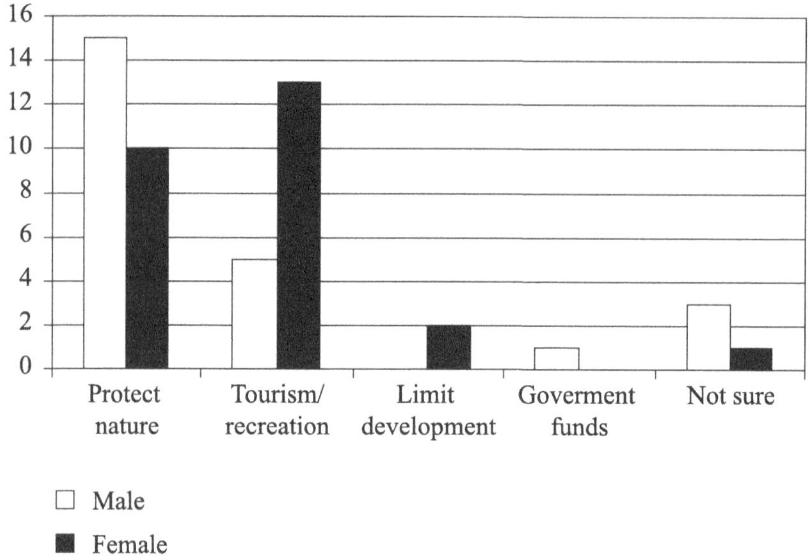

Figure 9.7 Residents' perception of the purpose of CNP by gender

Source: fieldwork, 1998.

legal status to make arrests of poachers, carried guns for protection and intimidation. They sometimes fired warning shots to scare off the offenders, usually poor residents of neighboring towns and, increasingly, squatters with easy access to the beaches. In May 1998, one of the guards informed me that he had recently shot at and wounded one of the more persistent poachers.

The challenge of regulating human activities in the park is amplified by the lack of institutional support. The park director and her staff all agreed that the most pressing need for park management was more staff and funding. With eight people on the payroll, only three or four individuals are usually in the park at the same time. Daily maintenance, attending to visitors, collecting fees, occasional meetings, and limited patrolling account for the bulk of the staff's activities. The staff, who averaged less than one year of tenure at CNP, expressed a desire for more training in service and science so they could better address the needs and questions of visitors. For example, none of the park personnel claimed any knowledge of the reef, offering only the opinion that it drew too many visitors. The park administrator of three years hoped to address some of the needs through international funding and increased involvement of university resources for training and scientific research (G. Cuza Jones, conversation, January 1998). A member of the Management Committee, she also welcomed the emerging constructive relationship between her contingent and the community of Cahuita. She pointed out that community–park interactions were encouraged and facilitated by a strong commitment to more participatory models of conservation on the part of regional and national conservation offices. Finally, she and her staff were all aware of the need to settle the land payment issues as an important step in healing community–park relations. As a sign of solidarity with the dispossessed owners, the staff displays a map at the Puerto Vargas entry indicating private holdings within park boundaries.

The new co-administration agreement for CNP is an important mechanism for easing the longstanding tensions between the community and government officials. There is an increased sense of ownership and identification with the park on the part of Cahuita residents. However, the new mechanisms for communication are not being utilized. There also remains much to accomplish in meeting the conservation challenges laid out at the beginning of this chapter. The economic value of the park in an economy dominated by tourism is well understood. But local people still do not express an appreciation for the scientific and biological value of the park. The new arrangement, while addressing many obstacles to effective administration of a recreation area, does little to directly address issues of conservation of biological diversity.

Conclusions

The establishment of Cahuita National Park was based on a two-pronged rationale. The area was recognized for its potential as a recreation site and tourist attraction that could attract revenue for the state and local economy. The site was also chosen as one of the earliest national parks, because it represented an important and unique piece of the richly diverse biological landscape of Costa Rica. The history of the park over the last three decades has been largely a history of politically and economically-based tension between the community and the national government's attempts to first take and then maintain administrative control over the area. In this contested area, socio-political events and processes have continually overshadowed the conservation of the park's biodiversity as an active agenda. The scientific community has engaged in very limited research and provided workshops for local guides and a few park personnel but has had little long-term impact. The current administrative agreements indicate an easing of the tensions between various stakeholders and create mechanisms for engaging the community in the caretaking of the park. As such, it helps creates conditions under which the park can be further developed to meet conservation goals, especially when they dovetail with tourism development. It is a necessary but not sufficient arrangement.

Cahuita is not alone in its struggle to reconcile the objectives of tourism, conservation and development. Despite the widespread articulation of integrative conservation and development policies that suggest local people should or must be involved in conservation of biodiversity and natural landscapes, in practice protected areas largely remain spaces of exclusion, greatly restricting livelihood activities of local residents (Colchester 1997; Ghimire and Pimbert 1997; Pretty 2002). In spatial terms, the nature/human dichotomy is not readily dissolved, even where local people have a relatively low impact on their immediate environment. Ecotourism and the inclusion of local people in co-management arrangements are two evolving instruments for reconciling conflicting interests among an increasingly diverse set of stakeholders involved in biodiversity conservation. These options should neither be touted as panaceas nor readily dismissed as failed initiatives. Both approaches must be considered within specific contexts, such as Cahuita, in order to understand their limits and potential. By articulating the varied impact of national and international environmental policy on local residents, the study may serve as a basis for more effective and culturally informed conservation policies.

Notes

1 Castro justified the fee hike in terms of park self-sufficiency, but the rationale for the 1,200 per cent increase was reportedly based on a flawed tourist survey that asked foreign visitors if they would be willing to pay US$15 to enter national parks. Many respondents mistook this to mean a one-time fee for any and all parks and found it reasonable. Castro further reasoned 'To go to the movies in the United States costs $6, so if two people go to a movie that lasts two hours, that's what they would pay to come here and see it live and in full color' (*Tico Times*, 9 September 1994).

2 The law, in principal, eliminated all private property rights within 200m of the shore.

3 As general rule, conservation biologists favor areas that are large, round and connected to other areas of high diversity (Meffe et al. 2002). CNP's land area fails on all three points.

4 CATIE (Centro Agronómico Tropical de Investigaciones Ensenanza) scientists first confirmed the presence of the disease in December 1978. The outbreak first occurred north of Cahuita near the Rio Estrella ('Monilia Disease of Cacao in Costa Rica', *Turrialba*, 1978).

5 By 1978, when CNP was established, only three people occupied the remaining buildings and only on a seasonal basis. Kutay (1991) uses the curious term 'Cahuita Indians' to describe these remaining occupants.

6 As of 1997, only 15 of 71 claims had been settled (MINAE 1997).

7 Shelford introduced the concept for conservation areas in 1933 but the term did not gain currency until the 1970s.

8 The lobster are still caught by a few divers who complained to me that they were becoming difficult to find and that they were being taken in smaller sizes. Wellington (1975) had documented their decline on the reef area in the mid-1970s due to spear fishing.

9 According to Weitzner and Fonseca Borrás (1999), the Defensoría do los Habitantes de la República acted as a vital and trusted mediator in the negotiations.

10 The committee is comprised of two government officials (the park administrator and the conservation area director) and three community representatives elected by the Chamber of Tourism and the Development Association.

11 This conclusion is corroborated by a Weitzner and Fonseca Borrás (1999) who conducted a survey in May 1998, that focused on community knowledge of the new arrangement.

References

Biot, Y., Blaikie, P.M., Jackson, C. and Palmer-Jones, R. (1995), 'Rethinking Research on Land Degradation in Developing Countries', Washington, DC: The World Bank.

Boza, M. (1993), 'Conservation in Action: Past, Present, and future of the National Park System of Costa Rica', *Conservation Biology*, 7, pp. 239–47.

Boza, M. and Cevo, J. (1998), 'Parques nacionales y otros areas protegidas Costa Rica/Costa Rica National Parks and Other Protected Areas', San José: Incafo Costa Rica.

Budowski, G. (1977), 'Turismo y conservación ambiental: ¿Conflicto, coexistencia o simbiosis?', *Parques*, 1, pp. 3–6.

Cahn, R. (1984), 'An Interview with Alvaro Ugalde', *Nature Conservancy News*, 34, pp. 8–18.

Carr, A. (1956), *The Windward Road: Adventures of a Naturalist on Remote Caribbean Shores*, New York: Knopf.

Colchester, M. (1997), 'Salvaging Nature: Indigenous Peoples and Protected Areas', in K. Ghimire and M. Pimbert (eds), *Social Change and Conservation*, London: Earthscan Publications, pp. 97–130.

Cortés, J. and Risk, M.J. (1985), 'A Reef Under Siltation Stress: Cahuita, Costa Rica', *Bulletin of Marine Science*, 36, pp. 339–56.

Franke, J. (1993), *Costa Rica's National Parks and Preserves: A Visitor's Guide*, Seattle: The Mountaineers.

Gámez, R. and Ugalde, A. (1988), 'Costa Rica's National Park System and the Preservation of Biological Diversity: Linking Conservation with socio-economic development', in F. Almeda and C. Pringle (eds), *Tropical Rainforests: Diversity and Conservation*, San Francisco: California Academy of Sciences, pp. 125–42.

Ghimire, K. and Pimbert, M. (eds) (1997), *Social Change and Conservation: Environmental Politics and the Impacts of National Parks and Protected Areas*, London: Earthscan Publications.

Hands, M.R., French, J.R. and O'Neill, A. (1993), 'Reef Stress at Cahuita Point, Costa Rica: Anthropogenically Enhanced Sediment Influx or Natural Geomorphic Change?', *Journal of Coastal Management*, 9, pp. 11–25.

Kutay, K. (1991), 'Cahuita National Park, Costa Rica: A Case Study in Living Cultures and National Park Management', in P.C. West and S.R. Brechin (eds), *Resident Peoples and National Parks*, Tucson: University of Arizona Press.

Lemieux, G. (1969), 'Oportunidades para el desarrollo turístico del litoral atlántico al sur de Puerto Limón, Costa Rica', MSc thesis, Instituto Interamericano de Ciencias Agrícola de la OEA, Turrialba, Costa Rica.

McNeely, J.A. and Miller, K.R. (1984), 'National Parks, Conservation, and Development: The Role of Protected Areas in Sustaining Society', in *Proceedings of the World Congress on National Parks Bali, Indonesia, 11–22 October 1982*, Washington, DC: Smithsonian Institution Press, p. 825.

Meffe, G., Nielson, L., Knight, R.L. and Schenborn, D. (2002), *Ecosystem Management: Adaptive, Community-based Conservation*, Washington, DC: Island Press.

Palmer, P. (1993), *'What Happen': A Folk-history of Costa Rica's Talamanca Coast*, San José, Costa Rica: Publications in English.

Pretty, J. (2002), 'People, Livelihoods and Collective Action in Biodiversity Management', in T. O'Riordan and S. Stoll-Kleeman (eds), *Biodiversity, Sustainability and Human Communities*, Cambridge: Cambridge University Press.

Purcell, T. (1993), *Banana Fallout: Class, Color, and Culture among West Indians in Costa Rica*, University of California, Los Angeles: Centre for Afro-American Studies.
Stone, R. (1992), *The Nature of Development*, New York: Alfred A. Knopf.
Turrialba (1978), 'Monilia Disease of Cacao in Costa Rica', 28 (4), pp. 339–40.
Wallace, D. (1992), *The Quetzal and the Macaw: The Story of Costa Rica's National Parks*, San Francisco: Sierra Club Books.
Weir, C. (1998), '"Blue Flag" Flying on More Clean Beaches', *The Tico Times*, San José, Costa Rica, 26 February, p. 13.
Weitzner, V. and Fonseca Borrás, M. (1999), 'Cahuita, Limón, Costa Rica: From Conflict to Collaboration', in D. Buckles (ed.), *Cultivating Peace: Conflict and Collaboration in Natural Resource Management*, Ottowa and Washington DC: IDRC/World Bank.
Wellington, G.R. (1975), 'The Galapagos Coastal Marine Environments', Report to Ministry of Agriculture and Livestock, Ecuador.

Chapter 10

Nature, People and Planning on the Coast of Belize*

Roger Few

The research reported in this chapter is not the first to point out ambiguities and impediments in the practical application of participatory planning in developing countries. Neither is it the first to note that community participation in externally-initiated projects often ends up as highly managed by the agencies pursuing such a policy. The persistence of top-down managerialism and the misrepresentation of public involvement have been evident both in the wider context of participation in rural development and resource management (e.g. Quarles van Ufford 1993; Cline-Cole 1997; Gauld 2000) and within conservation itself (Taylor and Johansson 1996; Pimbert and Pretty 1997; Hulme and Murphree 1999).

This study's departure from much previous critique is to analyse the fine detail of power relations in a planning arena in order to reveal socio-political processes shaping community involvement and ultimately substituting for participatory rhetoric. Such detailed research on the mechanisms of community involvement in environment/development interventions is important both for building a theoretical understanding of the complex social dynamics within participatory arenas and for uncovering the structural constraints that so often seem to hinder participation in practice. Thrift and Walling (2000) note that as decentralization and community empowerment have become central themes in the environmental sustainability agenda, so critical studies relating to such themes should gain increasing importance in development geography. Critical analysis of this kind has already informed much recent work in industrialized nations focussing on participatory planning and deliberative democracy (e.g. Healey 1997; Forester 1999; Dryzek 2000). These approaches give due recognition to stakeholder diversity, conflicts of interest and the fine-grain of power relations in decision-making arenas, but attempt to move beyond interest-based tensions in the search for genuinely collaborative and inclusive concensus-building practices.

This chapter addresses a topic in which the tensions of participation are particularly evident: biodiversity conservation in developing countries (Ghimire and Pimbert 1997; Brandon et al. 1998). It reports on research conducted in Belize on community involvement in the planning of protected areas (national parks and nature reserves), employing an actor-oriented style of analysis increasingly applied in political ecology research on natural resource management (Bryant and Bailey 1997; Brown and Rosendo 2000; Doornbos et al. 2000). Through close examination of the power relations between actors, the case study revealed that planner/community interactions were dominated by a process identified as 'containment', together with its twin opposing process referred to as 'counter-containment'. The principal purpose of this chapter is to analyse the actions and interactions that constituted these processes.

Following a brief discussion of the notion of containment and a summary of the case study findings, the chapter sets out in detail the containment mechanisms of avoidance, exclusion and control and the counter-containment actions juxtaposed with them. It then develops an analytical framework of containment to help explain differences in planning events between the study sites.

The Concept of Containment

Containment here refers to the strategic management of public involvement in planning so as to minimize disruption to preconceived planning goals. It presumes the existence of potential forces that might disrupt achievement of those goals. But containment is of necessity a subtle activity because it also presumes a need to accommodate involvement in some form – otherwise planning could be a coercive and solely technical process rather than a containing, social process. Successful containment therefore ensures that a project ostensibly engaging local involvement progresses to completion on time and within predefined parameters.

The idea of containment has its parallels in literature from the wider context of community participation in developmental and environmental programmes. The discussions of Hildyard et al. (1998) with respect to forest management converge strongly with this theme. They explicitly refer to development agencies as sometimes strategically using participation itself as a means for controlling, managing and 'containing' dissent:

> Far from being a transformative process in which local people are able to exert control over decision-making, participation becomes a well-honed tool for engineering consent to projects and programmes whose framework has already been determined in advance. (Hildyard et al. 1998: 32)

Other authors refer to cases where participatory fora act as rhetorical exercises and to the discursive management of public consultations (Nelson and Wright 1995; Brohman 1996; Peterson 1997). White (1996) notes how agencies can define what constitutes legitimate participation, and stresses that conflict should be expected in a process that cedes people a genuine voice. A reported absence of conflict should therefore raise suspicions of suppression:

> The bland front presented by many discussions of participation in development should itself suggest questions. What interests does this 'non-politics' serve, and what interests may it be suppressing? (White 1996: 15)

The pressure to contain community involvement in protected area planning derives partly from bureaucratic considerations of efficiency and authority common to projects in many fields. The work of conservation professionals is oriented toward meeting career-oriented and bureaucratic objectives relating to spending budgets and the completion of projects on time (Taylor and Johansson 1996; Pimbert and Pretty 1997). And participation is widely regarded as a costly and time-consuming exercise (GEF 1998). Sharpe (1998) suggests that planning for conservation in developing countries is typically confined to short-termism by the project cycles of donor agencies. Moreover, a colonial legacy of top-down planning and management of national parks and wildlife reserves commonly remains ingrained in the public institutions responsible for establishing protected areas in developing countries (Gbadegesin and Ayileka 2000).

But the containment pressure in conservation projects also relates to the specific design and function of protected areas. It is argued in depth elsewhere (Few 2000; 2000a) that containment is inherent in conventional protected area planning, because parks and reserves are designed to set regulations on human access to sites and the natural resources within (Ghimire and Pimbert 1997). Even when participation is a stated planning objective, the primary purpose of such projects remains biodiversity protection through spatialized access restrictions – a priority likely to be contested by resource-dependent people in developing countries (Little 1994; Sanjayan et al. 1997). If the protected area model is to be the end-result of planning, local stakeholder involvement inevitably has to be managed.

In conservation debate, the ideas of containment find clearest expression in reviews of integrated conservation-development projects (ICDPs) and other cases where rural development initiatives have been incorporated as part of protected area projects. ICDPs include compensation measures for lost access to resources and social and economic development measures to provide alternative incomes and alternative resources for communities surrounding protected areas. Schroeder (1999) claims that such initiatives typically have been highly circumscribed, have seldom involved agencies ceding effective control over resources to communities, and have been instituted with the aim of neutralizing opposition through distributing economic benefits. Again they reveal pre-determined agendas and raise constraints on what is considered legitimate participation (Richard and O'Connor 1997). Ghimire and Pimbert (1997: 34) also question the values and parameters that typify such initiatives: 'most of them have been initiated with the simple intention of reducing organized opposition to the establishment and expansion of protected areas'. West and Brechin (1991: 396) point to a similar role public participation can take within general protected area planning and management: 'even when park adminstrators and planners really do listen to local concerns, it is often to let them blow off steam in the hopes of deflating conflict'.

Case Study

The empirical research on which this chapter is based was conducted in Belize in 1996 and 1997. The case study set out to examine community involvement in the planning of statutory protected areas designated for biodiversity conservation within the country's coastal zone. During the 1980s and 1990s the Government of Belize established a chain of parks and reserves covering parts of coral islands (cays) and surrounding waters along the Belize Barrier Reef. Two such sites in the northeast were selected for detailed study (see Figure 10.1): the Bacalar Chico Marine Reserve and National Park, declared in 1996; and a proposed marine/terrestrial protected area off the island of Caye Caulker, which was still being planned at the time of the research.

The establishment of the protected areas was the joint responsibility of government agencies: specialist divisions of the Ministry of Agriculture and Fisheries (for the marine sections) and the Ministry of Natural Resources (for the terrestrial portions). In the case of Bacalar Chico these planning agencies worked in collaboration with international non-governmental organizations (INGOs), particularly the International Tropical Conservation Foundation.

Both case study sites encompass forest, mangrove, sea grass and coral reef habitats, and both lie on inhabited cays with settlements and tourist resorts occupying neighbouring sections of the islands. At the time of the research, the marine areas had a history of usage by small-scale fishing operations and by tour guides offering snorkel/dive or sports fishing tours, and potential landowners and developers had expressed interest in the terrestrial areas. In both protected area projects the marine portions only were to be multiple-use reserves, permitting limited access to specific zones for local fishermen and reef tour groups (August 1996; Gibson et al. 1996).

Using qualitative methodology, the study inductively analysed forms of public participation in planning for the protected area projects and examined the power relations and mechanisms in operation between the diverse actors involved. A total of 76 semi-structured interviews with local stakeholders, planning officials and other commentators provided the principal source of data. Complementary sources included informal meetings with actors, observations of planning events, and secondary materials such as official planning documents, maps, minutes of meetings, unofficial reports, newsletters and journal articles.

The research revealed a similar pattern of community involvement in planning for both main study sites. Planning team members from government agencies and INGOs had undertaken questionnaire surveys of local stakeholders, held informal conversations with user groups, arranged public consultation meetings in neighbouring settlements, and, in the case of Bacalar Chico, set up an advisory committee with local representation (see Table 10.1). However, these involvement activities were set within closely defined parameters. Local people had the opportunity to provide information and express viewpoints on the emerging proposals, but this input was more reactive than active, and all the spatial planning decisions were ultimately taken by the planning officials. The official channels of involvement equated to 'participation by consultation', in which citizens provided information and expressed opinions on proposals but did not take an active role in decision-making (Pimbert and Pretty 1997).

Even within such parameters, the consultation fora staged by the government and INGO planning teams proved ineffective in engaging and giving voice to a broad

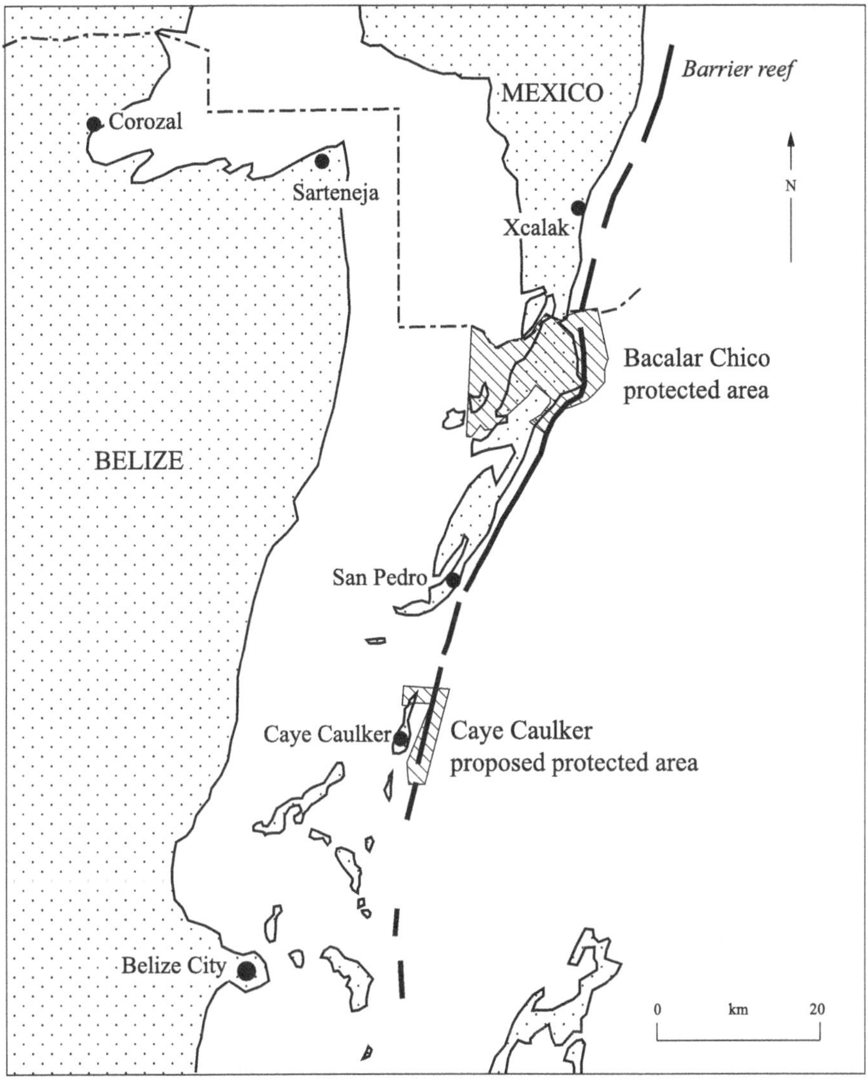

Figure 10.1 Case study sites in northeast Belize (1997)

cross-section of stakeholders, and local actors provided minimal direct input into plans. When proposals were presented to the public there was little evidence of feedback from local stakeholders leading to modifications in the plans. Despite widespread overall support for the creation of a protected area, specific concerns relating to resource use within the sites remained evident, as did discontentment with the consultation process itself. There was even evidence of exclusion of certain user groups from participation in the pattern of interaction between planners and the communities. This operated in

Table 10.1 Principal planning events in the two case studies

	Bacalar Chico
1994	Advisory committee appointed
1994	Draft management plan completed
1995	Surveys and public meetings in San Pedro, Corozal and Sarteneja
1995	Surveys of user groups in Bacalar Chico area
1996	Public meeting in San Pedro
1996	National Park and Marine Reserve declared
	Caye Caulker
1993–94	Questionnaire surveys in Caye Caulker village
1993–96	Consultation meetings in Caye Caulker village (1994–96 Village Council opposes land portion)
1996	Draft management plan prepared
1997	Former landowner announces legal challenge and presents new proposal for land portion

tandem with the selective inclusion of certain actors noted by authors such as Brohman (1996) and Desai (1996).

However, other channels of involvement existed alongside the official channels. Some local stakeholders undertook independent actions of the type identified in other actor-oriented studies, including informal liaison with project planners and political lobbying (e.g. Arce et al. 1994; Brown 1998; Brown and Rosendo 2000a). These actions too arguably constituted forms of 'participation' in planning. They also underline the important point that social differentiation exists within 'communities' (Leach et al. 1997), with different local actors possessing different participatory capacities as well as interests in the outcomes of planning.

Planning for the two sites therefore was not at all as populist in approach as the official rhetoric of participation might suggest. But at the same time neither did it fit a top-down model of imposed 'fortress conservation' (Blaikie and Jeanrenaud 1997). The emerging plans were manifestly shaped by socio-economic factors (gauged in part through consultations), some local actors achieved an indirect influence on plans, and the progress of planning was also subject to local influence. A decidedly more complex process was therefore at work.

The socio-political process of planning can perhaps best be conceived in terms of webs of social power exercised by actors in a negotiating arena (Quarles van Ufford 1993). Given the centralized role of the planning teams in protected area design, the process was dominated by attempts to alter power relations between them and the communities, both on the part of planners and of stakeholders. Through a detailed analysis of the motives, resources and actions of different actors and actor-groups, presented in Few (2000b), it was possible to characterize their tactical applications of power in the negotiating arena in terms of strategies and effects. Echoing the style of presentation adopted by Brown and Rosendo (2000a), Table 10.2 provides a generalized typology of local stakeholders from both study sites categorized in terms of their power relations with planners. Columns three to five in the table refer to the relative strength of their power in negotiation with planners, their principal reaction to planning proposals, and the response of planners to these reactions. (Note that although distinctions between individual planning team members existed – see later under 'The Balance of Containment' – their functional role vis-à-vis community participation was essentially unified and they are therefore represented as a 'collective actor' for the purposes of this first stage of analysis.)

Containment Actions

Strong patterns therefore emerged in the skewed relations between planning agencies and community members. But the differential responses of planners to different actors can be conceptualized further – as strands of a broader strategy of containment. The planning teams in Belize were engaged in an overarching process of containment, or more precisely *attempted* containment, that shaped their approach to negotiations in the power arena. The planners endeavoured to manage public involvement so as to minimize social conflict, dissent and overall disruption to a primary goal of producing and completing protected area plans fundamentally oriented toward biodiversity protection. As argued elsewhere (Few 2000; Few 2000a), the bureaucratic, political and discursive background to conservation planning channelled the actions of planners into such a mode of operation.

The key interest of this chapter is in the mechanics of containment: in the constituent social actions of the containment process. A focus on these, often tacit, actions is crucial in forging an understanding of the socio-political nature of participation. The containment actions of planners could be categorized into themes of:

- avoidance of conflict;
- exclusion of dissent; and
- control over both knowledge and procedure.

But, just as social power is almost inevitably twinned with resistance (Giddens 1985; Scott 1990; Crush 1995), so containment had its binary opposite: some of the actions of other actors had the effect of counter-containment.

Avoidance and Exclusion

Through the consultative forums, the planners in Belize were able to gain data on economic usage of the sites and repeatedly gauge opinions on the emergent plans. Using this supply of information, the planners took calculated 'avoidance' actions – strategic planning decisions designed to reduce or circumvent possible adverse

Table 10.2 Generalized typology of local actors

Actor type	Description	Power rating	Response to plans	Planners' response
Bridge-builders	Actively supportive individuals who took on an intermediary role between planners and community	Medium	Support	Encouragement, enrolment
Passive supporters	Snorkel/dive tour guides who expressed support for the marine reserve but had little active involvement in consultations	Low	Support	Accommodation, targeting of consultations
Semi-excluded	Lobster/beachtrap fishermen with some concerns over continued access but little opportunity to voice them	Very low	Qualified support	Partial accommodation
Excluded	'Outsider' fishermen viewed with antipathy in the main communities and given no opportunity of involvement	Very low	–	No accommodation
Low-power opponents	Spearfishers and sports fishing guides who expressed opposition to marine restrictions in consultation fora	Low	Opposition	No accommodation
High-power opponents	Groups with land development interests who used lobbying power to try to reduce the terrestrial coverage	High	Opposition	Partial accommodation

reactions from local stakeholders. Planning policy for both sites was always intended to promote sustainable development by taking socio-economic considerations into account (Programme for Belize 1996). But data from the study – including interviews with planning officials – explicitly refers to decisions that were motivated by tactics of avoidance rather than positive benefit to communities. They included decisions to accommodate certain usage of marine resources in selected zones and some of the public demands for future landholdings. Such actions typically involved a degree of compromise on the part of planners, but in turn they not only helped avoid controversy but also helped forge support and cooperation from key user groups. They reflect the same strategic neutralization of opposition that some authors associate with ICDP projects (Ghimire and Pimbert 1997; Schroeder 1999).

In terms of the typology of actors outlined in Table 10.2 avoidance actions tended to be used most in relation to the concerns of 'passive supporters' and the 'high-power opponents'. Planners recognized limitations to the likelihood of successfully imposing measures strongly opposed by high-power actors concerned with land resources or to numerically-large, low-power groups concerned with marine resources. As one stakeholder claimed:

> I think the scientists wanted to do more. But because of the pressure of the people, their hands were tied. They wouldn't be able to do it because it would be chaos, it would be civil unrest or something like that. (Interview with public official, San Pedro, December 1996)

In the resulting plans for Bacalar Chico the planners offered a compromise on the land boundary in negotiations with the politically influential cay development lobby, and the only strict no-take zones for marine users were in the northernmost section of the reserve – a stretch of reef seldom visited by tour guides and fishermen. The one location where potential conflict over marine restrictions was a real threat was Rocky Point, a spawning site for Nassau grouper (*Epinephelus striatus*). The seasonal concentration of these large fish attracts both commercial fishing boats and sports fishing tours, and the planners believed there was a need to place key restrictions on this activity. Initially, they suggested a two to three month closure of the area during the spawning season, but after strong public reaction planners recognized the need to compromise and endorsed a 10-day closure instead. As one sports fishing guide suggested, 'if they close that place probably they would have to take half of the village in gaol' (interview with tour guide, San Pedro, December 1996).

Compromise, however, could only go so far. The plans could diverge from an optimum for biodiversity conservation only if they remained within acceptable parameters for a credible protected area. Avoidance therefore had its limitations. If planners perceived that accommodating local concerns was unacceptable, and if power relations permitted, they could try to negate opposition or potential opposition through exclusion.

At Caye Caulker, given the power of the land development lobby and the landholding aspirations of the wider local community, planners acted to minimize opposition to the emerging plans by including only the far north of the cay within the protected area – a site known as North Point. At 50–60 ha., they were planning to conserve a terrestrial area minuscule by comparison with most of the world's national parks. The 1994–1996 Caye Caulker Village Council nevertheless remained concerned that too much land was being set aside for conservation. But the planners were not prepared to compromise still further to placate opponents. They regarded a size below 50 ha. as ecologically deficient. They also perceived that the counter-proposals of the land lobby were weakly supported both locally and in national political circles, and at that stage ceased negotiation and simply proceeded with planning. Instead of allowing a stalemate to continue putting the project on hold, the planners blocked off the channel of consultation with the Council.

'Exclusion' actions had to be subtle in application – reserved for relations in which the blocking of concerns was tactically feasible. They operated largely through the closure or attempted closure of avenues through which potential issues could be communicated – one of the fundamental dimensions of social power long recognized by social theorists (Hardy and Leiba-O'Sullivan 1998). They appeared to be used most easily and effectively in relation to the lowest-power actors – mostly the 'semi-excluded', the 'excluded' and the 'low-power opponents' noted in Table 10.2 – those who had the least power to resist and complain of their denial of a voice. Fishermen, as a whole, did not feel empowered to speak out and tended not to be targeted for consultations. The exclusion of the fishing cooperatives was particularly striking, their capacity for political lobbying blunted by blockage of information from government agencies. As the manager of the local fishermen's cooperative explained:

> We do not know enough about what the reserve's about, how many of the fishermen are going to be affected, whether it will have an effect on our operations. Once these things become clear, and it's starting to hurt us, then obviously we would set up the necessary lobbying methods .... This interview that we're doing right now is an eye-opener for me. (Interview with fishing cooperative officer, Belize City, February 1997)

The stakeholders given no opportunity to take part in consultations were plainly subject to exclusion. They comprised visiting fishermen from the mainland village of Sarteneja in the case of Caye Caulker, and fishermen crossing the border from Mexico in the case of Bacalar Chico. Had they been permitted a voice these fishermen would likely have raised objections to planned strict regulations for marine areas they utilized. In a sense blockage of their concerns enabled the avoidance of others, for, in order to meet national protected area guidelines, planners had to include core conservation zones ('no access' and 'no take' zones) somewhere within the marine reserves (CZMP 1996).

Exclusion and avoidance also proceeded hand in hand in the case of spearfishing at Caye Caulker, an activity over which local stakeholders held diverging opinions. One of the planners indicated that Caye Caulker's relatively powerful and large tourism lobby would not accept continuing spearfishing near snorkel tour sites along the reef. Dissent from the small number of commercial spearfishers was easy for the planners to block, and the emerging restrictions avoided conflict with the tourism lobby by heavily restricting the activity. Spearfishing was also implicated as a major cause of reef fish decline, and its prevention could be justified with reference to biodiversity arguments. It was one form of 'multiple use' that was not accomodated and that was not negotiable.

A more subtle form of exclusion was in evidence in the case of sports fishing guides at Bacalar Chico. Having been seen to compromise over restrictions at Rocky Point and having defused most opposition, the planners then mis-represented public support for the 10-day closure proposal as unanimous. They closed off further discussion at that stage, despite the continuing opposition of sports fishing guides.

Control over Procedure and Knowledge

The containment actions of avoidance and exclusion designed to neutralize opposition and deflect delay themselves hinged on further containment actions: the attempted control of planning procedure and the circulation of knowledge.

The planning agencies were in a commanding position to exert control at least over the official channels of public involvement. They arranged and conducted the meetings and surveys, drew up the agendas and reported on the outcomes. They were able to steer the discussions and selectively encourage the participation of stakeholders perceived as supportive of the emerging plans, such as reef tour guides. Such control rendered public participation as reactive and consultative, rather than pro-active and executive.

Yet there were dangers that containment of participation itself would too-conspicuously run counter to planning or funding policy of government and external donors. Expectations of comprehensive community involvement were, after all, written into the planning guidelines for protected areas. In order to avoid such a danger, planners conveyed the impression that the process had been more open to participation: they created a 'semblance' or illusion of active local participation presented both to legitimize projects in bureaucratic and donor circles and to defuse local tensions. As Arnstein (1969: 219) noted, such 'window-dressing' can simultaneously give stakeholders a sense that they have participated and give agencies evidence that 'they have gone through the required motions' of involving people. Hildyard et al. (1998: 32) suggest:

> Often it turns out that local people become a ghostly presence within the planning process – visible, heard even, but ultimately only there because their involvement lends credibility and legitimacy to decisions that have already been made .... Participation becomes a means for top-down planning to be imposed from the bottom-up.

In an interview, one member of the planning team for Bacalar Chico openly admitted that it was easy to represent the planning process as driven by grassroots input. Reports produced by the team demonstrated that consultation efforts were in place, but statements such as 'boundaries for the parks and the zones encompassed are set on the basis of discussion with local communities' (CZMP, personal communication, December 1995) gave little insight into the planning input actually resulting from participation. Contrary to the claims of, for example, the tour guides president at Caye Caulker, the researcher found that local actors had played little or no role in defining the boundaries, and that their input into zoning decisions had been primarily informational. Indeed, the confidence in the consultation process expressed by some key local actors – the 'bridge-builders' in Table 10.2 – is to some extent testament to their successful 'enrolment' by planners (Murdoch and Marsden 1995).

The constructed image of planning as bottom-up in character was one example of how planners also attempted to control knowledge processes. By actively promoting selected ideas and representations of the protected area sites and emerging plans, the planners further hoped to guide local opinions and smooth the course of planning. This constitutes attempted control of the 'public transcript' – another key dimension of social power, especially within environmental contexts (Bryant and Bailey 1997; Hardy and Leiba-O'Sullivan 1998).

The tactical mobilization and manipulation of ideas and discourses was amply illustrated in the case study. In their public promotion of Bacalar Chico, for example, planners drew heavily on local representations of Mexican fishermen crossing into Belizean waters as environmental 'villains'. The focus on curbing Mexican fishing enhanced support among fishermen in the communities. However, it is noteworthy that the chair of the fishing cooperative in San Pedro saw the key overfishing problem not in terms of foreign incursions but as the use of gill-nets on beachtraps set by Belizeans.

Across both sites, planners also placed emphasis in their consultations on the (unproven) potential of the protected areas to generate ecotourism. Again this tapped local-scale aspirations and wider, national discourses promoting Belize's economic future as a tourism destination. In effect, the planners were promoting the protected area as a development project rather than a biodiversity conservation project. Indeed it could be argued that the planners were not just trying to build support by invoking the promise of tourism, but were discursively manoeuvring stakeholders into acquiescence through the type of 'social contract' implicit in ICDPs: 'if we do X for you, you will stop destroying this habitat' (Richard and O'Connor 1997: 413).

The containment actions of planners had one last important element. As well as attempting to control their own exchanges with stakeholders, the planning teams also tried to control potentially disruptive interactions *within* the community. The clearest example of this was the stated preference of planning staff for setting up liaison and possible co-management relations with Caye Caulker village council rather than with two rival local NGOs. One official claimed:

> After speaking with a lot of people out there, you know, a lot of people know me out there, I think they are most satisfied with the village council actually playing the major role in it. They are satisfied. (Interview with government officer, Belize City, March 1997)

During interviews, however, the researcher found little interest in or knowledge of the co-management issue among ordinary local stakeholders. Instead, it appeared that, by supporting the council in its attempts to secure a role, the planners were hoping to circumvent the potentially obstructive problems of factionalism arising between the other two organizations. The same official complained of these tensions and went on to reveal 'if you don't be firm and give it good guidance then I think it could really become a mess, you know' (March 1997).

Counter-containment

Containment, however, was not an irresistible force in planning. The very fact that planners entered negotiations with stakeholders, sought their support and sought to demonstrate their involvement in planning, opened up the opportunities for conflict, dissent and disruption. Attention therefore also has to be given to the destabilizing capacities of those stakeholders subject to attempted containment – to the notion of counter-containment.

The existence of counter-containment is a logical consequence of planners' 'need' for containment, and it reflects the notions of power that emphasize the ubiquity of resistance (Clegg 1989). Scott (1990) details how even 'low-profile' actions or 'disguised' dissent can constitute forms of resistance that have an attritional impact on the seemingly dominant power of others. Giddens (1985: 11) stresses:

> No matter how great the scope or intensity of control superordinates possess, since their power presumes the active compliance of others, those others can bring to bear strategies of their own, and apply specific types of sanctions.

A number of authors have pointed out that local people are seldom 'powerless' in the face of agency control over involvement (White 1996; Peterson 1997; Pelling 1999). But the counter-containment concept relates not just to oppositional resistance. Its essence is action by non-planners that serves to undermine containment by disrupting or potentially disupting the progress of planning. It therefore includes incidentally disruptive actions as well as deliberate opposition. It is important to recognize the impact on community involvement of intra-community division and conflict (Leach et al. 1997; Sharpe 1998), and to acknowledge that, however stage-managed the participatory exercises might be, planning progress remains susceptible to such tensions.

In the case study, community involvement activities provided even low-power stakeholders with an opportunity to disrupt plans, although in the cases of Bacalar Chico and Caye Caulker their counter-containment role was minimal. For Bacalar Chico a small number of local people connected with sports fishing expressed overall disapproval with plans they saw as imposed from above and contrary to their interests, but failed to enrol a sufficient body of other stakeholders into their opposition. It may have been the case that the compromise tactic by planners over Rocky Point defused their potential for continuing effective dissent.

The capacity for counter-containment appeared greater for those 'high-power opponents' (see Table 10.2) concerned with the repercussions of the protected areas for land ownership and development. With their greater power resources they had a greater potential to stall planning progress, in part by lobbying other sectors of government. They could mobilize powerful discourses to strengthen their political position, for the planners by no means held a monopoly over the realm of ideas. One of the most potent was connected with the Belizean government's drive for external investment (GOB 1994). One stakeholder invoked the threat of a withdrawal of external investment should development restrictions be increased adjacent to Bacalar Chico:

> It's a little bit radical, it's a little bit extremist .... Say, you're looking at about 100 American investors that would have a problem with the stability of our country, with the development aspect, right. So it would definitely have a negative impact. (Interview with real estate manager, San Pedro, December 1996)

Some of the high-power opponents could also utilize a liaison role to misrepresent the views of general stakeholders. The chair of the 1994–1996 Caye Caulker Village Council, for example, claimed that their opposition to the terrestrial coverage of the Caye Caulker proposals was posited on behalf of ordinary villagers, yet there was little evidence of concern among villagers over the land portion. One local actor argued that the chair's lobbying actions had effectively been part of an ongoing attempt by potential landowners' to stall progress in designating the terrestrial portion, rather than achieve a compromise.

Moreover, as already suggested, counter-containment actions causing planning delays and forced changes against the will of planners were not limited to intentional acts. Delay in preparation of a management plan for Caye Caulker was an incidental effect of problems of intra-community factionalism, according to two planning officials from different ministries. The most striking example of counter-containment of all was the incidental action of a stakeholder at Caye Caulker who announced a legal claim to land formerly confiscated from him by the government and destined to be included in the planned protected area. His claim to the land at North Point was, ostensibly at least, an issue between himself and other sectors of government, rather than a response to the protected area plans. However, it immediately forced a rethink of the terrestrial extent of the protected area by planners and stalled progress in planning for both marine and terrestrial components. As a response, some planners regretfully suggested they might have to designate the marine reserve separately, and another feared long delay over the land portion might even result in its omission through political pressure.

The Balance of Containment: A Comparative Analysis

The case study revealed key similarities in the planning process for the two protected area sites. Yet there was also clear divergence between them in the course of planning events. Those differences can be articulated in terms of an analytical framework of containment. This chapter contends that attempted containment of stakeholder involvement was a feature common to both sites, and that differences in their planning progress can be explained in part by comparing the efficacy with which containment was practised. In so doing, it draws on the context-dependence of local stakeholders' motives and power resources, and underlines that the contingencies of place have a crucial bearing on the planning process.

Containment actions are conceptualized here as taking place at the local scale in the interactions between planners and local stakeholders. But the influence of wider contexts means that the efficacy of containment is also related to factors external to planner-stakeholder interactions: factors operating at the national and global scales. In comparing planning events for the two sites it is therefore necessary to look first at external factors influencing planning. They are referred to here as 'preconditions' because they help shape the potential for containment actions to succeed.

For Bacalar Chico, the preconditions of planning were comparatively strong. External resources provided by INGOs proved crucial in securing a strong financial package for the project from the European Union (EU) (Dotherow 1995). The incoming funding commitment, in turn, set up outgoing channels of responsibility in the form of progress reports to the EU. The Bacalar Chico project therefore had extra pressure laid upon it not only to demonstrate planning performance, but also to bring the project to fruition within the 28-month funding window.

There was also concerted political and administrative impetus for the project from within Belize. The proposed reserve was included in the government's application for World Heritage Site status, an application that proved a spur to the establishment of several protected areas. It was also promoted as the Belizean component of a potential transboundary reserve. Political and bureaucratic commitment to the project was considerable, providing the ministerial support seen as key to planning progress. All in all, the project had powerful momentum from the top down.

Caye Caulker had far less external finance and apparently weaker governmental support. The resources of a Coastal Zone Management Programme (funded by the Global Environment Facility) substantially aided planning (August 1996), but Caye Caulker did not attract the INGO involvement comparable with that of Bacalar Chico that might have helped secure external funds dedicated to the project. Funding for the site was difficult to justify on the basis of high biodiversity richness, the attribute most likely to attract conservation-oriented INGOs.

Moreover, the creation of a protected area at the site did not appear to figure so highly in national biodiversity priorities. Under conditions in which political and economic motives, including the push for investment, precluded guaranteed cross-governmental support for protected areas, at times cracks appeared in the unity of purpose between different arms of government. For Caye Caulker, governmental disunity emerged most strongly in differences in opinion among officials over the protection status of the land portion.

Many local stakeholders expressed cynicism over government handling of the project at Caye Caulker, and, owing to delays, more scepticism over the political and administrative momentum for designation. One supportive local stakeholder complained 'you know they talk about it but they don't really act, and we want someone to act' (interview with tour guide, Caye Caulker, January 1997). Altogether, the planning momentum for the Caye Caulker project showed faltering signs from the top down.

Differences in the preconditions of planning between the two sites combined with local-scale actions in the power arenas of planning to create different outcomes in terms of containment of community involvement.

For Bacalar Chico, the strong preconditions for planning progress were matched by a tendency for the project to generate relatively little counter-containment activity. Comments from stakeholders overall suggested their support for a reserve was conditional on plans having no perceived negative effect on individual livelihoods. In the absence of negative effects, support would be expressed. The chosen location of the reserve away from heavily visited fishing and tourism areas made it relatively uncontroversial in this respect. There was also minimal existing settlement close to the site, few local stakeholders expressed any substantial concerns about the terrestrial portion and most of the public land included was of low development potential. Referring to the entire western portion of the land area, one stakeholder remarked:

> Who the heck wants to go back there .... Unless somebody puts in a lot of money that land is probably going to sit like that for ever. (Interview with resident, San Pedro, November 1996)

Individual concerns existed over fishing access and restrictions on land use, differences of opinion existed over fish stocks, and interviews with local stakeholders revealed dismay over a perceived inadequacy of consultations and lack of knowledge of the plans. Yet these issues and others that might have arisen were, in this case, effectively contained by the avoidance, exclusion and control actions described earlier. In pursuing these actions, planners drew on the preconditional planning base built from adequate finance and governmental commitment, which enhanced the power resources of knowledge, authority and institutional capacity available for containment. Containment helped the reserve to be declared within a time span of four years from initiation of the project. From the point of view of planners, the project proceeded smoothly and swiftly to designation within its funding schedule, and any impediments were effectively circumvented.

By contrast, the weaker preconditions for containment at Caye Caulker were matched by more prominent instances of counter-containment. The proximity of the protected area to the village helped to raise more local interest and active support, but also provoked more concern and controversy. The proposed marine reserve was not only heavily visited by fishermen and tour guides, but the terrestrial portion was on land apparently coveted for development by certain people from the island and from the mainland. The planning process there became embroiled in disputes over the land portion, and was even affected by rivalries between groups within the community.

Controversy and debate over the land portion were identified as major obstructions both in the early stages and after the late emergence of the ownership issue. The planners' selection of a small portion of newly-acquired crown land in the north of the island (North Point) appeared to be an avoidance action, but opposition still arose at an early stage and brought about delay followed by the subsequent containment action of exclusion. As the then Village Council chair put it, the negotiations 'broke down right there' (interview with resident, Caye Caulker, January 1997). Later delays surrounded the organization of consultation meetings and completion of the management plan. Little progress on either took place during the fieldwork period. Further delaying issues arose over future local management responsibilities and, ultimately, the former landowner's claim to North Point, which also threatened an enforced downgrading of the plans in conservation terms.

In contrast with experience at Bacalar Chico, the Caye Caulker project was therefore characterized by planning impediments and both deliberate and incidental counter-containment actions. Its weaker preconditions were epitomized by the demonstrable differences in opinion aired at the institutional level. Power strategies were prominent at the local level. It was not only the planning agencies that tried to persuade, manipulate, enrol and control: local actors in turn actively deployed power tactics and some even tried to enrol the planners. And, finally, plans were disrupted by the threat of litigation from a former landowner – a threat against which planners appeared to have neither the financial resources nor the political clout to battle. The planning team could not effectively contain public involvement, the planning process did not proceed smoothly and declaration of the protected area was repeatedly delayed.

Figure 10.2 summarizes in diagrammatic form how different factors helped determine the balance of containment versus counter-containment in the case study sites.

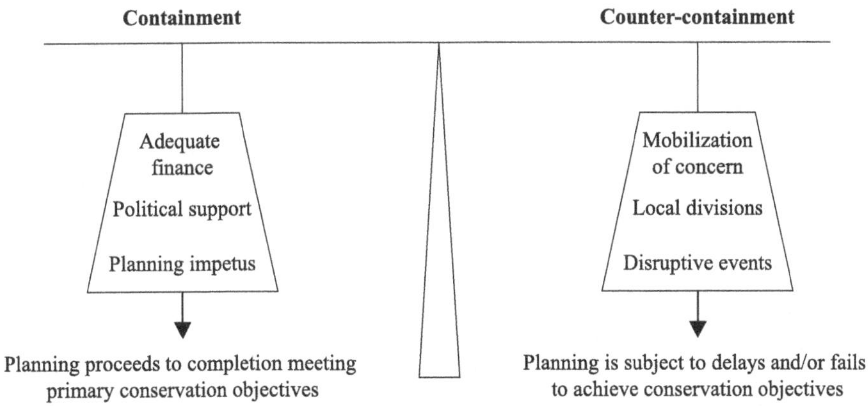

Figure 10.2 The balance of containment

Conclusion

The detailed argument in this chapter reflects a growing body of work critically assessing public participation in resource management projects (e.g. Hildyard et al. 1998; Gauld 2000; Pelling 1999). In particular, it echoes the critical analyses of protected area conservation by authors such as Pimbert and Pretty (1997) and Schroeder (1999). It suggests that long-established discourses of conservation combined with an institutional inertia to restrict the agencies' approach to community involvement in protected area planning at the case study sites in Belize. Planners made concessions toward, but could not embrace the ideals of, a people-oriented conservation.

What is new in the argument here is the recognition that planners consequently became engaged in an overarching process of attempted containment, via their power relations with other actors in the negotiating arena of planning. The key components of that process were avoidance and exclusion actions and the control of knowledge and procedure. But the actions of planners did not necessarily achieve intended outcomes. Some of the actions of non-planners in the power arenas can be conceptualized in terms of counter-containment, the binary opposite of containment. The concept of counter-containment can encompass mechanisms of resistance, but it does not necessarily result from opposition. Its definition is action that serves to undermine containment, whether or not that effect is intentional.

The concepts of containment and counter-containment may prove useful as analytical tools not just to elucidate actors' roles and interventions but to examine the whole pattern of community involvement in the power arena of planning. The concepts provide a framework for comparing planning 'progress' between different sites. The containment framework combines analysis of containment and counter-containment actions with analysis of wider contextual factors that influence the power resources available to planners and thereby shape their potential to contain effectively.

Lest the foregoing should imply that containment forges greater progress in terms of achieving conservation goals, it is important to stress one final analytical point. Clearly, containment stifles the objectives of participatory democracy as envisaged by writers such as Healey (1997) and Forester (1999). But successful containment does not even ensure ultimate project 'success' in the narrowly-defined terms of maximizing biodiversity protection. Public concern over the participation process surrounding both sites in Belize was by no means negligible: many people had expectations raised that were not fulfilled. Bacalar Chico may have proceeded swiftly to designation, but the pressures to do so meant that the final consultation stages were shelved. The finalized boundaries of the reserve were officially declared without the 'approval' of the communities. Just as the enthusiastic promotion of the tourism potential of protected areas by planners could fall foul if tourism were to enter a decline, so the circumscription of participation and the misrepresentation of the process risked fomenting future dissent during the project's implementation phase. Open and broad-based community participation has a practical as well as ethical role to play in conservation (Ghimire and Pimbert 1997; Gbadegesin and Ayileka 2000). Containment is no sustainable substitute for inclusive decision-making.

Acknowledgements

The author owes thanks to Clare Madge for comments on the initial drafts of this chapter. Gratitude is also due to staff at the Department of Geography, University of Leicester for research support, and to all those in Belize who took part in the study. The field research was financed in part by the Dudley Stamp Memorial Trust and the Developing Areas Research Group of the Institute of British Geographers.

Note

* This chapter was originally published as 'Containment and Counter-containment: Planner/Community Relations in Conservation Planning' in *The Geographical Journal*, 167 (2), June 2001, pp. 111–24 (© 2001 The Royal Geographical Society).

References

Arce, A., Villarreal, M. and de Vries, P. (1994), 'The Social Construction of Rural Development: Discourses, Practices and Power', in D. Booth (ed.) *Rethinking Social Development: Theory, Research and Practice*, Harlow: Longman, pp. 152–71.

Arnstein, S.R. (1969), 'A Ladder of Citizen Participation', *Journal of the American Institute of Planners*, 35, pp. 216–24.

August, A.P. (1996), *Caye Caulker Marine Reserve and National Park Preliminary Draft Management Plan*, Belize: Government of Belize.

Blaikie, P. and Jeanrenaud, S. (1997), 'Biodiversity and Human Welfare', in K.B. Ghimire and M.P. Pimbert (eds), *Social Change and Conservation: Environmental Politics and Impacts of National Parks and Protected Areas*, London: Earthscan, pp. 46–70.

Brandon, K., Redford, K.H. and Sanderson, S.E. (eds) (1998), *Parks in Peril: People, Politics, and Protected Areas*, Washington: Island Press.

Brohman, J. (1996), *Popular Development: Rethinking the Theory and Practice of Development*, Oxford: Blackwell.

Brown, K. (1998), 'The Political Ecology of Biodiversity, Conservation and Development in Nepal's Terai: Confused Meanings, Means and Ends', *Ecological Economics*, 24, pp. 73–87.

Brown, K. and Rosendo, S. (2000), 'The Institutional Architecture of Extractive Reserves in Rondonia, Brazil', *The Geographical Journal*, 166, pp. 35–48.

Brown, K. and Rosendo, S. (2000a), 'Environmentalists, Rubber Tappers and Empowerment: The Politics and Economics of Extractive Reserves', *Development and Change*, 31, pp. 201–27.

Bryant, R.L. and Bailey, S. (1997), *Third World Political Ecology*, London: Routledge.

Clegg, S.R. (1989), *Frameworks of Power*, London: Sage.

Cline-Cole, R. (1997), 'Promoting (Anti-)Social Forestry in northern Nigeria?', *Review of African Political Economy*, 74, pp. 515–36.

Crush, J. (ed.) (1995), *Power of Development*, London: Routledge.

CZMP (1995), Personal communication, December 1995.

CZMP (1996), *Protected Area Management Plans and Zoning Schemes*, Belize City: Coastal Zone Management Programme.

Desai, V. (1996), 'Access to Power and Participation', *Third World Planning Review*, 18, pp. 217–42.

Doornbos, M., Saith, A. and White, B. (2000), 'Forest Lives and Struggles: An Introduction', *Development and Change*, 31, pp. 1–10.

Dotherow, M. (1995), *Bacalar Chico Interim Report April–December 1994*, Marin-Neuchatel: International Tropical Conservation Foundation.

Dryzek, J. (2000), *Deliberative Democracy and Beyond: Liberals, Critics, Contestations*, Oxford: Oxford University Press.

Few, R. (2000), 'Conservation, Participation and Power: Protected-area Planning in the Coastal Zone of Belize', *Journal of Planning Education and Research*, 19, pp. 401–8.

Few, R. (2000a), 'Participation or Containment?: Community Involvement in Protected Area Planning', paper presented at *Environmental Resources: Conflict, Co-operation and Governance* (conference of the Development Studies Association), University of Bradford, Bradford, May 2000.

Few, R. (2000b), 'Conservation, Participation and Power: Community Involvement in Protected Area Planning in Belize', Unpublished PhD thesis, Department of Geography, University of Leicester, Leicester.

Forester, J. (1999), *The Deliberative Practitioner: Encouraging Participatory Planning Processes*, Cambridge, MA: MIT Press.

Gauld, R. (2000), 'Maintaining Centralized Control in Community-based Forestry: Policy Construction in the Philippines', *Development and Change*, 31, pp. 229–54.

Gbadegesin, A. and Ayileka, O. (2000), 'Avoiding the Mistakes of the Past: Towards a Community-oriented Management Strategy for the Proposed National Park in Abuja-Nigeria', *Land Use Policy*, 17, pp. 89–100.

GEF (1998), *Project Performance Report 1998* ,Washington: Global Environment Facility.

Ghimire, K.B. and Pimbert, M.P. (eds) (1997), *Social Change and Conservation: Environmental Politics and Impacts of National Parks and Protected Areas*, London: Earthscan.

Gibson, J., Azueta, J., Gomez, D. and Somerville, M. (1996), *Bacalar Chico Final Report*, Marin-Neuchatel: International Tropical Conservation Foundation.

Giddens, A. (1985), *The Nation-state and Violence*, Cambridge: Polity Press.

GOB (1994), *Belize Medium-term Economic Strategy Paper 1994–1997*, Belize: Government of Belize.

Hardy, C. and Leiba-O'Sullivan, S. (1998), 'The Power behind Empowerment: Implications for Research and Practice', *Human Relations*, 51, pp. 451–83.

Healey, P. (1997), *Collaborative Planning: Shaping Places in Fragmented Societies*, Houndmills: Macmillan Press.

Hildyard, N., Hegde, P., Wolvekamp, P. and Reddy, S. (1998), 'Pluralism, Participation and Power', *Forest, Trees and People*, 35, pp. 31–5.

Hulme, D. and Murphree, M. (1999), 'Communities, Wildlife and the 'New Conservation' in Africa', *Journal of International Development*, 11, pp. 277–85.

Leach, M., Mearns, R. and Scoones, I. (1997), 'Challenges to Community-based Sustainable Development: Dynamics, Entitlements, Institutions', *IDS Bulletin*, 28, pp. 4–14.

Little, P.D. (1994), 'The Link between Local Participation and Improved Conservation: A Review of Issues and Experiences', in D. Western, R.M. Wright and S. Strum (eds.), *Natural Connections: Perspectives in Community-based Conservation*, Washington: Island Press, pp. 347–72.

Murdoch, J. and Marsden, T. (1995), 'The Spatialization of Politics: Local and National Actor-spaces in Environmental Conflict', *Transactions of the Institute of British Geographers*, 20, pp. 368–80.

Nelson, N. and Wright, S. (eds) (1995), *Power and Participatory Development: Theory and Practice*, London: Intermediate Technology Publications.

Pelling, M. (1999), 'The Political Ecology of Flood Hazard in Urban Guyana', *Geoforum*, 30, pp. 249–61.

Peterson, T.R. (1997) *Sharing the Earth: The Rhetoric of Sustainable Development*, Columbia: University of South Carolina Press.

Pimbert, M.P. and Pretty, J.N. (1997), 'Parks, People and Professionals: Putting "Participation" into Protected Area Management', in K.B. Ghimire and M.P. Pimbert (eds), *Social Change and Conservation: Environmental Politics and Impacts of National Parks and Protected Areas*, London: Earthscan, pp. 297–330.

Programme for Belize (1996), *National Protected Areas Systems Plan for Belize: Synthesis Report*, Belize: NARMAP Project/Inter-American Development Bank.

Quarles van Ufford, P. (1993), 'Knowledge and Ignorance in the Practices of Development Policy', in M. Hobart (ed.), *An Anthropological Critique of Development*, London: Routledge, pp. 135–60.

Richard, A.F. and O'Connor, S. (1997), 'Degradation, Transformation and Conservation: The Past, Present and Possible Future of Madagascar's Environment', in S.M. Goodman and B.D. Patterson (eds), *Natural Change and Human Impact in Madagascar*, Washington: Smithsonian Institution, pp. 406–18.

Sanjayan, M.A., Shen, S. and Jansen, M. (1997), *Experiences with Integrated Conservation-development Projects in Asia*, Washington: The World Bank.

Schroeder, R.A. (1999), 'Geographies of Environmental Intervention in Africa', *Progress in Human Geography*, 23, pp. 359–78.

Scott, J. (1990), *Domination and the Arts of Resistance: Hidden Transcripts*, New Haven: Yale University Press.

Sharpe, B. (1998), '"First the Forest": Conservation, "Community" and "Participation" in South-west Cameroon', *Africa*, 68, pp. 25–45.

Taylor, G. and Johansson, L. (1996), 'Our Voices, Our Words and Our Pictures: Plans, Truths and Videotapes from the Ngorongoro Conservation Area', *Forest, Trees and People*, 30, pp. 28–39.

Thrift, N. and Walling, D. (2000), 'Geography in the United Kingdom 1996–2000', *The Geographical Journal*, 166, pp. 96–124.

West, P.C. and Brechin, S.R. (eds.) (1991), *Resident Peoples and National Parks: Social Dilemmas and Strategies in International Conservation*, Tucson: University of Arizona Press.

White, S.C. (1996), 'Depoliticising Development: The Uses and Abuses of Participation', *Development in Practice*, 6, pp. 6–15.

Chapter 11

Dis Da Fu We: Conservation, Development and Empowerment in San Pedro Town, Belize

Brandon Kitagawa and Janet Momsen

Reconciling Conservation and Development

In the years following World War II, decolonization led to an increased awareness of, and focus on, international development among former colonial powers (Isbister 2001; Klaren and Bossert 1986; Escobar 1995). At the same time as resources were invested in economic development, an independent movement sparked by environmental concerns worldwide began to unfold, resulting in a growing network of new national parks, preserves, reserves, and other conservation areas (Neumann 1998; Brown 2002).

Traditionally, each movement saw the other as an obstacle. On the one hand, many of those interested in economic development found that conservationist's methods for protecting the environment often hindered 'progress' and exacerbated conditions of poverty by denying access to the very resources needed to develop (see Martin chapter). Environmentalists, on the other hand, saw economic development and modernization as non-sustainable and counterproductive as they encroached on the fragile and pristine ecosystems that all life is dependent upon (Brown 2002; Barrett and Arcese 1995; Alpert 1996).

As a result of this conflict, many project outcomes fell into one of three categories: *exploitation*, *limitation*, or *disruption*. Large-scale, macro-development policies without regard for either local communities or the environment often led to the *exploitation* of both. While community-centered development often showed short-term success, without attention to ecological processes, many community-based projects ultimately failed because of the ecological *limitation* reached through unsustainable resource use. Conservation efforts, on the other hand, aimed at protecting nature from human impact. The *disruption* of this 'fortress' or 'fences and fines' conservation further alienated and marginalized border communities by restricting access to traditionally used resources (Neumann 1998; Newmark and Hough 2000; Alpert 1996; Barrett and Arcese 1995; Stocking and Perkin 1991). We argue here that such conflict between planning approaches is not necessary.

While each movement had some successes, a fourth option that attempts to reconcile community and ecological processes has emerged: *integration* (see Figure 11.1). This paradigm, generally referred to as integrated conservation and development

(ICD), is based on the idea that conservation and development are neither independent nor antagonistic (Alpert 1995). Rather, conservation must embrace local populations and development must account for the local environment (Wells, Brandon, and Hannah 1992; Stocking and Perkin 1991). By emphasizing the interconnections between the two, successful projects utilizing this strategy can achieve effective environmental protection and sustainable community development (Brown 2002; Mayaka 2002; Salafsky and Wollenberg 2000; Abbot and Thomas 2001).

ICD projects move away from expert-driven, top-down policies towards a participatory model (Wainwright and Wehrmeyer 1998). By engaging stakeholders in collective decision-making, ICD builds social solidarity and empowers the community (Jha 2000). Further, ICD helps define conservation in local terms, linking conservation and community benefits (Wells, Brandon, and Hannah 1992) and creating a sense of responsibility, pride, and ownership for the project (Wainwright and Wehrmeyer 1998). The fundamental idea is that ICD creates a space for participation that ensures decision-making power is in the hands of communities, providing an incentive to local people for building a sustainable relationship with their surrounding environment (Stocking and Perkin 1991).

Because ICD is a relatively new strategy, it is unclear how effective it has been over the long term. Most research has focused on economic or conservation outcomes,

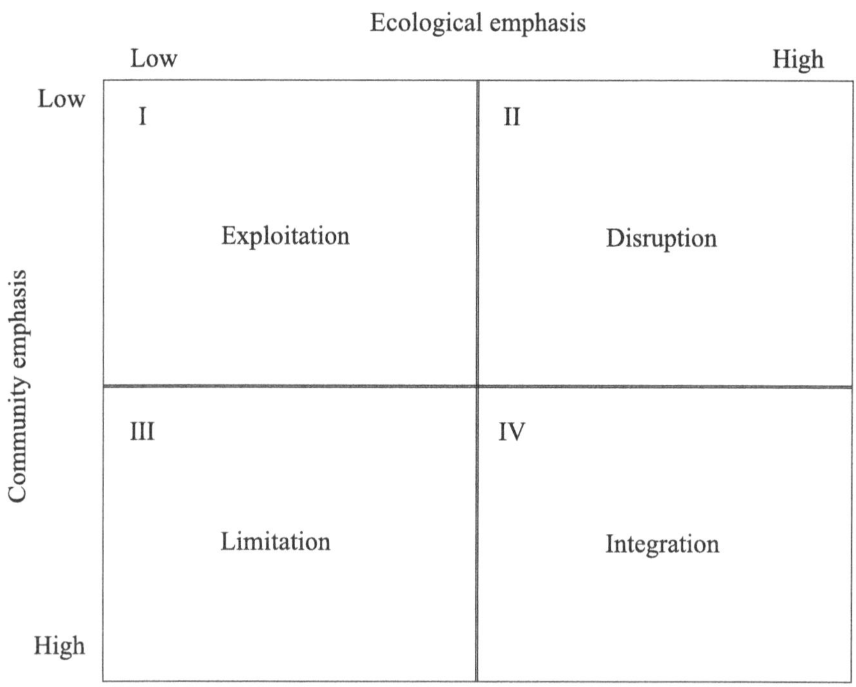

Figure 11.1 Dimensions of sustainable development

pointing to mixed results at best (Brown 2002; Barrett and Arcese 1995; Marcus 2001; Newmark and Hough 2000; Kremen, Merenlender, and Murphy 1994). Using the experience of San Pedro Town, Belize, we extend the research on ICD to community empowerment and conservation attitudes. Fifteen years after the establishment of the nearby Hol Chan Marine Reserve (HCMR), does San Pedro show signs of empowerment? How do *San Pedranos* view their relationship with their natural environment? And what factors are associated with differences in these perceptions? Consistent with the logic of ICD, the people of San Pedro report both individual and community empowerment and hold a positive outlook on the environment. These findings highlight the importance of the local context in which ICD strategies are implemented.

Research Location: San Pedro Town, Ambergris Caye, Belize

Belize is a small, Central American nation bordering Mexico, Guatemala, and the Caribbean Sea (see Figure 11.2). The country is sparsely settled with about 250,000 people in an area roughly the size of the state of Massachusetts (8,866 square miles or 23,657 km^2). San Pedro Town is the only settlement on Ambergris Caye, Belize's largest and northernmost barrier island on the largest barrier reef in the western hemisphere (and second in the world).

Commercial and subsistence fishing were the traditional mainstays of the community's economy. However, after a marked initial success following the founding of the Caribeña Producers Co-operative Society Limited (Caribeña) in 1963, the effects of intensive fishing began taking their toll (a clear example of *limitations*). The fishermen worked longer hours, covering more distant waters, yet their catch continued to decline, bringing less money back to the island. Similarly, the coral reef itself was beginning to show signs of stress (Godfrey 1996; Alamilla and Kitagawa 2001).

As a means of establishing better management of the fishery and boosting the inchoate tourism industry, the HCMR was established in 1987 (Young and Bilgre 2001). As one of the pioneering efforts in actively engaging the local community in protecting the natural environment in Belize (Carter 1990; Carter, Gibson and Azueta 1994), the HCMR provides an excellent example from which to examine the effect of participatory resource management on the community as a whole (see Few chapter). Furthermore, San Pedro has become Belize's leading tourist destination and is rapidly growing, highlighting the tensions between conservation and development.

The Hol Chan Marine Reserve and the San Pedro Community

This chapter examines the impact of the Reserve on community structure and empowerment, almost two decades after its establishment. It thus provides an assessment of the grassroots impact of a conservation project on the top-down planning noted by Few (Chapter 10). The two years spent as a Peace Corps Volunteer by the first author living in San Pedro and working for the HCMR (1999–2001) provided

Figure 11.2 Map of Belize

Source: Foundation for the Advancement of Mesoamerican Studies, Inc., <http://www.famsi.org/maps/belize.htm>.

significant insights about community processes. A return visit in the summer of 2002 built on the earlier period of participant observation in the community and enabled the collection of data measuring empowerment within the community using both surveys and in depth interviews with key informants.

As important decision-makers, the leaders of community organizations were targeted for these interviews. Interviewees included the presidents of the San Pedro Tour Guide Association (SPTGA), the San Pedro Lions Club, Green Reef (a local environmental watchdog), and Caribeña,[1] and both the current and original managers of the HCMR.

The survey instrument used key community indicators (gender, age, income, education, place of origin, and membership in local organizations), to create indices measuring perceptions of individual and community empowerment (McMillan et al. 1995; Itzhaky and York 2000; Speer and Peterson 2000; Zimmerman 1995), These indices also measured attitudes towards conservation and tourism (Lindberg and Enriquez 1994; Alexander 2000; Belsky 1999; Fiallo and Jacobson 1995; Parry and Campbell 1992). Members of the community were also asked open-ended questions about conservation and development. This same series of questions was asked of the key informants. Congruence between the answers of the general community and community leaders would suggest a broad level of empowerment.

A total of 89 surveys were collected, although not all respondents were able to answer every question. The sampling was not completely random, but theoretically based, similar to that used by Reininger et al. (2001). As a result, tour guides and, by extension, men were over represented in the sample. However, only five questions revealed a significant difference linked to gender or status as a tour guide. Given the focus of this research, the information gained through the theoretical emphasis in the methodology appears to outweigh the loss of a truly random sample.

To determine relationships between dependent and independent variables, data were cross-tabulated using chi-square to measure significant correlations. A Chronbach's Alpha test has been widely used to measure the reliability of indices (Speer and Peterson 2000; McMillan et al. 1995; Itzhaky and York 2000) and is used in this study. Scores of .72 and .79 for individual and community empowerment, respectively, are consistent with the range found in the previously mentioned studies, suggesting the questions making up each index are strongly interrelated.

Empowerment: The Ability to Achieve Goals

Empowerment as a process and empowerment as an outcome emerge as main themes in the empowerment literature (Reininger et al. 2001; Perkins and Zimmerman 1995; McMillan et al. 1995; Lyons, Smuts and Stephens 2001). As a multi-level process (individual, organizational and/or community), researchers point to the act of participating and working towards a goal as empowered, whereas an empowered outcome is identified by the attainment of increased control over one's individual or collective life (Reininger et al. 2001; Lyons, Smuts, and Stephens 2001; Zimmerman

1995; Perkins and Zimmerman 1995; McMillan et al. 1995; Zimmerman and Rappaport 1988). Using these elements and borrowing from Fetterman (2002), for the purpose of this study, empowerment is defined as an increased ability to achieve self-determined goals through self-determined means. It is essential for the long term success of conservation projects that the local residents feel involved and supportive. Community empowerment is a measure of the local impacts of such projects.

Previous studies have shown that sense of community, participation, and feelings of control are strong indicators of empowerment (McMillan et al. 1995; Lyons, Smuts and Stephens 2001; Reininger et al. 2001; Itzhaky and York 2000; Julian et al. 1997; Speer and Peterson 2000; Chavis and Wandersman 1990; Zimmerman and Rappaport 1988; Zimmerman 1995). Building on this earlier research, 5-point Likert Scale questions (strongly disagree, disagree, neutral, agree, strongly agree) were developed to measure perceptions of individual and community empowerment. Responses were coded from one to five with an increasing indication of empowerment. The sum of individual questions was used to create an index for individual and community empowerment. Respondents were labeled as 'high' or 'low' with the sum of neutral (three points) answers to all questions within the given empowerment index as the threshold.

Individual Empowerment

If ICD projects, such as the creation of the HCMR, serve as a means to achieve individual empowerment for local people, then, given the success of the marine reserve, one would expect the people of San Pedro to perceive themselves as empowered. The results illustrated in Tables 11.1 and 11.2 suggest that this is true. Average responses on the 5-point scale ranged from a high of 3.87 (I1) to a low of 2.51 (I4). Overall, a majority of those surveyed (56.5 per cent) indicated a sense of individual empowerment with an average seven-question index score of 21.2 out of 35 (SD = 3.89). Although this does not directly establish that the creation of the marine reserve is the source of this sense of empowerment, it is consistent with the logic justifying such participatory policies. It also refutes the null hypothesis that the Reserve has undermined feelings of control over their lives among residents of San Pedro.

While the results reveal that, in general, individuals in San Pedro believe they are empowered, it is important to recognize that a large portion of those surveyed (43.5 per cent) does not feel connected to the community, does not participate, and does not consider itself an influence on community decision-making. An important step towards addressing this disparity in perceived individual empowerment is to uncover factors that contribute to this empowerment as well as obstacles. This was done by examining relationships between individual empowerment scores and key community indicators.

Gender

Given the gender relationships observed during Brandon Kitagawa's time in San Pedro, we expected gender to influence how people perceive their own empowerment. Although girls and young women are increasingly attaining higher levels of education, have a strong presence in local businesses, and have been elected as both local and national political representatives, cultural attitudes often lag behind such social changes (Momsen 2004). Women are still expected to be responsible for household duties and sometimes are expected to forego careers to do so.

The results appear to be consistent with transforming gender rules. Among the women surveyed, 40.0 per cent indicated a high level of perceived individual empowerment as opposed to 61.5 per cent of men. The disparity between the experience of women and men is strongest in their sense of connection to the community. These differences demonstrate the tension between the increased opportunities afforded to women without the social acceptance allowing women to pursue those opportunities.

Age

Because adults tend to hold positions of power and only the older generation had had the benefit of participating in the success of both Caribeña and the creation of the HCMR, it was hypothesized that this generation would consider itself more empowered than those too young to have experienced these events. However, the findings do not indicate a relationship between age and perceived individual empowerment.

After conducting interviews with members of the community, the link between age and perceived empowerment seemed even less clear. Past successes that increased the power and autonomy of San Pedro and years of participation in community events may feed a sense of empowerment among those with more experience, yet issues of obsolescence can arise and erode these feelings as time passes and the next generation begins assuming positions of power. On the other hand, the younger generation benefited from the work of those that preceded them. They have grown up with increasing opportunities, allowing them to achieve their goals and bolster their sense of personal empowerment above what was possible for earlier generations.

Education and Income

Among those surveyed, education and income are not shown as reliable indicators of perceived individual empowerment. The fact that not one of the seven questions that make up the index of empowerment demonstrates even a weak association with these factors, further suggests that those with a low education and income are just as likely to perceive themselves as empowered as those with a high education and income.

Membership in Community Organizations

The willingness to be involved in community organizations suggests a belief in one's ability to affect change. Thus, it is reasonable to expect those actively engaged in organizations would be more likely to identify themselves as empowered than individuals not associated with local groups. In fact, over two-thirds (69.6 per cent) of those who were members of organizations scored high on the index as opposed to 41.0 per cent of those not involved in local associations, indicating a strong relationship ($p = .008$). Members are more active in and feel more connected to the community.

Table 11.1 Individual empowerment questions

Question (N)	SD (%)	D (%)	N (%)	A (%)	SA (%)	Empowerment average (SD)
I1) I feel like a member of the community (87)	0 (0.0)	7 (7.9)	8 (9.0)	61 (68.5)	11 (12.4)	3.87 (.73)
I2) I regularly attend community activities (85)	1 (1.1)	27 (30.3)	19 (21.3)	37 (41.6)	1 (1.1)	3.12 (.92)
I3) I volunteer my time to work at community activities (84)	2 (2.2)	33 (37.1)	16 (18.0)	32 (36.0)	1 (1.1)	2.96 (.95)
I4) I help organize community activities (84)	2 55 (2.2)	11 (61.8)	14 (12.4)	2 (15.7)	2.51 (2.2)	(.88)
I5) Leaders in San Pedro address my concerns (84)	2 (2.2)	24 (27.0)	23 (25.8)	35 (39.3)	0 (0.0)	3.08 (.89)
I6) I feel like I have a voice in the (80) community	0 (0.0)	33 (37.1)	13 (14.6)	33 (37.1)	1 (1.1)	3.02 (.94)
I7) I do not get involved in community affairs; I mind my own business (83)	1 (1.1)	26 (29.2)	14 (15.7)	39 (43.8)	3 (3.4)	2.80 (.97)

Table 11.2 Individual Empowerment Index

Individual Empowerment Index (N = 85; alpha = .72)					
	'Low'			'High'	
Index score	Frequency	%	Index score	Frequency	%
10.0	1	1.2	21.0	8	9.4
12.0	1	1.2	21.2	1	1.2
13.4	1	1.2	22.0	6	7.1
15.0	4	4.7	22.3	1	1.2
15.3	1	1.2	23.0	4	4.7
16.0	3	3.5	23.3	1	1.2
17.0	4	4.7	24.0	5	5.9
18.0	5	5.9	25.0	10	11.8
19.0	5	5.9	26.0	5	5.9
20.0	12	14.1	26.8	1	1.2
			27.0	5	5.9
			28.0	1	1.2
Total	37	43.5	Total	48	56.5

This connection is not surprising for San Pedro. From Caribeña, the SPTGA, and the HCMR to the Lions Club and Green Reef, *San Pedranos* have long used organizing as a mechanism for creating change. Those involved in these organizations have seen their efforts pay off. With recognition of their ability to influence local decisions, it seems logical that participants would consider themselves empowered.

Place of Origin and Length of Residence

Contrary to expectations, immigrants to San Pedro, with less shared experience with and connection to the community, were neither more nor less likely to identify themselves with high individual empowerment than 'true' *San Pedranos.* However, simply distinguishing between those born on the island and those who migrated may mask the relationship between place of origin and individual empowerment.

First, there may be a level of self-selection involved. For the most part, immigrants to San Pedro were not forced to leave their homes (refugees from civil unrest in neighboring countries aside), but instead, willingly chose to move to the island to take advantage of the economic opportunities present (41.1 per cent of immigrants migrated for economic reasons). The decision to take such drastic action to improve one's chance of success is indicative of individual empowerment. Similarly, 37.5 per cent of immigrants surveyed moved to San Pedro to be with family. The presence of familial relationships may dampen the effects of being new to a locale and help create a sense of solidarity with the community more easily, thus increasing the sense of empowerment.

In addition to self-selection, the fact that the length of residence on the island for immigrants ranged from six months to 33 years may have also obscured the relationship. Those that moved to San Pedro more than 15 years prior to this study[2] were somewhat more likely to score high on the index (84.6 per cent) than those who migrated 15 years ago or less (54.8 per cent). Immigrants with more than 15 years on the island were more likely to agree that they volunteered, helped organize community activities and became involved in community affairs. These findings are consistent with the notion that those who have lived on the island longer have had the time to build connections to the community and perceive themselves as more empowered than more recent immigrants, especially as they were there when the Reserve was established and so were able to participate in planning for the project.

Tour Guiding

Because of the tour guide's participation in the creation of the HCMR and the benefits they have received as tourism has grown in San Pedro, examining possible differences between tour guides' and non-tour guides' perceptions of individual empowerment seemed important. According to the surveys, such an association is unlikely. The general success of the tourism industry as a whole, and the fact that most people surveyed held jobs associated with the tourism industry (91.0 per cent), may explain why there is no significant differentiation between tour guides' and non-tour guides' self-reported sense of empowerment.

Community Empowerment

Besides perceptions of individual connectedness and control, empowerment can also be experienced on the community level. Like individual empowerment, the presence of a feeling of community empowerment in San Pedro would support the hypothesis that participatory ICD can empower communities. The results from a six-question index on community empowerment reveal that San Pedro is seen as empowered by those surveyed (see Table 11.3 and Table 11.4). On the 5-point scale, average answers ranged from 3.73 (C6) to 3.54 (C3). Overwhelmingly, 82.4 per cent scored high in the community empowerment index with an average six-question score of 21.7 out of 30 (SD = 3.35). Further, 40.0 per cent averaged at least four points per question, indicating a strong sense of community empowerment. Like individual empowerment, these findings are consistent with ICD in contrast to Few's (Chapter 10) fears concerning lack of grassroots involvement in conservation planning.

Despite the strong positive perceptions of community empowerment, it is necessary to acknowledge the portion of the community that does not believe San Pedro is an empowered community (17.6 per cent). Again, cross-tabulations and chi-square analysis and the same indicators used in the individual empowerment section were applied to uncover factors associated with this disparity in perception of community empowerment. No relationship was found with any of the indicators used in this study suggesting that an individual's perception of community empowerment is independent of their place in the community.

Even though significant associations were not found with the index score, two of the factors did correlate well with some of the individual questions within the index. Women were much more likely to believe it is a waste of time to attend community meetings than men (C5, $p < .001$). Having attended various formal community meetings during my time in San Pedro, I found that women tended to be underrepresented, if they were in attendance at all. This may be a reflection of the lingering effects of traditional power relations that limited women's sphere of influence to the household, leaving broader community issues to men. However, women's belief in the ineffectiveness of community meetings belies their participation in less formal community settings. Women are among the most active members of the Lions Club and other community oriented groups, each of which could be seen as a place for informal community meetings. Although gender barriers are being broken, the long exclusion of women from formal avenues of influence may have coloured their perception of those activities and their willingness to become involved.

Similarly, tour guides were more likely to disagree that it is a waste of time to attend community meetings than non-tour guides and to agree that people in San Pedro work together to solve problems. These results may reflect the tour guide's experience working together through community forums, including influencing the creation of the HCMR and successfully petitioning for its expansion in 1999. While few report regularly attending SPTGA meetings (25 per cent), when issues important to them arise, they tend to show up in numbers.

Participation in community organizations may also be seen as a form of social capital. Thus empowerment is linked to high levels of social capital.

Leaders and Community Concerns

The association between participation and empowerment is made tenuous by the conflicts within the concept of empowerment itself. The main difficulty is the distinction between the perception of control and actually gaining decision-making power (Perkins and Zimmerman 1995). Despite the critical link between the two, participation, in and of itself, does not necessarily lead to empowerment. Instead, it can just as easily be used as a guise to hide and legitimize top-down decision-making (Arnstein 1969; Valenzuela 1989; Lyons, Smuts, and Stephens 2001; Pimbert and Pretty 1997; Itzhaky and York 2000). As such, Zimmerman (1995) asserts that genuine empowerment must not only produce the sense of empowerment, but also contain a measure of actual socio-political authority. To address this aspect of empowerment, both the general community and community decision-makers were asked about their concerns regarding the HCMR and the marine environment, the natural environment in San Pedro, development on the island, and the growth of tourism.

The impact of increased visitation to Hol Chan was the most cited concern about the reserve by the community (20.2 per cent) and the presidents of Caribeña, the SPTGA, and Green Reef, with the need for more enforcement (14.6 per cent), the presence of irresponsible guides (11.2 per cent), the increase in cruise ship arrivals (7.9 per cent), and suspected illegal fishing (6.7 per cent) as the main sources of this

Table 11.3 Community empowerment questions

Question (N)	SD (%)	D (%)	N (%)	A (%)	SA (%)	Empowerment average (SD)
C1) People in San Pedro tend to cooperate to solve problems (86)	1 (1.1)	10 (11.2)	17 (19.1)	51 (57.3)	7 (7.9)	3.62 (.92)
C2) The people of San Pedro work together as a community (85)	0 (0.0)	8 (9.0)	18 (20.2)	50 (56.2)	9 (10.1)	3.71 (.78)
C3) The community generally accomplishes its goals (83)	2 (2.2)	8 (9.0)	16 (18.0)	57 (64.0)	0 (0.0)	3.54 (.77)
C4) There is a strong sense of community in San Pedro (84)	0 (0.0)	14 (15.7)	6 (6.7)	64 (68.7)	0 (0.0)	3.60 (.76)
C5) It is a waste of time to attend community meetings (85)	6 (6.7)	52 (58.4)	11 (12.4)	16 (18.0)	0 (0.0)	3.56 (.88)
C6) There is opportunity to address concerns to local leaders (83)	0 (0.0)	8 (9.0)	9 (10.1)	63 (70.8)	3 (3.4)	3.73 (.68)

Table 11.4 Community Empowerment Index

Community Empowerment Index (N = 85; alpha = .79)					
	'Low'			'High'	
Index score	Frequency	%	Index score	Frequency	%
12.0	3	3.5	19.0	5	5.9
13.0	1	1.2	19.25	1	1.2
15.75	1	1.2	20.25	1	1.2
16.0	3	3.5	21.0	7	8.2
17.0	2	2.4	22.0	13	15.2
17.75	1	1.2	23.0	11	12.9
18	4	4.7	24.0	20	23.5
			25.0	9	10.6
			26.0	2	2.4
			27.0	1	1.2
Total	15	17.6	Total	70	82.4

apprehension. According to the manager of the reserve, it is the goal of the staff to conduct carrying capacity studies to help guide new management strategies that may alleviate some of the pressure on the reserve.

Pollution (21.3 per cent), mangrove and lagoon loss (20.2 per cent), and dredging (16.9 per cent) were the greatest environmental concerns of the community. Together, the leaders of Green Reef, the SPTGA, Caribeña, and the HCMR placed enough pressure on operators to create a near moratorium on dredging. The main issue concerning all local leaders interviewed about development on the island was the lack of planning associated with development. This worry ranked second amongst the community (30.3 per cent). First were issues related to the number of vehicles in San Pedro (39.3 per cent). Both the presidents of Caribeña and the SPTGA, as well as the manager of the HCMR, felt vehicles were an important factor affecting development as a result of improper planning. Finally, all six local leaders interviewed expressed apprehension about the increase of crime and drug abuse, consistent with fears of the community (32.6 per cent).

While the growth in tourism was commonly seen as a factor underlying issues of conservation and development, 34.8 per cent of those surveyed and all of the local leaders not only say they had no concerns regarding tourism, but that its continued growth would be a good thing. Overall, the parity found between the concerns of leaders and the community suggests more than simply the perception of empowerment.

'*Dis Da Fu We*': Perceptions of Conservation and Tourism

When speaking to locals about issues of conservation and resource use, the Creole phrase, *dis da fu we*[3] was often used. Translated as 'this is for us' or 'this is ours', *dis da fu we* seems the most apt and appropriate way to capture the importance, pride, and responsibility many in San Pedro associate with their natural environment. Coupled with empowerment, ICD strategies are intended to promote sustainable development by connecting environmental protection to community well being. The ownership implied in *dis da fu we* suggests that many in San Pedro have made this link.

Previous work by Lindberg and Enriquez (1994), Alexander (2000), Blesky (1999), and Fiallo and Jacobson (1995) has examined conservation attitudes in relation to management interventions. Using a series of 5-point Likert Scale questions gauging attitudes towards conservation and tourism largely derived from their work, we found that most interviewed held a favourable outlook on environmental health and tourism development, supporting claims in favour of integrative approaches (see Table 11.5). Responses were coded from one to five with an increasing indication of a positive outlook on conservation and tourism.

Attitudes Towards Conservation and the HCMR

Average responses to questions about the HCMR and issues related to conservation ranged from a low of 3.48 (CT6) and a high of 4.60 (CT11). One of the keys to integrated approaches is to establish direct benefits from conservation efforts. The survey showed that most felt that the establishment of the HCMR had directly benefited their household (CT1, 3.82), San Pedro (CT2, 4.15) and Belize (CT3, 4.25). Likewise, when asked if the community benefits from conservation, the average score was 4.04 (CT15). Clearly, people in San Pedro have identified the value of protecting their environment.

Another important element consistent with this integrated strategy is the emergence of a feeling of ownership of and responsibility for natural resources. Perhaps more clearly than in any of the survey answers, one tour guide expressed his perception of who is responsible for the environment, claiming, 'Hol Chan da fu alla we ... da fu alla San Pedro an' fu alla Belize. Only fi we go'na protek it'.[4]

ICD is also geared to improve environmental protection through better management of resources. When asked to assess the management of Hol Chan assuming that proper management does produce increased environmental health, responses were relatively consistent suggesting people are satisfied with the management of the reserve.

Finally, by establishing the links between conservation and development, unified approaches should foster an increased awareness of environmental concerns. According to those surveyed, the establishment of the HCMR has had a positive influence on their conservation attitudes. Everyone agreed that it is important to protect the environment and most were concerned about the loss of mangrove around the island. Most significantly, those interviewed responded favourably to the idea of supporting conservation even without economic benefits. Other questions did not evoke universal agreement and therefore, like the empowerment indices, exploring for relationships can help identify factors that influence perspective on the HCMR and conservation. Again, cross-tabulations and chi-square analysis were used to determine significant associations.

Women surveyed generally held similar conservation attitudes to the men. However, women expressed more neutral feelings towards the benefits of the marine reserve on their households than men. This finding may be a reflection of the fact that women tend to have less direct contact with the reserve and experience fewer of its direct benefits, as the majority of tour guides are men.

As many tour guides derive at least a part of their livelihood from using the HCMR (95.7 per cent of those surveyed), it would seem reasonable that tour guides show more favourable attitudes towards the reserve and conservation. In fact, the data suggest that tour guides tend to perceive more household benefits from the creation of the HCMR than non-tour guides and appear to be somewhat more likely to pick up litter on the beach. This association may be explained by the fact that the tour guide's work is dependent on a clean and healthy environment, making them more conscious of various forms of pollution than non-tour guides.

Attitudes towards Tourism

Although not true for all ICD projects, in the context of San Pedro, tourism is the engine for development and a major mechanism linking economic benefits to conservation (see Chapter 9 in this volume). As a result, determining the attitudes towards tourism of individuals in San Pedro can also be used to assess the ICD strategy. Those surveyed acknowledge the benefits of tourism development consistent with integrated policies. In addition to recognizing the benefits of tourism, respondents demonstrated a complex understanding of the dynamics between tourism and the environment, stating that much of the environment gets protected for the purpose of attracting tourists, making tourism beneficial to nature. However, many also saw that increased visitation magnifies the impact of using the resource, which may in fact harm wildlife. In the end, most decided the benefits outweigh the costs.

Finally, those interviewed expressed a favourable attitude towards their children becoming tour guides. This suggests that tour guiding is considered a respectable occupation. Furthermore, the only significant relationship found among this group of questions is that tour guides are more likely than non-tour guides to be happy if their children became guides ($p = .022$). This difference could be a result of the fact that tour guides directly experience the benefits of their occupation, making them more likely to be happy if their children became involved in guiding. This finding also suggests that tour guides are proud of the work they do. In fact, many enthusiastically hoped that their children would become tour guides.

Table 11.5 Conservation and tourism questions

Question (N)	SD (%)	D (%)	N (%)	A (%)	SA (%)	Empowerment average (SD)
CT1) The establishment of Hol Chan has been good for my household (84)	0 (0.0)	8 (9.0)	4 (4.5)	67 (75.3)	5 (5.6)	3.82 (.68)
CT2) The establishment of Hol Chan has been good for my community (84)	0 (0.0)	0 (0.0)	2 (2.2)	67 (75.3)	15 (16.9)	4.15 (.42)
CT3) The establishment of Hol Chan has been good for Belize (83)	0 (0.0)	0 (0.0)	1 (1.1)	60 (67.4)	22 (24.7)	4.25 (.46)
CT4) The Hol Chan Marine Reserve belongs to the community (83)	0 (0.0)	7 (7.9)	3 (3.4)	68 (76.4)	5 (5.6)	3.86 (.65)
CT5) The management of Hol Chan represents the needs of San Pedro (81)	0 (0.0)	12 (13.5)	11 (12.4)	57 (64.0)	1 (1.1)	3.58 (.76)
CT6) Hol Chan is primarily run for tourists, not for me or the community (85)	2 (2.2)	59 (66.3)	3 (3.4)	20 (22.5)	1 (1.1)	3.48 (.92)
CT7) The Hol Chan staff is open to the community's input (83)	0 (0.0)	15 (16.9)	7 (7.9)	60 (67.4)	1 (1.1)	3.57 (.80)
CT8) I am satisfied with the management of the reserve (85)	0 (0.0)	12 (13.5)	11 (12.4)	58 (65.2)	4 (4.5)	3.65 (.78)
CT9) The establishment of Hol Chan has influenced my conservation attitudes (82)	0 (0.0)	9 (10.1)	1 (1.1)	63 (70.8)	9 (10.1)	3.88 (.74)
CT10) I would support marine conservation even if there were not economic benefits (85)	0 (0.0)	6 (6.7)	0 0 (0.0)	69 (77.5)	10 (11.2)	3.98 (.64)
CT11) It is important to protect the environment (86)	0 (0.0)	0 (0.0)	0 (0.0)	34 (38.2)	52 (58.4)	4.60 (.49)

Table 11.5 cont'd

Question (N)	SD (%)	D (%)	N (%)	A (%)	SA (%)	Empowerment average (SD)
CT12) I am concerned about the loss of mangrove around the island (82)	0 (0.0)	6 (6.7)	0 (0.0)	61 (68.5)	15 (16.9)	4.04 (.69)
CT13) I feel it is my responsibility to help protect the local environment (85)	0 (0.0)	0 (0.0)	3 (3.4)	70 (78.7)	12 (13.5)	4.11 (.41)
CT14) I pick up garbage on the beach when I see it (83)	0 (0.0)	7 (7.9)	10 (11.2)	55 (61.8)	11 (12.4)	3.84 (.76)
CT15) The community benefits from conservation (83)	0 (0.0)	2 (2.2)	3 (3.4)	68 (76.4)	10 (11.2)	4.04 (.50)
CT16) Tourism is beneficial for the protection of wildlife (82)	0 (0.0)	5 (5.6)	8 (9.0)	63 (70.8)	6 (6.7)	3.85 (.63)
CT17) Tourists will stop visiting San Pedro if the environment is degraded (86)	0 (0.0)	8 (9.0)	1 (1.1)	62 (69.7)	15 (16.9)	3.98 (.75)
CT18) Tourism has been good for my household (86)	0 (0.0)	3 (3.4)	1 (1.1)	67 (75.3)	15 (16.9)	4.09 (.57)
CT19) Tourism has been good for San Pedro (86)	0 (0.0)	1 (1.1)	2 (2.2)	57 (64.0)	26 (29.2)	4.26 (.56)
CT20) Tourism has been good for Belize (86)	0 (0.0)	0 (0.0)	2 (2.2)	61 (68.5)	23 (25.8)	4.24 (.48)
CT21) I would be happy if my children became tour guides (84)	0 (0.0)	15 (16.9)	5 (5.6)	47 (52.8)	17 (19.1)	3.79 (.97)

From Hooksticks to Snorkels: Implications from the Experience of San Pedro Town

Participatory ICD approaches emerged in response to the resistance to traditional environmental or development strategies. Where conventional top-down policies failed because they excluded locals and/or neglected environmental processes, ICD is intended to emphasize the connections between communities and their surroundings. By involving communities in ICD, projects aim to achieve successful resource management and sustainable development through an empowering process. This chapter follows the evolution of San Pedro Town, Belize, from a small fishing village to a rapidly growing tourist destination, as it investigates one such project. The establishment of the HCMR near San Pedro marks the transition from the days of catching lobster with hook sticks[5] to guiding visitors to view marine life armed only with snorkels, masks, fins, and an occasional camera. This intervention helped align the benefits of conservation to local development, increased environmental awareness, and improved the ability of the people and community of San Pedro to achieve self-determined goals through self-determined means, consistent with ICD rationale.

In San Pedro, gender, membership in community organizations, and length of residence of immigrants to the island emerged as important indicators of perceived empowerment. The prominent role gender plays in San Pedro supports Zweifel's (1997) appeal for an increased focus on women's relationship to participatory resource use. The fact that those who participate in community organizations report higher levels of empowerment than non-members validates Itzhaky and York's (2000) and Perkins, Brown, and Taylor's (1996) findings. Also, underlining the importance of identity as a *San Pedrano,* is the discovery that the longer immigrants have lived in the community tends to increase their perception of empowerment and is consistent with Perkins, Brown, and Taylor's (1996) work.

What emerged from this study is the importance of existing social structures on ICD projects. To understand the influence of the HCMR, one must understand the history into which it was inserted. Bringing established social networks with them, *mestizos* fleeing armed rebellion in Mexico's Yucatan Peninsula founded San Pedro in 1848. The close ties created through a cooperative and interdependent existence have continued over the years to influence the shape of participation in community events today. These bonds based on strong community social capital helped build and were strengthened by the formation of Caribeña. Similarly, the social ties created by participation in the cooperative fostered the success of the Lions Club and the SPTGA. Much of the accomplishments of the HCMR are due to these prior community activities, just as the reserve has had an impact on the achievements of Green Reef and other new community organizations.

While existing dynamics have been essential in facilitating successful ICD in San Pedro, they have been equally capable of fragmenting and eroding social solidarity. The early, common struggles of the community resulted in a strong identity as *San Pedranos*. This shared identity was a source of strength for the community as people had to work together to survive. However, the increased migration to San Pedro, as a result of the economic opportunities created by the fishing industry followed by tourism, threatens this identity. *San Pedranos* believe they have to protect their 'local' identity. Often, this has taken the form of scepticism towards non-*San Pedranos* that legitimizes their exclusion, which fragments and diminishes the potential benefits of ICD.

Another important issue to surface in this study is the effect of a lucrative tourism industry in San Pedro. Often, ICD programmes are implemented in areas with only nascent tourism potential. As a popular tourist destination with a viable natural attraction, San Pedro offers a unique opportunity to examine the influence of economic prosperity on ICD. By creating direct economic benefits to conservation, an active tourism sector helps make linking conservation and development more rewarding for those in San Pedro than in places where tourism has not met expectations (Belsky 1999; Alexander 2000). Furthermore, sharing in the success of the industry fosters the growth of the social solidarity that engenders empowerment.

On the other hand, as tourism development becomes more successful, it becomes more difficult to control (Kusler in Kusler 1991; Wilkinson 1992). The potential for profit creates economic incentives to capture and maximize those earnings, which often puts pressure on a community's commitment to ecological considerations. This tension is evidenced in San Pedro by increased dredging and clearing of mangrove habitat for new resorts as well as housing for the growing population. However, the fact that both the community and its leaders are concerned about rapid, unplanned development on the island demonstrates recognition of this dilemma. The challenge the community faces is to determine how to manage this kind of development.

The experience of San Pedro illustrates the complexity of ICD policies and identifies benefits and caveats of which policy makers should be aware. Knowledge of the existing community dynamics is essential to the success of ICD projects. With this understanding, leaders can take advantage of and build upon the strengths of communities by harnessing prior achievements. At the same time, they can repudiate the notion of homogenous communities and prepare to ameliorate potential conflicts by addressing social disparities and recognizing the diverse power relationships within communities (Agrawal and Gibson 1999; Belsky 1999; Brown 2002; Singleton 2000; Few 2001). Those engaged in ICD must also recognize the challenges that accompany 'success' or 'failure' in order to ensure local communities are able to determine acceptable growth or adjust to disappointing results. This research suggests that ICD, in and of itself, is not *the* answer to sustainable resource management. Instead, understanding how such policies interact with the community processes of participation, inclusion, and power is necessary to tailor strategies to the realities of specific communities.

Notes

1 This individual was elected to political office in 2003.
2 The establishment of the HCMR was used as a threshold.

3 The phrase *dis da fu we* carries nationalistic undertones associated with the end of colonization and independence. It connotes both a sense of sovereignty and pride. Applying the phrase to conservation signifies the importance given to environmental concerns and the conscious effort to connect the benefits of environmental protection to the future of Belize.

4 'Hol Chan is for all of us ... it's for all of San Pedro and for all of Belize. It is up to us to protect it.'

5 A hook stick is an instrument commonly used to snare lobster from crevices along the reef. It consists of a two to three foot rod with a large, four to six inch hook fastened to one end.

References

Abbot, J. and Thomas, D. (2001), 'Understanding the Links between Conservation and Development in the Bamenda Highlands, Cameroon', *World Development*, 29 (7), pp. 1115–36.

Agrawal, A. and Gibson, C.C. (1999), 'Enchantment and Disenchantment: The Role of Community in Natural Resources Conservation', *World Development*, 27 (4), pp. 629–49.

Alamilla Jr, M. and Kitagawa, B. (2001), *The Hol Chan Marine Reserve: Information Booklet*, funded by the World Conservation Union (IUCN) and the Government of Norway, Belize City: Angelus Press.

Alexander, S. (2000), 'Resident Attitudes towards Conservation and Black Howler Monkeys in Belize: The Community Baboon Sanctuary', *Environmental Conservation*, 27 (4), pp. 341–50.

Alpert, P. (1995), 'Applying Ecological Research at Integrated Conservation and Development Projects', *Ecological Applications*, 5 (4), pp. 857–61.

Alpert, P. (1996), 'Integrated Conservation and Development Projects: Examples from Africa', *Bioscience*, 46 (11), pp. 845–55.

Arnstein, S. (1969), 'A Ladder of Citizen Participation', *Journal of the American Institute of Planners*, 35 (4), pp. 216–24.

Barrett, C.B. and Arcese, P. (1995), 'Are Integrated Conservation-development Projects Sustainable? On the Conservation of Large Mammals in Sub-Saharan Africa', *World Development*, 23 (7), pp. 1073–84.

Belsky, J. (1999), 'Misrepresenting Communities: The Politics of Community-based Rural Ecotourism in Gales Point Manatee, Belize', *Rural Sociology*, 64 (4), pp. 641–66.

Brown, K. (2002), 'Innovations for Conservation and Development', *Geographical Journal*, 168 (1), pp. 6–17.

Carter, J. (1990), 'A delicate Balance', *Wildlife Conservation* 93 (1), pp. 56–67.

Carter, J., Gibson, J. and Azueta, J. (1994), 'Creation of the Hol Chan Marine Reserve in Belize: A Grass-roots Approach to Barrier Reef Conservation', *EnvironmentalProfessional*. 16 (3), pp. 220–31.

Chavis, D.M. and Wandersman, A. (1990), 'Sense of Community in the Urban Environment: A Catalyst for Participation and Commuit Development', *American Journal of Community Psychology*, 18 (1), pp. 55–82.

Escobar, A. (1995), *Encountering Development: The Making and Unmaking of the Third World*, Princeton: Princeton University Press.

Fetterman, D.M. (2002), 'Empowerment Evaluation: Building Communities of Practice and a Culture of Learning', *American Journal of Community Psychology*, 30 (1), pp. 89–102.

Few, R. (2001), 'Containment and Counter-containment: Planner/Community Relations in Conservation Planning', *Geographical Journal*, 167 (2), pp. 111–24.

Fiallo, E.A. and Jacobson, S.K. (1995), 'Local Communities and Protected Areas: Attitudes of Rural Residents towards Conservation and Machalilla National Park, Ecuador', *Environmental Conservation*, 22 (3), pp. 241–9.

Godfrey, G. (1996), *Ambergris Caye: Paradise with a Past*, Benque Viejo del Carmen, Belize: Cubola Productions.

Isbister, J. (2001), *Promises Not Kept: The Betrayal of Social Change in the Third World*, Bloomfield: Kumarian Press.

Itzhaky, H. and York, A.S. (2000), 'Empowerment and Community Participation: Does Gender Make a Difference?', *Social Work Research*, 24 (4), pp. 225–34.

Jha, S. (2000), 'Conservation and Preservation through Community Participation in two Indian Projects: A Policy Perspective', *AMBIO*, 29 (8), pp. 527–8.

Julian, T.A., Reischl, T.M., Carrick, R.V. and Katrenich, C. (1997), 'Citizen Participation Lessons from a Local United Way Planning Process', *Journal of the American Planning Association*, 63 (3), pp. 345–55.

Klaren, P.F. and Bossert, T.J. (1986), *Promise of Development: Theories of Change in Latin America*, Boulder, CO: Westview Press.

Kremen, C., Merenlender, A.M. and Murphy, D.D. (1994), 'Ecological Monitoring: A Vital Need for Integrated Conservation and Development Programs in the Tropics', *Conservation Biology*, 8 (2), pp. 388–97.

Kusler, J.A. (ed.) (1991), *Ecotourism and Resource Conservation*, selected papers from 1st International Symposium: Ecotourism, 17–19 April 1989, [and] 2nd International Symposium: Ecotourism and Resource Conservation, 27 November– 2 December 1990, Berne, NY: Ecotourism and Resource Conservation Project.

Lindberg, K. and Enriquez, J. (1994), *An Analysis of Ecotourism's Economic Contribution to Conservation and Development in Belize: Volumes I and II*, World Wildlife Fund and the Ministry of Tourism and the Environment, Belize.

Lyons, M., Smuts, C. and Stephens, A. (2001), 'Participation, Empowerment, and Sustainability: How do the Links Work?', *Urban Studies*, 38 (8), pp. 1233–51.

Marcus, R.R. (2001), 'Seeing the Forest for the Trees: Integrated Conservation and Development Projects and Local Perceptions of Conservation in Madagascar', *Human Ecology*, 29 (4), pp. 381–97.

Mayaka, T.B. (2002), 'Wildlife Co-management in the Benoue National Park-Complex, Cameroon: A Bumpy Road to Institutional Development', *World Development*, 30 (11), pp. 2001–16.

McMillan, B., Florin, P., Stevenson, J., Kerman, B. and Mitchell, R.E. (1995), 'Empowerment Praxis in Community Coalitions', *American Journal of Community Psychology*, 23 (5), pp. 699–727.

Momsen, J.H. (2004), *Gender and Development*, London and New York: Routledge.

Neumann, R.P. (1998), *Imposing Wilderness: Struggles over Livelihood and Nature Preservation in Africa*, Berkeley: University of California Press.

Newmark, W.D. and Hough, J.L. (2000), 'Conserving Wildlife in Africa: Integrated Conservation and Development Projects and Beyond', *Bioscience*, 50 (7), pp. 585–2.

Parry, D. and Campbell, B. (1992), 'Attitudes of Rural Communities to Animal Wildlife and its Utilization in Chobe Enclave and Mababe Depression, Botswana', *Environmental Conservation*, 19 (3), pp. 245–52.

Perkins, D.D., Brown, B.B. and Taylor, R.B. (1996), 'The Ecology of Empowerment: Predicting Participation in Community Organizations', *Journal of Social Issues*, 52 (1), pp. 85–110.

Perkins, D.D. and Zimmerman, M.A. (1995), 'Empowerment Theory, Research, and Applications', *American Journal of Community Psychology*, 23 (5), pp. 569–79.

Pimbert, M.P. and Pretty, J.N. (1997), 'Parks, People, and Professionals: Putting "Participation" into Protected Area Management', in K.G. Ghimire and M.P. Pimbert (eds), *Social Change and Conservation*, London: Earthscan, pp. 297–332.

Reininger, B., Martin, D.W., Ross, M., Smith Sinicrope, P. and Dinh-Zarr, T. (2001), 'Advancing the Theory and Measurement of Collective Empowerment: A Qualitative Study', *International Quarterly of Community Health Education*, 19 (4), pp. 293–320.

Salafsky, N. and Wollenberg, E. (2000), 'Linking Livelihoods and Conservation: A Conceptual Framework and Scale for Assessing the Integration of Human Needs and Biodiversity', *World Development*, 28 (8), pp. 1421–38.

Singleton, S. (2000), 'Co-operation or Capture? The Paradox of Co-management and Community Participation in Natural Resource Management and Environmental Policy-making', *Environmental Politics*, 9 (2), pp. 1–21.

Speer, P.W. and Peterson, A.N. (2000), 'Psychometric Properties of an Empowerment Scale: Testing Cognitive, Emotional, and Behavioral Domains', *Social Work Research*, 24 (2), pp. 109–18.

Stocking, M. and Perkin, S. (1992), 'Conservation-with-development: An Application of the Concept in the Usambara Mountains, Tanzania', *Transactions of the Institute of British Geographers*, 17 (3), pp. 337–49.

Valenzuela, E. (1989), *People's Participation and Environmentally Sustainable Development*, Manila: Asian NGO Coalition for Agrarian Reform and Rural Development (ANGOC).

Wainwright, C. and Wehrmeyer, W. (1998), 'Success in Integrating Conservation and Development? A Study from Zambia', *World Development*, 26 (6), pp. 933–44.

Wells, M., Brandon, K. and Hannah, L. (1992), *People and Parks: Linking Protected Area Management with Local Communities*, Washington, DC: World Bank.

Wilkinson, P. (1992), 'Tourism – The Curse of the Nineties? Belize – An Experiment to Integrate Tourism and the Environment', *Community Development Journal*, 27 (4), pp. 386–93.

Young, E. and Bilgre, B. (2002), *Hol Chan Marine Reserve Management Plan* (update), San Jose, Costa Rica: IUCN.

Zimmerman, M.A. (1995), 'Psychological Empowerment: Issues and Illustrations', *American Journal of Community Psychology*, 23 (5), pp. 581–99.

Zimmerman, M.A. and Rappaport, J. (1988), 'Citizen Participation, Perceived Control, and Psychological Empowerment', *American Journal of Community Psychology*, 16 (5), pp. 725–50.

Zweifel, H. (1997), 'The Gendered Nature of Biodiversity Conservation', *National Women's Studies Association (NWSA) Journal*, 9 (2), pp. 107–23.

Index

Abbot, J. 178
action research 93–101
Africa 5, 22, 34
Afshar, F. 73
Agrawal, A. 195
agro-biodiversity 33–5, 37, 38, 39, 42–9
agro-forestry 46, 67, 133, 134
agrochemical 33, 43, 44, 45, 46, 48, 80
Aitken, S. 101
Alamilla Jr, M. 179
Albrow, M. 73
Alexander, S. 22, 23, 181, 190, 195
Alpert, P. 177, 178
Amaral, A. 74
Anderson, Alexander 22
Anglophone Caribbean 1, 2, 7, 8, 9, 11, 12, 13, 15, 17, 18
Anguilla 8
Antigua 8, 9, 11, 23, 25, 115
appeals 11, 12, 17, 68, 105
Arce, A. 160
Arcese, P. 177, 179
Arnstein, S. 165, 187
Ash, J. 55, 114
Ashworth, G.J. 73
Asia 34
August, A.P. 158
Ayala, H. 111, 112, 115
Ayileka, O. 157, 172
ayuntamientos 56
Azueta, J. 174, 179

Bailey, C. 102, 155
Bailey, S. 166
Baldacchino, G. 59
Banana Export Company (BECO) 4, 42, 46
Bangladesh 53
Barbados 3, 9, 11, 12, 15, 17, 18, 23, 25, 58, 77
Barberia, L.G. 73
Barnes, T. 100
Barnett, C. 95
Baroni, S. 81
Barrett, C.B. 102, 177, 179
Barthell, D. 74
Bateson, Gregory 55, 64
Belize 1, 3, 155–72, 177, 179–80, 190, 193–4, 196
  Bacalar Chico 158, 160, 163–72
  Caribeña 179, 181, 183, 185, 187, 189, 194
  Caye Caulker 158, 160, 163–4, 166–71
  San Pedro 160, 163, 166–8, 170, 177, 179, 181–91, 193–6
Belsky, J. 181, 190
Benn, S. 114
Berleant-Schiller, R. 25
Besson, J. 25, 31
Bilgre, B. 179
biodiversity 4, 33–5, 37–8, 43–5, 47–50, 63, 113, 129, 132, 134, 151–2, 155, 157–8, 161, 163, 165–6, 169, 172
Biot, Y. 129
Blaikie, P. 13, 160
Blunt, A. 1
Bossert, T.J. 177
botanical gardens
  Carriacou 29
  Grenada 22, 26
  St Vincent 3–4
Bowermaster, J. 74
Boza, M. 132
Brandon, K. 155, 178
Brechin, S.R. 153, 157
Brett, D. 74
Britain 4, 37, 60, 67, 68
British Caribbean 24
British colonial administration 3, 21
British Colonial Office 9
British Guiana 9
British Honduras 9
British Virgin Islands 8, 25
Broadway, W.E. 22, 26, 27, 28
Brohman, J. 156, 160

Bromley, R.D.F. 73
Brookfield, H. 33, 34
Brown, B.B. 194, 195
Brown, K. 155, 160, 161, 177, 178, 179,
Brunn, S.D. 123
Bryant, R.L. 155, 166
Buchanan, Alphaeus 140, 147
Budowski, G. 132
Buisseret, D. 74
Burgess, J. 100
Burial Scheme Society, Jamaica 47
Burr, C. 77
Butler, R. 62, 112, 113, 114

Cahn, R. 133
Cahuita 2, 3, 129–52, 154
  Cahuita National Park (CNP) 2, 3, 129–32, 134, 140, 142–52
Campbell, B. 181
Canada 20, 60, 87, 116
Canessa, Guillermo 141, 142
Caribbean Community and Common Market (CARICOM) 68
Caribbean Development Bank 16
Caribbean Disaster Emergency Response Agency (CDERA) 68
Caribbean Tourism Organization (CTO) 55, 115
Caribeña Producers Co-operative Society Limited 179
Carr, W. 98, 144
Carriacou 1, 3, 4, 22–30
Carter, J. 16, 179
Castells, M. 94
Castro, Fidel 75, 152
Cayman Islands 8
Central America 2, 23
Centre for Population, Community and Social Change 97
Centro Agronómico Tropical de Investigaciones Ensenanza (CATIE) 152
Cevo, J. 132
Chambers, R. 96, 97, 106
Chavis, D.M. 182
chemical fertilizers 44, 45, 81
chemical pesticides 45
Chevannes, B. 94, 97, 103
Civil Contingencies Secretariat (CCS) 68
Clay, E. 4, 60
Cleaver, F. 93
Clegg, S.R. 167
Cline-Cole, R. 155
coastal erosion 54
Codrescu, A. 75
Cohen, E. 113
Colchester, M. 151
Colladom R, 83
colonialism 1
  colonial administrators 22, 25, 27, 29, 30
  colonial government 23, 24, 25, 26, 28, 29
  colonial officials 22, 25, 30
  colonial policies 29, 54
  colonial status 4, 54, 56, 60
community-based organizations (CBOs) 97, 99, 104, 117
Community Development Committees (CDCs) 104
conservation 1, 3, 10, 19, 21–6, 30, 34–5, 37, 43, 47–9, 57, 61, 67, 70, 89, 113, 122, 129, 131–5, 141–5, 148–52, 155, 157–61, 163–4, 166, 169, 171–2, 177–9, 181, 182, 186, 189–91, 193–6, 198
conservation areas 3, 134, 142, 145, 152, 177
containment 71, 156–7, 161, 165–72
Conway, D. 74, 113
Corbin, J. 102
Cordeiro, F. 55
Cornebise, M.W. 77
Cortés,J. 144
Cosgrove, D. 73
Costa Rica 1, 2, 129, 131–2, 134, 141–2, 145, 151
cotton 27–30
counter-containment 156, 161, 167–8, 170–72
Coyula, M. 73
Crain, J. 74
Crawley, H. 96
crop diseases 37
crop insurance 37
Crush, J. 13, 161
Cuba 1, 3–5, 55, 73–5, 77–8, 80–81, 83–5, 87, 116
  Baracoa 74, 84, 85, 86

Camagüey 74, 82
Havana 3, 74–5, 77–81, 84–5, 91
Santiago 74, 82, 84
Trinidad 74, 81–6
cultural identity 94
Cummings, Wayne 118
Curtin, V. 115
Cuza Jones, G. 150

de Albuquerque, K. 114
Denzin, N. 102
Department for International Development, UK (DFID) 5, 14, 19, 60, 61, 65, 67
Desai, V. 20, 108, 126, 160
desiccationism 4, 22
development agencies 8, 14, 114, 156
Development Control Authorities 9, 10, 11
development reform 12
development studies 1, 13, 14
Diallo, Tirmizion 67
Díaz-Briquets, Z. 77, 78, 81
Dicken, P. 73
Dodman, D. 3, 93, 98, 101
Dodman, J. 3, 93, 104
Dominica 8, 9, 10, 11, 12, 16, 23
donor agencies 7, 13, 14–18, 157
Doornbos, M. 155
Dornan, D'Arcy 4
Dotherow, M. 169
Doughty, P. 54
Drayton, Edward 28, 29
Dryzek, J. 155
Duncan, J.S. 100
Dunphy, D. 114
Duval, D.T. 113, 114, 115
Dyck, R. 83

Eade, D. 96
East India Trading Company 25
Eckstein, S. 75
ecotourism 38, 54, 62, 83, 84, 112, 113, 123–26, 129, 151, 166
Elinson, H. 77
Elliott, J. 98
emancipation 24, 25
empowerment 48–9, 93–4, 96–8, 104, 155, 179, 181–91, 194–5
Enriquez, J. 181, 190
environmental disasters 24
environmental impact 3, 74, 78, 114, 143
Environmental Impact Assessments (EIAs) 17, 114
Environmental Management and Land Use Project (EMLUP) 17, 18
environmental management system (EMS) 112, 117, 119, 122
environmental planning 7, 20, 54, 61, 63–5, 68, 70, 74, 77, 85–7, 105–6
environmental sustainability 111, 113–14, 121–3, 155
Escobar, Arturo 13, 14, 177
Esteva, G. 14
Europe 4, 5, 21, 22, 87, 114
European Union (EU) 5, 16, 87, 103, 169
Evans, S.L. 90, 100
Ewing, G. 112, 115
export crops 2, 35, 38
bananas 2, 4–5, 35, 37–40, 42–3, 45–6, 56, 132, 134, 144
cacao 2, 26–8, 133–5, 142–3
cocoa 26, 133, 141
coconuts 2, 35, 39, 44
coffee 26–8, 35, 39–40, 43, 55, 56, 84
tobacco 26, 27

Federal Emergency Management Agency (FEMA) 68
Fennell, D. 112
Fergus, Howard 56, 57, 58, 60
fertilizers 33, 34, 44, 45, 46, 81
Fetterman, D.M. 182
Few, R. 3, 155, 157, 160, 161, 179, 186, 195
Fiallo, E.A. 181, 190
Figueres, José Maria 129
Figueroa, M. 105
Fonseca Borrás, M. 142, 147, 148, 152
Ford, L. 75
Foreign and Commonwealth Office (FCO) 53, 60, 61
forest conservation 23, 24
Forester, J. 155, 172
forest reserves 4, 23, 24, 27, 29
Foster, D. 56
Fowler, C. 33
France 4

Francis, P. 31, 96, 102
Fraser, V. 74
Freire, P. 96, 97, 98
Freitag, T.G. 112
French, J.R. 147
funding agencies 18

'green imperialism' 3, 22
Gade, D. 75
Gámez, R. 143
Gancedo, N. 73
Gardner, K. 65
Gauld, R. 155, 172
Gbadegesin, A. 157, 172
Geertz, C. 64
George, V. 115
Ghimire, K. 151, 155, 157, 163, 172
Gibson, J. 120, 123, 125, 158, 179, 195
Gibson-Graham, J.K. 120, 123
Giddens, A. 161, 167
Gmelch, G. 114
Godfrey, G. 179
governing elites 2, 7, 8, 9, 12, 15, 16
Graham, B. 73
Green Globe 21 Standard 111, 112, 117
Green Reef 181, 185, 187, 189, 194
Greenwood, D. 95
Grenada 8–10, 12, 13, 22–3, 25–6, 28–30
Griffin, C.E. 19, 75
Griffiths, A. 114
Grove, R. 3, 21, 22, 23
Guadeloupe 1, 57
Guatemala 179
Guillén Martínez, F. 75
Gunn, G. 87
Gutiérrez, R. 73, 87
Gutman, M. 74
Guyana 12, 16

Haas, J. 68
Haiti 85, 97
Hall, B. 99
Hall, M.C. 112
Halsall, R. 99
Hamnett, C. 95
Hands, M.R. 147
Hannah, L. 178
Hansen, A.T. 75
Hardoy, J.E. 74
Hardy, C. 164, 166
Harrison, D. 112
Harvey, D. 28, 29, 31, 105
Haynes, J. 94
Haywood, K.M. 112
Hol Chan Marine Reserve (HCMR) 179, 181–3, 185–7, 189–91, 193–5
Healey, P. 155, 172
Heiman, M.K. 104
Henry, Burchill 118, 119, 120, 121
Hernández, G. 81
Hildyard, N. 156, 165, 172
Hill, D. 30
Hoffman, S. 64, 65
Holder, J. 55, 113
Home, R. 9
Hopkins, D. 98
Hough, J.L. 177, 179
Hudson, B. 115
Hulme, D. 155
Hurricane Hugo 4, 53, 54, 57, 58, 63

Ingold, T. 55, 64
institutional capacity building 2, 7, 8, 13, 15–18
institutional strengthening 17
integrated conservation and development (ICD) 142, 157, 163, 166, 178–9, 182, 186, 190–91, 194–5
integrated pest management (IPM) 2
integrated planning approach (IPA) 61, 62
Inter-American Development Bank 87, 90, 103
International Development Committee of the House of Commons 53
International Monetary Fund (IMF) 103
international non-governmental organizations (INGOs) 158, 169
International Tropical Conservation Foundation 158
Irarrázaval, I. 75, 85
Irwin, A. 95
Isaacs, M.C. 53
Isbister, J. 177
Itzhaky, H. 181, 182, 187, 194

Jacobson, S.K. 181, 190

Jafari, J. 77
Jamaica 1–4, 9, 10, 12, 23, 25, 34–8, 44, 46, 48–9, 54, 60, 93–4, 96–7, 100, 103, 106, 111–12, 115–16, 118–20
  Kingston 3, 22, 93, 98, 99, 101, 104, 105
  Portland 34–7, 103
  Rio Grande Valley 4, 34–40, 48–9
Jamaica Agricultural Society 45
Jamaica Hotel and Tourist Association (JHTA) 118, 122
Jamaica Social Investment Fund (JSIF) 93, 97, 103, 104
Jayawardena, C. 112
Jeanrenaud, S. 160
Jha, S. 178
Johansson, L. 155, 157
Johnson, V. 101
Johnston, R. 73
Jones, G.A. 73
Joseph, M. 38
Julian, T.A. 182

Kemmis, S. 98
Kesby, M. 102
Khan, J. 10
Kingsbury, P. 3, 111, 114, 115, 123, 124
Kitagawa, B. 3, 179, 182
Klak, T. 73, 114, 124
Klaren, P.F. 177
Kothari, U. 1, 105
Kremen, C. 179
Kusler, J. 195
Kutay, J.A. 132–4, 142–6, 152

Lambert, Leo 119, 120, 121
land-use stages 38–40, 42–3, 45
land degradation 34, 35
land management 21–2, 33–4, 38–9, 42–5, 49, 55, 63, 103
land reform 21, 25–9
Lash, S. 74
Latin America 15, 34, 73, 97
Lawton, L. 111
Leach, M. 160, 167
Leal, E. 77
Leiba-O'Sullivan, S. 164, 166
Lemieux, G. 133–6, 138–42, 144
Levin, M. 95
Levy, H. 94, 97, 103
Lewin, Kurt 98
Lewis, D. 65
Lezcano, J. 81
Lincoln, Y, 102
Lindberg, K. 181, 190
Linden, E. 73
Little, P.D. 157
local elites 7–9, 17–18
local knowledge 95, 96, 105
local planning policies 1
'local solutions to local problems' 7, 8, 13, 17, 18
Lowenthal, D. 74
Lundy, P. 102
Lyons, M. 181, 182, 187

Marcus, R.R. 179
Margalef species richness index 39
Marín, F. 74, 82
Marrero, L. 84
Marsden, T. 166
Martin, G. 2, 3, 129, 177
Martinique 1, 58
Marx, Karl 98
Matos, H. 56, 84
Mauer, B. 25
Mauritius 22, 23, 25
May, Richard 118, 122
Mayaka, T.B. 178
McDonald, W.A. 10
McElroy, J.L. 114
McGranahan, G. 105
McKernan, J. 98
McMillan, B. 181, 182
McNeely, J.A. 132
McTaggart, R. 99
Meffe, G. 152
Merenlender, A.M. 179
metayage 25, 28
Mexico 31, 54, 164, 179, 194
Miller, D. 107, 132
Mills, B. 3, 21, 29, 30
Milne, S. 112, 115
Milton, K. 55
Mohan, G. 93, 95, 105
Momsen, J. 1, 2, 3, 25, 114, 177, 183
monoculture 33–5, 37–9, 46, 49

Montserrat 1–4, 8, 25, 53–4, 57–61, 63–5, 67–8
  Galways Soufrière 57
Mooney, P. 33
Moreno Fraginals, M. 82
Morris, Anthony 119
Morrison, E. 44
Moseley, M. 53, 63, 64
Mowforth, M. 73, 111–14, 123–4
Mullings, B. 94, 96, 114
Munt, I. 73, 111, 112, 113, 114, 123, 124
Murdoch, J. 166
Murphree, M. 155
Murphy, P. 111, 179
Murrell, N. 94
Myers, G. 5

Nandy, A. 14
Nash, C. 1
natural disasters 4, 54–5
  earthquake 53–4, 58, 147
  erosion 4, 21, 29–30, 37, 39, 44, 54–6, 63, 64, 113
  firestorm 64–5
  flood 35, 37, 39, 43–4, 53, 56, 64
  hurricane 54–58, 60, 63–4, 68
  Hurricanes 55
  hurricane 24, 37, 55–6, 58, 63–4
  landslide 35, 37, 43–4
  tectonic disaster 54, 63, 65
  volcanic eruption 4, 53–4, 58–61, 64, 66, 68–9
natural hazards 34, 37, 65
Nelson, N. 156
Nettleford, R. 94
Neumann, R. 177
Nevis 8, 11, 15, 16
Newmark, W.D. 177, 179
non-governmental organizations (NGOs) 2, 57, 82, 87, 89, 97, 99, 122, 166
Nickel, A. 81
Núñez Jiménez, A. 82

O'Connor, S. 157, 166
O'Neill, A. 147
Oliver-Smith, A. 53, 54
Olwig, K.F. 24
Organization of Eastern Caribbean States 16
Overseas Development Institute (ODI) 5, 60
Overseas Territory of Britain 4, 60
OXFAM 97

Pain, R. 96, 102
Palmer, P. 133, 134, 140, 141, 142
Pantojas-García, E. 114
Parry, D. 181
participatory appraisal 93, 96–8, 103–4
participatory approach 3, 65, 101
Participatory Learning and Action (PLA) 103
participatory planning 1, 49, 98, 155
participatory research 93–6, 99, 102, 103, 104, 105, 106
Participatory Rural Analysis (PRA) 67
Pattullo, P. 55, 62, 75, 113, 114, 115, 120
Pearce, D.G. 70, 112, 114, 115
Peet, R. 95
Pelling, M. 93, 167, 172
Pender, J. 13, 14
People, Land Management and Environmental Change (PLEC) 34–6, 38, 42, 44–7
Pérez, L. 55, 77, 78, 81
Perkin, S. 177, 178
Perkins, D.D. 181, 182, 187, 194
pest control 33, 45–6, 54
pesticides 2, 33, 44–5
Peters, P. 73, 75, 82
Peterson, T.R. 156, 167, 181, 182
Pezzoli, K. 73
Physical Development and Control Planning Act (2002) Grenada 10
physical development planning 7, 8, 9, 11, 13, 15, 18
Physical Planning Act (2001) (Dominica) 10
Pimbert, M. 151, 155, 157–8, 163, 172, 187
Place, S. 114
planning discourses 8, 9, 15, 17, 18
political ecology 54, 68, 155
Poon, A. 115
Portes, A. 73
Possekel, A. 65, 66, 67, 68
Potter, R. 1
poverty reduction strategies 14
power relations 1, 93, 95, 105, 155, 158, 160–61, 163, 172, 187

Pretty, J. 151, 155, 157, 158, 172, 187
Puerto Rico 56, 57, 63, 68
Pugh, J. 1, 2, 7, 15, 17, 46, 111
Purcell, T. 133

Quarles van Ufford, P. 155, 160

Radcliffe, Sarah A. 1
Rahnema, M. 105
Rapid Rural Appraisal (RRA) 67
Rapoport, R.N. 98
Rappaport, J. 182
reforestation 28, 29, 33
Regulska, J. 87
Reininger, B. 181, 182
Richard, A.F. 157, 166
Richardson, B. 23, 24, 25, 26, 74
Rigau, J. 74
Rio Earth Summit 15, 111
Robinson, M. 73
Rocheleau, D. 100
Rodríguez, E.L. 74
Rohter, R. 83
Rojas, E. 73
Rojeck, C. 74
Rose, G. 1, 95
Rosendo, S. 155, 160, 161
Rubenstein, H. 48
Rural Agricultural Development Agency (RADA) 46

Salafsky, N. 178
Sandals Resorts International 111–24
Sandals Training and Development Institute (STDI) 121
Sanjayan, M.A. 157
San Pedro Lions Club 181, 185, 187, 194
San Pedro Tour Guide Association (SPTGA) 181, 185, 187, 189, 194
Savage, Frank 53
Scarpaci, Joseph L. 3, 5, 73, 74, 75, 77, 80, 81, 82, 83, 85
Schroeder, R.A. 157, 163, 172
Schwartz, S. 56, 68
Scott, J. 161, 167
Segre, R. 81
sharecropping 25
Sharma, S. 114
Sharp, J. 95
Sharpe, B. 157, 167
Sheller, M. 114
Sheppard, E. 87
Sidaway, J.D. 13
Singleton, S. 195
Skinner, J. 2, 4, 53, 55, 58, 60, 65
slavery 21, 24–5, 56, 74, 84
small farmers 1, 4
Small Island Developing States Programme of Action (SIDsPOA) 15
Smith, H. 45
Smuts, C. 181, 182, 187
Social Development Commission (SDC) 97, 104
Social Investment Fund (SIF) 93, 97, 103
soil erosion 4, 21, 44, 56, 63, 113
soil loss 30, 35
Sontag, S. 101
soufrières 58
Soviet Union 75, 83
Spanish-American War 55
Speer, P.W. 181, 182
Spence, B. 1, 3, 4, 33, 35, 38, 44, 46, 47, 48, 50, 103
Stanislawski, D. 75
Starick, S. 114
St Christopher 8
Stephens, A. 181, 182, 187
Steward, J. 55
Stewart, Gordon 'Butch' 116, 119, 120
St Kitts 9, 11, 15–16, 25
St Lucia 8–12
Stocking, M. 50, 177, 178
Stone, R. 133
Strauss, A. 102
St Vincent 4, 8, 9, 22, 23, 25
Suddard, R.W. 12
Sugar Duties Act (1846) 24
sustainable development 15, 63, 83, 104, 108, 115, 143–4, 149, 163, 178, 190, 194
Sustainable Development Plan 61, 64, 66
Swarbrooke, J. 90, 112

Taylor, G. 155, 157
Taylor, P. 89,
Taylor, R.B. 194

Tewarie, B. 113
Theodorson, G.A. 75
Thin, N. 55
Thomas, D. 178
Thomas-Hope, E. 1, 3, 4, 33, 35, 38, 44, 46, 47, 48, 103
Thrift, N. 155
Tillmann, Hermann 67
Timms, B. 74
tourism 3, 5, 30, 38, 54–5, 62, 70–71, 73–5, 77–8, 81–91, 111–16, 118–20, 122–7, 131–4, 141–2, 145, 147, 149, 151–2, 164–6, 170, 172, 179, 181, 186–7, 189–91, 193, 195
  alternative 111–14, 116
  heritage 3, 5, 73, 74, 75, 77, 81, 82, 85, 86
  mass 111–14, 116
  tourism 3, 54, 112, 114–15
Tourtellot, J.B. 87
Town and Country Planning Act 9 (1932) (England)
Town and Country Planning Act (1971) (St Lucia) 9, 11
Town and Country Planning Act (1981) (Barbados) 11
Town and Country Planning Act (1990) (England) 11
Town and Country Planning Act (1995) (England) 10
Trinidad 2, 9, 11–13, 25, 30, 106
tropical deforestation 4, 22
Trumball, C. 77
Tung, A. 74
Turks and Caicos 8, 115
Turner, L. 55, 114

Ugalde, Alvaro 141, 142, 143
UNESCO 3, 73, 81–5
Union Island 25
United Kingdom 4, 116
United Nations 4, 5, 8, 53, 68, 111
United Nations Development Programme (UNDP) 8, 58
United States of America 2, 55–57, 60, 63 68, 75, 82, 85, 87, 116, 118, 152
University of the West Indies (UWI) 50, 97, 122
Urry 55, 74
USAID 2

Varley, A. 73
Venezuela 4, 60
Virgin Islands 8, 25, 57
visual methods 93, 100, 101
Von Humboldt, Baron Alexander 23, 75

Wacker, C. 104
Wadge, G. 53
Wainwright, C. 178
Walker, R. 101
Wallace, A. 71, 132, 133, 134, 142, 144
Walling, D. 155
Wandersman, A. 182
Ward, P. 73
water pollution 54, 77
Watts, D. 34
Weaver, D.B. 111, 112, 113
Wehrmeyer, W. 178
Weiler, B. 112
Weir, C. 147
Weis, Tony 5
Weitzner, V. 142, 147, 148, 152
Wellington, G.R. 90, 152
Wells, M. 28, 178
West, P.C. 157
Western funding agencies 18
Western planning discourses 8, 9, 15, 17, 18
West Indies Royal Commission of 1897 25, 26
White, G. 68, 156, 167
Wilkinson, P.F. 112, 113, 114, 195
Williams, G. 12, 13
Willis, Katie 1
Wills, J. 1
Windward Islands 21, 23, 29, 30
Wingate, J. 101
Wollenberg, E. 178
World Bank 14, 87, 97, 103, 114
World Conservation Union (IUCN) 131–2, 135, 140
World Heritage 3, 81–3, 85, 169
World Tourism Organization (WTO) 5, 37, 114
World Trade Organization 5, 37
World Travel and Tourism Council (WTTC) 111, 118

Wright, R.M. 156

Yeoh, Brenda 1
York, A.S. 181, 182, 187, 194
Young, R. 58, 102, 179

Zaman, M. 53
Zarin, D.J. 39
Ziller, R. 101
Zimmerman, M.A. 181, 182, 187
Zweifel, H. 194